THE WHOLEFOOD COOKBOOK

GAIL DUFF

Marshall Cavendish

Editor: **Pepita Aris**
Designer: **Rob Burt**

Published by Marshall Cavendish Books Limited
58, Old Compton Street,
London W1V 5PA

©Marshall Cavendish Limited, 1980, 1981

First printing 1980
Second printing 1981

Printed in Hong Kong

ISBN 0 85685 819 6

**All recipes serve 4 people
unless otherwise specified**

Why Eat The Natural Way?

The answer is that you will increase both your health and your enjoyment of eating. Whole means something complete — nothing added and nothing taken away. When this is applied to food, it is easy to see why **wholefoods** are better for you.

Prepackaged, processed food requires a battery of preservatives, colourings and chemical additives. Worse — the natural goodness of the food is often diminished at the same time.

Wholefood eating is a return to sensible eating — it is also a return to gusty, pleasurable dining. Food in its natural state, that has not been tampered with, taste so much better than a succession of 'quick foods'.

Wholefoods is about choosing well: food at its freshest and best. It is also about cooking intelligently, selecting methods that will show off the natural virtues and characteristics of the ingredients, rather than disguising them.

Contents

An Introduction to Wholefoods

What exactly are natural or wholefoods? This is a question that confuses many people who feel they would like to live on as healthy a diet as possible, but do not know quite how to begin. They go into a health food shop and look at the bewildering array of ingredients with strange-sounding names and, unless there is a knowledgeable assistant on hand to help, they either run out without buying anything or buy just a pack of nuts. They then go away still more confused—perhaps with their original enthusiasm for healthy eating dampened.

Whole foods and eating foods the natural way are, in fact, far more simple than you think. The word 'whole' means something that is complete, with nothing added and nothing taken away. Apply this to food and it means good, basic ingredients, grown and produced in as natural a way as possible: foods that have not been processed and have had nothing taken away from them or nothing added to them.

This can apply to any of the basic ingredients that are used in wholefood cookery. Wheat is one of the best examples of a natural or whole food. If you follow it through from the field to the loaf that you eventually eat, it will give you the right idea. Wheat can be grown organically or with the aid of chemical sprays and fertilisers. Organically-grown wheat is preferable in a healthy diet. Once it has been harvested, the wheat has to be ground. The whole of the grain can be ground together to make what we call wholewheat, wholemeal or whole grain flour, or much of the fibre and the good-

ness can be taken away to make white flour which is then chemically bleached and 'enriched' with artificial vitamins.

The same story could be told of other ingredients. Fruit and vegetables can be organically or chemically grown. A large proportion of any fruit crop goes for freezing, canning and drying, three processes which usually include the use of chemicals and artificial colourings and flavourings. Meat can be 'factory' reared and then sent to food processors for making up into such things as luncheon meats and sausages which nearly all contain artificial flavourings and colourings and also preservatives. Fish can be coated in batter and coloured crumbs, milk can be condensed and dried, while eggs can be produced in batteries and everywhere there are highly-coloured and highly-sugared desserts and confections.

All this sounds a bit like science fiction, but your food need not necessarily be like this at all. There is a wide variety of good, wholesome foods available to everyone who cares to seek them out and this book is intended as an introduction to them.

Whether a food is natural or not is not solely influenced by what happens to it before you buy it: foods can also be spoiled at home. Their nutritive qualities can be reduced through poor storing, preparation and cooking. So as well as descriptions of the ingredients, you will find recipes which will give you the best idea of how natural foods can be used to give you the optimum goodness and enjoyment.

The other question often asked is, 'Why eat

unprocessed foods at all?' Well, contrary to what we have been led to believe, our Western society is not one of the most healthy. Our starchy, sweet, high-fat over-refined diet has produced quite a frightening list of modern illnesses and many people, although not actually ill, often feel slightly below par. Vitamin deficiencies are still found in children and not just in those from deprived communities; and allergies to food additives are also found.

The 'permitted' list of food additives (colourings, flavourings, preservatives, fortifiers, stabilizers, etc.) is constantly changing; old ones are found harmful and banned and new ones added. It is difficult to estimate just how many food additives have been used and discarded and how much harm they did before they were banned, as sometimes the effects can take years to trace. Although one additive in one food may not be significant, if you constantly eat a lot of foods with additives, there could be a build-up. Surely the best thing for us to do is to avoid as many foods as possible with additives, buy food in its natural state and make it into whatever dish we like?

When you compare the goodness contained in some whole, natural products with that in their refined counterparts, the difference may not seem significant. For example, weight for weight, besides the extra fibre, brown rice contains a little more goodness than white. The amounts may seem very tiny, but the amount of vitamins and minerals that we need is small (although without them we can quickly become ill). Eat brown rice instead of white once and the effect will be nil, but if you ate rice once or twice a week for a year, the difference in the amount of goodness you obtained would be measurable. And if you did the same thing with all your foods, then you can see how the nutritional benefits would start to snowball.

Many people, when they first change to a natural diet, find that they quickly feel healthier and such things as indigestion tablets and aspirins are forgotten. Those overweight lose it naturally, while those underweight put on a little.

Beside all these health reasons, there is one big reason why many cooks, both at home and in restaurants, choose to buy whole and natural ingredients: they taste far better. Whereas processed products generally dictate the use to which they can be put, basic natural ingredients can be turned into as many different dishes as you can discover or invent. For example, a sausage can be served only as that, but a fresh piece of lean pork has many possibilities. Frozen vegetables cannot offer the advantages of fresh vegetables, full of flavour, which can be lightly boiled or steamed or made into more interesting roast, braised simmered or stir-fried dishes. Fresh vegetables can also be served raw, which gives them another dimension and this is rarely true of frozen vegetables. Eating vegetables raw is a sure way of getting as much goodness as possible.

Many people have the idea that health food eating is frugal eating, or that it is boring; but you only have to look at the range of ingredients available and the different ways of cooking them to see that this is not so. The most boring diet of all is the 'meat plus one starch and one green vegetable' every day. A natural food diet will not exclude this menu, if the meat is of good quality and the vegetables are fresh and well-cooked, but you can experience a far wider variety of culinary pleasures if you also base meals on pulses (dried legumes), grains and dairy products. Many processed foods contain identical flavour-enhancers, even when the food type differs, and so, whatever you eat, it all tastes very similar. Every food in its natural state has

an individual flavour and you can appreciate this alone or combine it with others to produce an infinite variety of tastes and types of dishes.

As well as the enjoyment we get from eating whole and natural ingredients, the cook in the family will also derive much pleasure in preparing it and she will never be bored with the same daily routine.

Health food eating is not necessarily vegetarian, although many vegetarians pay extreme care to the quality of the food that they eat. Meat-eaters can eat a whole or natural food diet too. They will have the same fresh, basic ingredients and the same variety, the only difference being that meat will be included. You will often find, though, that because of the large number of foods from which to choose, meat eaters on a natural diet will inevitably include some days when meat is not consumed.

You have really only to look at and taste different foods to realise that they must be made up of varying constituents and you will most probably balance your meals through common sense. For example, fish, potatoes and a selection of green vegetables will provide you with different flavours but they will also provide protein, carbohydrate and different vitamins. It is highly unlikely that you would ever choose to have fish, eggs and meat together. You will therefore be naturally producing balanced meals. You do not have to sit down every day with a vitamin and mineral chart, but it may help to know just a little about the constituents of foods. For this reason, a very brief description has been included.

As well as the basic ingredients that are dealt with in the following chapters, do not forget to pay attention to detail when it comes to the flavourings, seasonings, oils and other ingredients that are included in your dishes. As you are not relying on artificial flavourers, herbs are invaluable and it is always best, if you can, to grow your own so you will have them fresh for most part of the year and your own dried ones (which will probably be fresher and tastier than bought ones) for the rest of the time. If you do not have a garden, try growing them in window boxes or in pots on a sunny window-ledge. Herbs will supply countless different flavours and you can use them separately or in mixtures.

All the basic spices such as paprika or nutmeg can be used to great advantage in wholefood cookery and they are similar wherever you buy them. When it comes to salt, use a sea salt or natural coarse salt. These contain many essential minerals and have had no chemical added to make them flow easily. If you have trouble when using them, it is worth investing in a salt mill. It is best if you are sparing in your use of salt when cooking. Certain foods, such as grains and potatoes, need a little; but other vegetables, contrary

to what we have been led to believe, need little or none.

If you use oil in cooking, make sure it is a good one. The best are the cold-pressed oils which have been obtained from their natural vegetables, fruits and seeds by simply pressing. Their colour will be a deep amber and they will have a definite flavour. The best for general use are olive oil, sunflower, safflower, groundnut and corn oils. For a special occasion salad, try sesame or walnut oil. The worst oils are those labelled simply 'vegetable oil'. They have been produced by a chemical extraction process and because they contain a whole mixture of oils such as rape and linseed, their taste is unpleasant.

Drinks can also come into consideration. Tea, coffee and cocoa contain caffeine and are quite powerful stimulants. They should really only be drunk in moderation in a natural food diet. Interchange them with the wide range of herb teas or tisanes that are now available. Give up sugary, artificially-coloured fizzy drinks for natural, unsweetened fruit juices and mineral waters.

Natural eating need not be more expensive than a diet of convenience or so-called 'junk' foods. Admittedly, some of the commodities such as raw sugar or wholemeal (whole grain) bread and flour are going to be more expensive than their unrefined couterparts, but you are not going to be buying any ready-made products, such as frozen meat dishes, sweet biscuits (cookies), cakes or instant dried meals. You will probably also be eating more of the cheaper things,

like eggs, or dried peas and beans, instead of meat on some days in the week. If you enjoy the luxuries of life then an unprocessed, additive-free diet will probably cost about the same as an over-processed, convenience food one. If you have simple tastes, then it will be cheaper.

Now that you are enthusiastic about the idea of natural foods, how can you convince your family? The best way is not too fast and not too forceful. Gradually introduce whole grain products into the diet, add the occasional salad, substitute fresh fruit for rich desserts and replace the usual processed breakfast cereal with muesli. Do not say they have got to eat natural foods or else, but offer the new foods as something exciting to try. They will then increasingly become a part of an, enjoyable way of life. Your family will be a lot healthier and probably happier too.

The constituents of foods

Foods are made up of proteins, carbohydrates and fats with small, but absolutely necessary amounts of vitamins and minerals.

Proteins are the body builders. They are important for growing children and are also needed by adults to help replace the $\frac{1}{2}\%$ of body tissue that is lost every day. Proteins are made up of amino acids, and different types of protein foods include them in different combinations. Amino acids can be divided into two main groups: essential and non-essential amino acids.

Essential amino acids cannot be made by the body

and have to be present in the diet for the body to make new protein. Non-essential amino acids, although no less necessary for making protein, can be made from other amino acids that are present in excess. The quality of the protein, therefore, depends on its ability to provide all the essential amino acids needed by the body.

Animal proteins are made up of a combination of amino acids with a pattern of essential amino acids very similar to that making up the protein in our own bodies. Meat, fish, cheese, milk and eggs provide us with high-quality protein, which can be used to make new proteins for the body with the minimum of waste.

Vegetables such as soya beans, pulses, cereals and nuts have a high protein content. However, vegetable proteins which are made up of different combinations of amino acids all have a relative lack of one essential amino acid. The amino acid that is low varies between different vegetables, so that these vegetables can be combined to complement one another and produce a protein of enhanced quality. For example, cereals are low in the essential acid amino called lysine and pulses are low in the essential amino acid called methionine. Cereals contain plenty of methionine, while pulses have amply lysine, so when these two foods are combined they provide both acids in the proportion we need. Examples of how this works in practice are baked beans on toast and lentil curry with rice.

The protein quality of cereals can similarly be enhanced by combining them with animal protein rich in lysine; for example cheese on toast, milk with breakfast cereals and pasta with meat sauce. The amino acid which is most lacking in nuts varies in different types, but as a general rule the protein quality can be improved by eating them in combinations with cereals and/or dairy products; for example a peanut butter sandwich.

Many people may be over-concerned about getting enough protein, but the amounts that we actually need are surprisingly low. The average man needs 60-70g (2½-3oz) a day and the average woman 50-60g (2-2½oz). To obtain this from meat alone we would have to eat around 275g (10oz) in one day, but as so many different foods contain protein we can obtain it from many different sources, and cut down on meat.

Carbohydrates are needed to give us energy for basic body functions as well as general activities. There are basically two types, refined and unrefined. Refined foods such as white flour and sugar were once associated with luxury. They are, by one definition, 'pure', but this means that they are all sugar or all starch and other nutrients and fibre are considerably reduced. Refined sugar gives us quick bursts of energy, but it is very quickly used up, so we may eat more to compensate. We need more white bread to satisfy us than we do whole grain. Therefore, by eating the refined products, we are eating more calories than we need and less goodness and bulk. The healthiest sources of carbohydrates are the whole grain products such as wheat and brown rice, fresh vegetables and fruit.

Fats: the word 'fats' has become rather a dirty one in recent years but we would not be healthy without them. They provide a concentrated source of energy in the diet and contribute a slow digestibility to food. Fats protect our body tissues, organs and nerves, help to maintain our temperature, assist in our general metabolism and carry the vitamins A, D, E, F and K round the body. As well as the visible fats such as butter, margarine, cooking oils and the fat on meat, there are also invisible types such as that in oily fish, in the structure of meat and in nuts and seeds. Fats are composed of a mixture of fatty acids of which there are three types: saturated, mono-unsaturated and poly-unsaturated. All products that contain fats generally carry a mixture of these. Saturated fats are found predominantly in animal products, hard cooking fats and margarines. Mono-unsaturated fats are high in olive oil and are widely distributed in all foods. Polyunsaturated fats are found in soft margarines, cooking oils such as safflower and sunflower and in nuts and seeds. Saturated fats have been implicated in the causes of heart disease, while polyunsaturated fats are thought by some to have a protective effect. The main point is: too much fat of any one type is not good for us, but it is best to cut down all round rather than get too worried about any one particular item.

Vitamins: although we know more about vitamins than we did twenty years ago, there is still much research to be done in this field. Vitamins are contained in only very small amounts in food, but a deficiency in any one of them could lead to serious illness.

Vitamin A is essential for growth and healthy eyes and skin and is found mainly in yellow fruit, green vegetables, carrots, oily fish and liver.

There are a large number of vitamins in the B complex group; the most important ones are thiamin (B_1) riboflavin (B_2), pantothenic acid, pyridoxine (B_6) cynocobalamine (B_{12}), biotin, folic acid and nicotinic acid. They are needed for growth, for healthy skin, to help in the digestion of carbohydrates and protein and for the health of the nervous system. Choline and inositol are needed to prevent the build-up of fats in the blood. The foods most rich in B vitamins are yeast, liver, other meats, whole grains, soya beans, green vegetables, eggs and fish.

Vitamin C (ascorbic acid), the fresh fruit and vegetable vitamin, is essential for the health of our body tissues, teeth and gums and for the healing of wounds. Vitamin D is found mainly in oily fish, butter, margarine, eggs and milk, and is also obtained by the action of sunlight on the skin. It is needed for healthy bones and teeth.

The purpose of vitamin E is still not known, but it is thought to be needed for fertility and prevent premature ageing. It is found in vegetable oils, wheat-germ, whole grains, eggs, green vegetables and nuts. Vitamin K, which aids in the clotting of the blood, is found in green vegetables, especially spinach, soya beans, liver, some oils and the white part (pith) of citrus fruits.

Minerals are found in foods in even smaller amounts than vitamins, but iron, sodium, calcium, chlorine, phosphorus, potassium and magnesium are absolutely essential for good health. Most foods contain a selection of minerals and if you eat a varied, natural food diet you should have no problem in obtaining them all in sufficient amounts.

Vegetables

Walk into any vegetable market or even into the vegetable department of a supermarket at any time of the year and you will always find a superb selection of fresh vegetables, both seasonal local produce and produce grown elsewhere, which may be foreign and exotic. There are leafy green vegetables such as curly, ruffled kale or spring greens, tightly-packed ones like cabbage or baby Brussels sprouts, solid root vegetables, crunchy stalks such as celery or Florence fennel, cucumbers, or a pumpkin, the many varieties of onions and those vegetables in a class of their own such as mushrooms and asparagus. Their colours and flavours, shapes and sizes must be an inspiration to any cook. Who needs to resort to cans and frozen packages when there is all this variety?

Fresh vegetables, as well as supplying us with many different flavours and culinary possibilities, also contain a whole range of valuable vitamins and minerals, and it is for these that vegetables are mainly valued. Each type, and indeed each individual vegetable, contains a different combination. So, to obtain as much goodness as possible from vegetables, it is best if we can eat a selection in at least two meals a day. There are so many kinds and ways of serving and presenting them that we need never be bored.

The protein content of vegetables is highest in peas and beans, but all vegetable types contain a certain amount. It is, however, small in most other vegetables and they should not, apart from occasionally avocados, be regarded as the main protein part of the meal. Carbohydrate is also present in all vegetables, but the amounts vary tremendously. It is lowest in the leafy types, in moderate amounts in root vegetables and onions and highest in potatoes, parsnips, beetroot (beets), peas and broad (fava) beans. There are little or no fats in all vegetables but avocados. The fat content only creeps up when a significant amount is added during cooking, such as with fried onions or potato chips. Vegetables are also high in fibre content, so from every aspect they are a very valuable inclusion in a natural diet.

Shopping for vegetables

The goodness in vegetables is highest when they are freshly picked. Canned vegetables have nearly always been first frozen and then cooked (and very often coloured), thus destroying many of their essential nutrients and doctoring them with dubious chemicals. They should definitely not feature in a wholefood diet. Frozen vegetables are slightly better nutritionally than canned but, even so, have been blanched, while colouring is added in some cases. Whenever possible it is best to avoid buying these also.

Minerals & Vitamins

Each vegetable contains a selection of vitamins, some in larger amounts than others. Carotene, which is converted by the body to vitamin A, is very often contained in vegetables which are red- or orange-coloured. Carrots are the obvious example, for they are exceptionally high in vitamin A, but so are pumpkins, red (bell) peppers and tomatoes. Other green vegetables with large amounts of vitamin A are broccoli, curly endive (chicory), kale, spinach, cress and watercress.

Some vegetables high in thiamine (vitamin B_1) are avocados, globe and Jerusalem artichokes, asparagus, broccoli, Brussels sprouts, cauliflower, kale, mushrooms, parsnips, peas, potatoes, spinach and watercress. Nicotinic acid, another B vitamin, is found mainly in asparagus, broad (fava) beans, broccoli, kale, mushrooms—it is particularly high in these—parsnips, peas, potatoes and swedes (rutabagas). Riboflavin (vitamin B_2) is found in asparagus, runner (green or snap) beans, broccoli, cauliflower, curly endive (chicory), peas and spinach.

Vitamin C is present in nearly all vegetables and, looking at a nutritional table, it is difficult to know which ones to pick out as containing the most. Those with really large amounts are broccoli, Brussels sprouts, kale and green (bell) peppers. This group is closely followed by cabbage, cauliflower, mustard and cress, spinach and watercress. Potatoes, which are often thought of as a starchy, filler food, are in fact a very good source of vitamin C. Most other vegetables, however, have significant amounts. Vitamin K is present in varying amounts in all green vegetables. Vegetables are high in minerals as well as vitamins. The main mineral is calcium. This is found in the greatest quantities in cabbage and the leafy greens, carrots, celery, spinach and parsnips. Iron is present in large quantities in mushrooms, peas, spinach and watercress. Vegetables also contain significant amounts of potassium.

When you go out to buy vegetables, always look for those that are crisp and fresh. Tired, limp examples have been picked for too long and their goodness has already started to break down. Supermarkets sell a good variety of vegetables, many of which are of excellent quality, but the plastic wrappings which are so often used have been found, in some cases, to destroy flavour and goodness. So it is worth looking around in local markets and shops and finding out where you can buy direct from the farm.

The best vegetables you can possibly have are those that have been organically grown (that is, without the use of chemical sprays and fertilizers), but these may

be difficult to find except in specialist health food shops. Of course, the best way to keep yourself supplied is to grow your own but, if this is not possible, buy unwrapped, loose vegetables from specialist shops or farmers.

For quality and also for cheapness it is always best to use vegetables that are in season. Seasonal vegetables also match our seasonal moods and feelings. A hearty stew with root vegetables will warm us up on a winter's night. A light dish of baked courgettes (zucchini) or simmered summer cabbage is more suitable for the warm evenings of summer.

If you grow your own vegetables, you will be lucky enough to go into the garden every day and pick just enough for one meal. If you are relying on shopping for supplies, then there will be the problem of how many vegetables to buy at once and how to store them. If this is practical, shop for vegetables twice or more times a week. Then you will be eating them as fresh as possible.

Storing vegetables

Most vegetables should be kept cool and preferably in the dark. Root vegetables and potatoes should be left unscrubbed and stored in a paper sack or thick paper carrier bag in a dark cupboard. Onions are also best treated in this way. Tomatoes are best left in a bowl in a cool cupboard. They keep more flavour when stored this way than if kept in the refrigerator. All types of cauliflowers, cabbage and leafy greens, on the other hand, are best refrigerated. Put them into a plastic bag and store them in the crisper compartment. The same treatment is best for leeks and spring onions (scallions), lettuces, endive, chicory, celery and Florence fennel. Cucumbers can be refrigerated unwrapped, and Brussels sprouts, courgettes (zucchini), squash, aubergines (eggplants) and green (bell) peppers are best in the refrigerator in a paper bag. Mushrooms lose a lot of water during storage and they are best put first into a paper bag and then in a plastic one.

Asparagus, broad (fava or lima) beans, peas and mange tout (snow or sugar peas) should never be stored for long. They are all best eaten on the day of purchase. These are the basic rules for storing, but obviously 'fresh picked and soon eaten' is the best motto in order to obtain the maximum goodness.

Preparation

The nutritional content of vegetables will be reduced if they are badly handled and prepared. Much of their goodness lies just under the surface, so the less you peel and scrape them, the better. Most root vegetables, if they are fresh, should only need a good scrub—unless of course they are blemished. Celeriac (celery root) is the one root vegetable which does always need to be peeled, because it has such a tough outer layer. A peeled vegetable will lose far more goodness during cooking than an unpeeled one and this is never more true than of potatoes. A quick scrubbing is all they need. If you wish to serve them plainly boiled or steamed or perhaps mashed with butter or yogurt, then boil them in their skins and peel them when they are cooked.

Leafy vegetables need to have the tougher stems removed, but the smaller, more tender ones will cook

down with the rest. The outer leaves of cabbage must be trimmed away and, once this is done, there will probably be no need to wash the heart. The same applies to Brussels sprouts. When you are preparing these, there is no need to cut a cross in the base.

It is worth remembering that many of the vitamins contained in vegetables, vitamin C in particular, are water-soluble. This means that they dissolve during the cooking process but also if the vegetables are immersed in cold water for too long. A quick rinse and chop just before they go into the pot is far better nutritionally than preparing them in advance and leaving them to soak, or leaving peeled and chopped vegetables exposed to the air for too long.

When you are chopping or slicing vegetables, always use a sharp knife. A blunt one will squash and damage the plant cells, again lowering the vitamin content.

Raw vegetables

Is it better to cook vegetables or always to eat them raw? No matter how careful you are in preparation or how quick and efficient your chosen cooking method, significant amounts of vitamins are always lost during the cooking process. Vitamin A is one of the most stable in water and heat, but you can lose up to 40% of the riboflavin and thiamin content and 60% of the vitamin C. However, raw vegetables at every meal could become monotonous, while there are some vegetables, such as spring greens, broccoli or aubergines (eggplants) which are not at all pleasant to eat in their raw state. To get the best in both nutrition and enjoyment, serve raw vegetables with one meal in the day and carefully cooked ones with the other.

Salads

A large plateful of raw vegetables, completely ungarnished and unflavoured, would probably be rather

unappealing, so make them into imaginative, colourful and tasty salads. There are basically three different types of salads: those to be served as at the beginning of a meal, salads to accompany the main dish and main course salads.

A salad is an ideal way of starting the meal as it refreshes your palate and stimulates your taste buds. Make it small but delectable and very attractive. It can consist of a small amount of vegetables with a little protein, such as diced, hard cheese, a spoonful of cottage or curd (farmer's) cheese, a few nuts and dried fruits, shellfish such as prawns (shrimp), a little diced chicken, some cooked, dried beans such as haricot beans or chick-peas or diced avocado.

The salad ingredients can be combined in a variety of different ways. Salad and protein ingredients can both be mixed together into the salad dressing; an example is chopped hazelnuts with raisins, mixed with finely diced celery and apple into a yogurt dressing. Alternatively, the salad can be dressed, with the additions placed decoratively on top; an example is a tomato and watercress salad with a vinaigrette dressing, topped with a portion of cottage cheese. A third type is a plain salad with the protein and dressing mixed together on top; for example a base of shredded lettuce or curly endive (chicory) topped with chopped hard-boiled eggs and prawns (shrimp) in mayonnaise.

All kinds of vegetables can be combined at different times of the year to make side salads and the combinations that you can devise are practically endless. To obtain as much variety in goodness, flavour and colour as possible, mix different types of vegetables, taking care that the flavours and textures go together. For added enjoyment you can also add diced fresh fruits, dried fruit, a small amount of chopped nuts or poppy or sesame seeds, finely-chopped pickled onions, gherkins or walnuts or a very little grated cheese.

Make the flavour of your chosen dressing comple-

ment the flavour of the vegetables. To a basic vinaigrette dressing made with 60ml (4tbls) oil and 30ml (2 tbls) vinegar, you can add chopped herbs, crushed garlic, spices such as paprika or cinnamon, tomato paste, Worcestershire or Tabasco sauce, tamari (Shoyu) sauce, mustard powder or a little prepared mustard, or a little tahini or peanut butter. You can also change the type of vinegar that you use (cider, red wine, white wine, malt or herb), or use lemon or orange juice instead. Yogurt makes a good base for a salad dressing. Simply mix chopped herbs and crushed garlic into a 150ml ($\frac{1}{4}$pt) or $\frac{2}{3}$ cup of yogurt. Thicken the dressing by beating in 30ml (2tbls) olive or sunflower oil. Use 90ml (6tbls) dairy sour cream mixed with the juice of half a lemon to make a light-flavoured creamy dressing.

Main course salads can be made on the same principles as those for a first course, but the quantity of most of the ingredients is increased. Use a wide selection of ingredients and present them attractively.

Cooked vegetables

If you want plainly-cooked vegetables with no additional flavourings, then boiling and steaming are the best methods.

Boiling is the method which causes the greatest loss of goodness but, provided you are careful, you can still finish with a nutritional dish. The first thing to remember is not to use too much water. You need only just enough to barely cover the vegetables. Salt is not essential when boiling green vegetables, although a little is needed for potatoes and the sweeter roots such as carrots and parsnips.

Vegetables which contain vitamin C also contain an enzyme which can destroy the vitamin. This is released by any physical damage to the vegetable and so destruction begins with preparation. Damage is minimized by putting the vegetable directly into

water which is already boiling so the enzyme will be destroyed. Therefore bring a pan of water to the boil and put in the vegetables. Then turn down the heat, cover and simmer gently until the vegetables are barely tender. Drain them immediately and serve them as soon as you can. A rolling boil tends to destroy even more vitamins, and so does keeping the cooked vegetables warm for long periods and cooling them and reheating them later.

Steaming takes slightly longer than boiling, but it retains a fresher and more definite flavour. Chop or slice the vegetables into smaller pieces than you would for boiling, or grate root vegetables and put them into a perforated vegetable steamer or a large colander. Bring a little water to the boil in a saucepan and set the steamer above it. Cover the vegetables with a lid or foil and cook them until they are barely tender. Chopped herbs or a bouquet garni can be added to steaming vegetables, or a little spice such as freshly-grated nutmeg. You can also steam combinations of vegetables such as cabbage or spring greens with leeks, thinly-sliced potatoes with sliced onion, or cauliflower florets with strips of green (bell) pepper.

Vegetables can also be steamed in a closed container such as a bowl in a pan of water or a double boiler. This takes rather a long time, but brings out a very strong flavour and keeps in all the goodness.

Baking vegetables can be another light and nutritious cooking method, provided not too much fat is used. The obvious example is large potatoes, simply baked in their skins on the oven rack. Similar treatment can be given to Jerusalem artichokes and parsnips. Root vegetables and also pumpkins can be cut into large dice and baked in a dish containing a little stock; mushrooms and tomatoes can be baked in lightly-greased dishes. Wrapping vegetables in lightly-greased foil before baking keeps in all their goodness and flavour. This method is particularly successful for

15

diced root vegetables with chopped herbs or grated nutmeg and also for whole aubergines (eggplants) and courgettes (zucchini). When baked they can then be served exactly as they are, or hollowed out and stuffed.

Grilling or broiling is a very quick and efficient cooking method which requires the minimum of fat or oil. It is excellent for large mushrooms, tomato halves and slices of courgettes (zucchini) and aubergines (eggplants). Parboiling and then grilling (broiling) vegetables tends to destroy too much goodness.

Simmering: if a richer, more flavoursome dish is required, then try simmering your vegetables. Only a very little liquid, which can be water, stock, wine, beer or cider, is needed for this process and usually a small amount of butter or oil. The result is a glossy vegetable, full of flavour. The liquid is either absorbed or evaporated so that no goodness is thrown away at the end. Vegetables can be simmered alone or in various combinations—cabbage and celery, for example, or carrots and swedes (rutabagas)—and you can flavour them with chopped herbs, garlic, a little spice, tomato paste, mustard, Worcestershire sauce or tamari (Shoyu) sauce.

A little butter or oil is heated in a large saucepan and the vegetables are then stirred in this. The liquid and flavourings are added, the lid put on and the vegetables simmered for 10-20 minutes, depending on the variety. The amount of liquid that you use also varies. Carrots and other root vegetables need 225ml (½pt) or 1¼ cups per 450g (1lb). Spring greens, broccoli, kale, peas, broad (fava or lima) beans and the tougher kinds of cabbage need 150ml (¼pt) or ⅔ cup, while the lighter kinds of cabbage, leeks and celery need 90ml (6tbls) or ⅓ cup and spinach and the summer cabbages none at all.

Braising vegetables is a similar process to simmering. The main difference between them is that a braised dish is finished off in the oven to give a slightly richer flavour and texture. Once again butter or oil is melted in a casserole and the vegetables are stirred in. Liquids and flavourings, the same as for simmering, are added and the casserole is covered and put into a moderate oven for 30-50 minutes. Braised vegetables can easily form the base of a main dish. When they are cooked, chopped nuts or grated cheese, together with wholemeal (whole grain) breadcrumbs, can be sprinkled over the top to give you a well-balanced protein meal.

Stir-frying and stir-braising are two Chinese methods of cooking which are becoming increasingly popular in wholefood kitchens. The vegetables are cooked very rapidly in hot oil and served immediately so the minimum amount of goodness is lost, the flavours are fresh and strong and the colours enhanced.

In order to stir-fry successfully, all the vegetables must be finely chopped or thinly sliced before you start. You can stir-fry cabbage, Brussels sprouts, cucumbers, marrows (summer squash), green and red (bell) peppers, carrots, onions, leeks, celery, Florence fennel, Chinese cabbage, runner (string) and French (green) beans and also finely-chopped spinach. The oil is first heated on a high heat in a large frying-pan or wok (the Chinese round-based pan), very often with a chopped clove of garlic. When the garlic sizzles, the vegetables are put in and stirred around on the heat for 2 minutes. Then a little liquid is added and reduced and the vegetables are served immediately. The liquid consists of one or a mixture of sherry, tamari (Shoyu) sauce and stock. No more than 90ml (6tbls) liquid are needed per 450g (1lb) vegetables. Spinach receives slightly different treatment. It is finely chopped and turned in butter until it is soft, sprinkled with nutmeg and served.

For tougher vegetables, such as spring greens, kale or button (shallots and pickling) onions and sometimes more crunchy ones such as carrots, celery or cauliflower, the cooking is taken further. Called stir-braising, the process is also very quick and nutritious. After the vegetables have been stirred in the oil for about 2 minutes, slightly more liquid is added— usually 150ml (¼pt) or ⅔ cup per 450g (1lb). They are then covered and cooked over a moderate heat for 10 minutes. Most of the liquid will be evaporated or absorbed and the vegetables will be bright and glossy and just tender.

RECIPES

Three Root Soup

Blended root vegetables can form the base of smooth and creamy soups which need no added flour, cream or egg yolks. In this one, half the vegetables are puréed and the other half left in pieces to give an interesting texture.

METRIC/IMPERIAL	AMERICAN
225g (½lb) swede	½lb rutabaga
225g (½lb) parsnips	½lb parsnips
225g (½lb) carrots	½lb carrots
1 medium-sized onion	1 medium-sized onion
25g (1oz) butter	2tbls butter
850ml (1½pt) stock	3½ cups stock or broth
large bouquet garni	large bouquet garni
sea salt	sea salt
freshly ground black pepper	freshly ground black pepper
15ml (1tbls) chopped parsley	1tbls chopped parsley
15ml (1tbls) chopped chervil	1tbls chopped chervil

Dice all the vegetables into small, even-sized cubes. Melt the butter in a saucepan on a low heat, stir in the vegetables, cover them and let them sweat for 10 minutes. Pour in the stock and bring it to the boil. Put in the bouquet garni and season. Cover and simmer for 20 minutes. Remove the bouquet garni.
Put half the soup into a blender and blend until it is smooth, or alternatively, rub it through a food mill. Stir the puréed soup back into the remaining vegetables. Mix in the herbs and reheat.

Cooking time: 50 minutes

Chunky Leek Soup

This is a colourful, unblended soup which, despite its chunky texture, makes a very light starter to a meal.

A light but warming soup for early spring, chunky leek soup has tomatoes in it for extra colour.

METRIC/IMPERIAL	AMERICAN
450g (1lb) leeks	1lb leeks
1 medium-sized onion	1 medium-sized onion
25g (1oz) butter	2 tbls butter
15ml (1tbls) flour	1tbls flour
5ml (1tsp) mustard powder	1tsp dry mustard
30ml (2tbls) tomato purée	2tbls tomato paste
700ml (1¼pt) stock	3 cups stock or broth
4 small, firm tomatoes	4 small, firm tomatoes
150ml (¼pt) dry white wine	⅔ cup dry white wine
30ml (2tbls) chopped chives	2tbls chopped chives

If the leeks are thin, cut them into 2cm (¾in) lengths, if thick cut them into 1cm (½in) pieces. Slice the onion into rings. Melt the butter in a large saucepan on a low heat. Stir in the leeks and onion, cover them and let them sweat for 10 minutes. Stir in the flour and mustard and cook them for 1 minute, stirring. Stir in the tomato paste and then the stock, bring the soup to the boil and simmer, uncovered, for 15 minutes.
Scald, skin and chop the tomatoes. Add the tomatoes and wine to the soup and reheat. Scatter the chives over the top before serving.

Cooking time : 40 minutes

Potato and Garlic Soup

This potato soup has a beautiful, creamy texture and colour. It is made all the better if you use a really large bunch of herbs for flavouring.

METRIC/IMPERIAL	AMERICAN
450g (1lb) potatoes	1lb potatoes
2 medium-sized onions	2 medium-sized onions
25g (1oz) butter	2tbls butter
850ml (1½pt) stock	3½ cups stock or broth
2 cloves garlic, crushed with	2 cloves garlic, crushed with
2.5ml (½tsp) sea salt	½tsp sea salt
1 large bouquet garni	1 large bouquet garni
freshly ground black pepper	freshly ground black pepper
150ml (¼pt) natural yogurt	⅔ cup plain yogurt
30ml (2tbls) chopped parsley	2tbls chopped parsley

Peel and thinly slice the potatoes. Finely chop the onion. Melt the butter in a saucepan on a low heat. Stir in the potatoes and onions, cover them and let them sweat for 8 minutes. Pour in the stock and bring it to the boil. Add the garlic and bunch of herbs and season with the pepper. Cover and simmer for 20 minutes. Remove the bouquet garni and either purée the soup

Celery and carrot boats

in a blender until it is smooth or rub it through the fine blade of a vegetable mill. Stir in the yogurt and reheat the soup if necessary, without boiling. Serve it with the chopped parsley sprinkled over the top.

Cooking time : 50 minutes

Lemon Mushroom Appetizer

Mushrooms, simply cooked with tomato paste and lemon juice make a warming and tasty first course.

METRIC/IMPERIAL	AMERICAN
450g (1lb) button mushrooms	1lb mushrooms
1 large onion	1 large onion
1 large clove garlic	1 large clove garlic
60ml (4tbls) olive oil	4tbls olive oil
juice of 1 lemon	juice of 1 lemon
30ml (2tbls) tomato purée	2tbls tomato paste
30ml (2tbls) chopped lemon thyme (or common thyme)	2tbls chopped lemon thyme (or common thyme)

If the mushrooms are small, leave them whole, if not, halve or quarter them depending on their size. Quarter and thinly slice the onion and finely chop the garlic. Heat the oil in a saucepan on a low heat. Stir in the mushrooms, onion and garlic, cover the pan and cook them gently for 10 minutes. Add the lemon juice, tomato paste and lemon thyme. Cover again and cook for a further 5 minutes. Serve in warm bowls with wholemeal (whole grain) bread.

Cooking time : 25 minutes

Celery and Carrot Boats

Salads to start the meal can be made to look really attractive. In this recipe, celery stalks are used as containers for a light mixture of carrots and curd cheese, which are attractively presented to look like small sailing ships.

METRIC/IMPERIAL	AMERICAN
175g (6oz) carrots	1½ cups shredded carrots
25g (1oz) raisins	¼ cup chopped raisins
125g (¼lb) curd cheese	1 cup farmer's cheese
1 clove garlic, crushed with a pinch sea salt	1 clove garlic, crushed with a pinch sea salt
juice ½ lemon	juice ½ lemon
freshly ground black pepper	freshly ground black pepper
4 large sticks celery or the wide ends of 8 small ones	4 large stalks celery
1 lemon for garnish	1 lemon for garnish

Finely grate the carrots and chop the raisins. Mix them into the cheese with the garlic and lemon juice. Season with the pepper. Cut the large stalks of celery across into two and use both ends. Keep the small stalks as they are. Pile the carrot filling into the celery boats.

Cut the lemon into 8 thin slices and stand these upright in the cheese to resemble sails.

Preparation time : 25 minutes

Peanut Butter Salad

Refreshing tomatoes and peppers go superbly with a nutty peanut butter dressing. The salad is a simple one but very effective.

METRIC/IMPERIAL	AMERICAN
450g (1lb) tomatoes	1lb tomatoes
2 medium-sized green peppers	2 medium-sized green bell peppers
30ml (2tbls) peanut butter	2tbls peanut butter
60ml (4tbls) oil	4tbls oil
30ml (2tbls) white wine vinegar	2tbls white wine vinegar
30ml (2tbls) chopped basil	2tbls chopped basil
1 clove garlic, crushed with a pinch of sea salt	1 clove garlic, crushed with a pinch of sea salt
freshly ground black pepper	freshly ground black pepper

Chop the tomatoes and divide them between four small plates. Cut the peppers in half lengthwise and remove stalks and seeds. Cut the peppers into half-moon, crosswise slices. Surround the tomatoes with the slices of pepper. Beat the peanut butter with the oil, vinegar, basil, garlic and pepper and spoon this dressing over the tomatoes.

Preparation time : 15 minutes

Avocado and Black Grape Salad

METRIC/IMPERIAL	AMERICAN
4 ripe avocados	4 ripe avocados
175g (6oz) black grapes	about 1 cup Concord grapes
125g (¼ lb) chopped walnuts	1 cup chopped walnuts
juice ½ lemon	juice ½ lemon
juice ½ orange	juice ½ orange
45ml (3tbls) olive oil	3tbls olive oil
1 clove garlic, crushed with a pinch sea salt	1 clove garlic, crushed with a pinch sea salt
freshly ground black pepper	freshly ground black pepper
4 boxes cress	2lb jar of sprouted alfalfa seeds or 4 bunches watercress
30ml (2tbls) chopped tarragon	2tbls chopped tarragon

Stone (pit), peel and chop the avocados. Halve and seed the grapes. Put the avocado and grapes into a bowl with the walnuts. Mix together the lemon and orange juices, oil, garlic and pepper.
Arrange a bed or cress, alfalfa sprouts or watercress, on a serving dish, pile the salad on top and scatter over the tarragon.
Serve with a burghul (bulgar) salad or with wholemeal scones (whole grain biscuits) for a main course.

Preparation time : 30 minutes

Stir-Braised Kale with Worcestershire Sauce

Stir-braised kale is very succulent and satisfying. Instead of the traditional tamari (Shoyu) sauce, Worcestershire sauce and parsley are added to give western flavours to an oriental method.

METRIC/IMPERIAL	AMERICAN
450g (1lb) curly kale	1lb kale or other greens
1 medium-sized onion	1 medium-sized onion
150ml (¼ pt) stock	⅔ cup stock or bouillon
20ml (2tbls) Worcestershire sauce	2tbls Worcestershire sauce
45ml (3tbls) oil	3tbls oil
30ml (2tbls) chopped parsley	2tbls chopped parsley

Tear the kale or greens into small pieces about 3cm (1in) square and thinly slice the onion. Mix the stock and sauce together. Heat the oil in a large frying-pan on a low heat. Mix in the onion and cook it until it is soft. Raise the heat to moderate and put in the kale—it will be quite bulky at first but will soon cook down. Stir it about for 2 minutes. Pour in the stock and sauce and bring them to the boil. Add the parsley. Cover and keep on a moderate heat for 10 minutes.

Cooking time : 30 minutes

Hot Cucumber Salad with Dill and Capers

The stir-frying method can be adapted to make hot salads. Instead of adding tamari (Shoyu) or another savoury sauce, vinegar and other salad dressing ingredients are put into the pan after frying.

METRIC/IMPERIAL	AMERICAN
1 medium-sized cucumber	1 medium-sized cucumber
6 small spring onions	6 scallions
30ml (2tbls) white wine vinegar	2tbls white wine vinegar
5ml (1tsp) Dijon mustard	1tsp Dijon-style mustard
15ml (1tbls) chopped capers	1tbls chopped capers
60ml (4tbls) olive oil	4tbls olive oil
5ml (1tsp) dill seeds	1tsp dill seeds

Wipe the cucumber and cut it into 6mm (¼in) slices. Chop the onions into 1cm (⅜in) lengths. Mix the vinegar, mustard and capers together. Heat the oil in a large frying-pan on a high heat. Put in the cucumber onions and dill seeds and stir-fry them for 2 minutes. Pour in the vinegar mixture and let it bubble. Serve the salad immediately.

Cooking time : 15 minutes

Green salads are synonymous with summer—and make the ideal side dish at any time of the year. Grow your own herbs—in a pot in the window if you have no garden. Use a variety of herbs together, as in this mixed herb salad, or a different herb each day.

20

Cabbage, Fennel and Celery Salad

Cabbage, fennel and celery make a refreshing and crunchy winter salad.

METRIC/IMPERIAL	AMERICAN
½ small white cabbage	½ small white cabbage
1 small bulb fennel weighing about 175g (6oz)	1 small Florence fennel bulb weighing about 6oz
4 sticks celery	4 stalks celery
50g (2oz) sultanas	¼ cup white raisins (muscats)
50g (2oz) chopped walnuts	½ cup chopped walnuts
60ml (4tbls) sour cream	4tbls sour cream
15ml (1tbls) cider vinegar	1tbls cider vinegar
sea salt	sea salt
freshly ground black pepper	freshly ground black pepper

Shred the cabbage and finely chop the fennel and celery. Put them into a salad bowl with the sultanas or raisins and walnuts. Beat the sour cream with the vinegar and seasonings and fold into the salad.

Cooking time : 15 minutes

† A clove of crushed garlic can also be added to the dressing.

Mixed Herb Salad

This is a salad for summer when all the herbs are fresh and tender. It is based on an old-fashioned 16th century recipe.

METRIC/IMPERIAL	AMERICAN
1 small lettuce	1 small lettuce
½ small curly endive	½ small chicory
½ small cucumber	½ cucumber
1 lemon	1 lemon
60ml (4tbls) chopped chives	4tbls chopped chives
30ml (2tbls) chopped mint	2tbls chopped mint
15ml (1tbls) chopped tarragon	1tbls chopped tarragon
10 chopped sage leaves	10 chopped sage leaves
60ml (4tbls) olive oil	4tbls olive oil
30ml (2tbls) tarragon vinegar	2tbls tarragon vinegar
sea salt	sea salt
freshly ground black pepper	freshly ground black pepper

Tear the lettuce and curly endive (chicory) into small pieces and chop the cucumber without peeling it. Cut the rind and fibre from the lemon and finely chop the pulpy flesh. Put the lettuce, endive (chicory), cucumber and lemon into a salad bowl with the herbs. Beat the oil, vinegar and seasonings together and fold them into the salad.

Cooking time : 15 minutes

† Chopped apricots may be used instead of the lemon.
† An orange may be used instead of the lemon.
† A creamy dressing, such as the one given above, may be substituted for the vinaigrette.

Savoury baked potatoes.

Mixed Root Vegetables in a Bowl

When vegetables are cooked in a closed steamer, you can be sure no flavour or goodness will escape. The vegetables soften but maintain all the strength of flavour and bulk that they had when raw. Consequently you will find that you need less than the normal amount for cooked vegetables.

METRIC/IMPERIAL	AMERICAN
125g (¼lb) carrots	1 cup carrots, grated
125g (¼lb) white turnips	1 cup white turnips, grated
125g (¼lb) swede	1 cup rutabaga, grated
little freshly grated nutmeg	little freshly grated nutmeg
30ml (2tbls) chopped parsley	2tbls chopped parsley
sea salt	sea salt
freshly ground black pepper	freshly ground black pepper
15ml (1tbls) tomato purée	1tbls tomato paste
25g (1oz) butter	2tbls butter

Grate the vegetables and put them into a large pudding bowl. Mix them together and mix in the nutmeg, parsley, seasonings and tomato paste. Bury the butter in the middle. Bring a saucepan of water to the boil, lower in the bowl and cover the pan. Steam the vegetables for 1½ hours. During the last 45 minutes stir the vegetables several times to ensure even cooking.

Cooking time : 1 hour 45 minutes

Savoury Baked Potatoes

Potatoes baked in their skins can be a delicious accompaniment to a meal; or they can be hollowed out and stuffed to make them into a light lunch or supper dish. The eggs in this recipe make the filling light-textured and fluffy. Serve the potatoes with a green salad.

METRIC/IMPERIAL	AMERICAN
4 medium-to-large baking potatoes	4 medium-to-large baking potatoes
15g (½oz) butter	1tbls butter
100g (¼lb) grated farmhouse Double Gloucester cheese	1 cup grated Longhorn or Cheddar cheese
2 eggs, beaten	2 eggs, beaten
30ml (2tbls) chopped parsley	2tbls chopped parsley
30ml (2tbls) chopped chives	2tbls chopped chives
6 chopped sage leaves	6 chopped sage leaves
30ml (2tbls) tomato purée	2tbls tomato paste
sea salt	sea salt
freshly ground black pepper	freshly ground black pepper

Heat the oven to gas mark 6 / 200°C (400°F). Scrub the potatoes, prick them twice on both sides with a fork and bake them on the oven rack for 1½ hours.
Cut a 1cm (½in) slice from the long side of each potato and scoop out the inside into a bowl. Beat in the butter, cheese, eggs, herbs, tomato paste and seasonings. Pile the filling back into the large potato shells

and put the potatoes onto a heatproof serving dish. Put the potatoes back into the oven for 20 minutes or until the filling is browned and risen.

Cooking time: 2 hours

Marrow (Summer Squash) with Nut Stuffing

Marrows or summer squash are excellent vegetables for stuffing as they have such a convenient shape. This mixed nut stuffing is well-flavoured with herbs and lemon.

METRIC/IMPERIAL	AMERICAN
1 medium-sized marrow	1 medium-sized summer
50g (2oz) almonds	squash
50g (2oz) walnuts	½ cup almonds
1 large onion	½ cup walnuts
1 clove garlic	1 large onion
60ml (4tbls) oil	1 clove garlic
100g (¼lb) fresh wholemeal	4tbls oil
breadcrumbs	3-4 cups whole grain
30ml (2tbls) chopped parsley	breadcrumbs
15ml (1tbls) chopped thyme	2tbls chopped parsley
grated rind and juice 1 lemon	1tbls chopped thyme
1 egg, beaten	grated rind and juice 1 lemon
	1 egg, beaten

Heat the oven to gas mark 6 / 200°C (400°F). Cut the top off the vegetable to make a lid and scoop out the seeds from the lid and the main part. Half fill a large saucepan with water. Bring the water to the boil, put in both halves of the vegetable and simmer for 5 minutes. Lift it out and drain it well.

Blanch and skin the almonds and grind them in a blender, food processor or clean coffee mill with the walnuts. Finely chop the onion and garlic. Heat the oil in a frying-pan on a low heat. Mix in the onion and garlic and cook them until they are soft. Take the pan from the heat and mix in the breadcrumbs, nuts, herbs, lemon rind and juice and egg. Fill the vegetable with the stuffing and replace the lid, anchoring it with cocktail sticks (picks) if necessary.

Lightly butter a large casserole and put in the stuffed vegetable. Cover it and bake for 1 hour.

Cooking time: 1 hour 30 minutes

† Any mixture of nuts, or just one type, can be used instead of the walnuts and almonds.

† For brown rice stuffing, cook 225g (½lb) or 1 cup brown rice. Fry 1 medium-sized onion and 1 garlic clove, then add the rice with 50g (2oz) or ⅓ cup chopped raisins, 50g (2oz) or ½ cup chopped almonds. Flavour with 5ml (1 tsp) cinnamon, the rind and juice 1 lemon, seasoning and 15ml (1 tbls) tomato purée (paste) and 30ml (2 tbls) chopped parsley.

Stuffing adds flavour to marrow or summer squash.

Steamed Cauliflower with Tomatoes and Hazelnuts

Plainly-steamed vegetables can be dressed with melted butter or with a sauce for a special occasion. This cauliflower is good with egg and fish dishes and, with a few extra nuts added, it can help to stretch a small main course.

METRIC/IMPERIAL	AMERICAN
1 medium-sized cauliflower	1 medium-sized cauliflower
30ml (2tbls) chopped parsley	2tbls chopped parsley
15ml (1tbls) chopped thyme	1tbls chopped thyme
225g (½lb) tomatoes	½lb tomatoes
little butter or oil for greasing	little butter or oil for greasing
50g (2oz) chopped hazelnuts	½ cup chopped hazelnuts

Break the cauliflower into small florets and put them into a vegetable steamer or colander. Scatter them with half the herbs. Scald, skin and roughly chop the tomatoes. Lightly grease a small saucepan and put in the tomatoes and the remaining herbs. Steam the cauliflower, covered, for 15 minutes. Cover the tomatoes and set them on a low heat for 3 minutes. Turn the cauliflower into a serving dish, scatter it with the hazelnuts and spoon the tomatoes over the top.

Cooking time: 20 minutes

† To make a satisfying main dish, use a large cauliflower, 450g (1lb) tomatoes and up to 275g (10oz) or 2½ cups mixed, chopped nuts.

Vegetable Curry

With the addition of creamed coconut, a dish of curried vegetables can be made into a substantial main meal. Serve the curry with a savoury rice.

METRIC/IMPERIAL	AMERICAN
1 medium-sized cauliflower	1 medium-sized cauliflower
225g (½lb) carrots	½lb carrots
2 medium-sized courgettes	2 medium-sized zucchini
2 medium-sized green peppers	2 medium-sized green bell peppers
2 medium-sized onions	2 medium-sized onions
2 cloves garlic	2 cloves garlic
4 green chillis	4 green chilli peppers
25g (1oz) fresh ginger root	2tbls fresh ginger
25g (1oz) butter	2tbls butter
5ml (1tsp) curry powder	1tsp curry powder
5ml (1tsp) ground turmeric	1tsp ground turmeric
75g (3oz) creamed coconut	1 cup canned, moist coconut
150ml (¼ pt) stock	⅔ cup stock or broth

Cut the cauliflower into small florets. Thinly slice the carrots and courgettes (zucchini). Core, and seed the peppers and cut them into 3cm (1in) strips. Thinly slice the onions and finely chop the garlic. Remove the stalks and seeds and finely chop the chillis. Peel and grate the ginger root.

Melt the butter in a saucepan on a low heat. Mix in the onion, garlic, chillis and ginger and cook them until the onions are soft. Stir in the curry powder and turmeric and cook for 1 minute more. Put in the coconut and break it up so it melts. Fold in the vegetables and pour in the stock. Cover and cook on a moderate heat for 20 minutes.

Cooking time: 40 minutes

Simple Sprouts with Garlic

Boiling is one of the simplest ways of cooking vegetables. So they cook quickly, these Brussels sprouts are thinly sliced before cooking and then flavoured with garlic.

METRIC/IMPERIAL	AMERICAN
450g (1lb) Brussels sprouts	1lb Brussels sprouts
1 clove garlic	1 clove garlic
freshly ground black pepper	freshly ground black pepper
water to barely cover	water to barely cover

Trim the sprouts and slice them 6mm (¼in) thick. Finely chop the garlic. Bring the water to the boil in a saucepan. Put in the sprouts and garlic and season with the pepper. Cover and cook gently for 10 minutes. The sprouts should still be slightly crunchy and most of the water will have been absorbed.

Cooking time: 25 minutes

Carrots with Caraway

Simmering is the best way of cooking carrots. It keeps in all their goodness and gives them a bright glaze. Caraway seeds are added here for extra flavour but, for a plainer dish, they can be omitted.

METRIC/IMPERIAL	AMERICAN
450g (1lb) carrots	1lb carrots
25g (1oz) butter	2tbls butter
10ml (2tsp) caraway seeds	2tsp caraway seeds
275ml (½ pt) stock	1¼ cups stock or broth

Thinly slice the carrots. Melt the butter in a saucepan on a low heat and stir in the carrots and caraway seeds. Pour in the stock and bring it to the boil. Cover and cook on a moderate heat for 20 minutes so all the liquid is absorbed and the carrots are slightly glazed.

Cooking time: 30 minutes

Tomato Eggplants

Aubergines or eggplants are one of the few vegetables that can be grilled (broiled) without par-boiling. These succulent, orange-red slices are gently flavoured with tomato and cinnamon. They can be served as an

accompaniment or as a course to begin a meal.

METRIC/IMPERIAL	AMERICAN
2 medium-to-large aubergines	*2 medium-to-large eggplants*
15ml (1tbls) sea salt	*1tbls sea salt*
60ml (4tbls) olive oil	*4tbls olive oil*
45ml (3tbls) tomato purée	*3tbls tomato paste*
2.5ml (½tsp) ground cinnamon	*½tsp cinnamon*
1 clove garlic, crushed with a pinch of sea salt	*1 clove garlic, crushed with a pinch of sea salt*
freshly ground black pepper	*freshly ground black pepper*

Cut the eggplants into 1cm (⅜in) slices. Put them into a colander and sprinkle them with the salt. Leave them to drain for 30 minutes. Beat the remaining ingredients together. Rinse the eggplant slices under cold water and pat them dry with absorbent paper. Brush one side of the slices with half the tomato mixture. Preheat the grill (broiler) to high. Lay the slices on the hot rack, tomato side up, and grill (broil) them close to the heat for 2 minutes. Turn them over, brush them with the remaining tomato mixture and cook them for a further 2 minutes.

Cooking time : 45 minutes

A curry sauce and creamed coconut lend interest to a variety of mixed vegetables and make them into a substantial main course dish.

Green Cabbage Simmered with Paprika and White Wine

This is a very light and fresh recipe for green cabbage.

METRIC/IMPERIAL	AMERICAN
1 medium-sized green cabbage	*1 medium-sized green cabbage*
1 clove garlic	*1 clove garlic*
25g (1oz) butter	*2tbls butter*
5ml (1tsp) paprika	*1tsp paprika*
60ml (4tbls) dry white wine	*4tbls dry white wine*

Shred the cabbage and finely chop the garlic. Melt the butter in a saucepan on a moderate heat. Stir in the paprika and then the cabbage and garlic. Pour in the wine. Cover the pan and cook on a very low heat for 10 minutes.

Cooking time : 20 minutes

Courgettes (Zucchini) Stuffed with Cheese

These courgettes (zucchini) are first simply baked wrapped in oiled foil. They can be served as an accompaniment or as a first course.

METRIC/IMPERIAL	AMERICAN
6 small-to-medium courgettes	6 small-to-medium zucchini
little oil for greasing	little oil for greasing
125g (¼lb) grated Cheddar cheese	1 cup grated Cheddar cheese
25g (1oz) wholemeal breadcrumbs	2tbls whole grain bread crumbs
15ml (1tbls) chopped thyme	1tbls chopped thyme
15ml (1tbls) chopped parsley	1tbls chopped parsley
15ml (1tbls) browned wholemeal crumbs	1tbls toasted whole grain crumbs

Heat the oven to gas mark 4 / 180°C (350°F). Lightly oil a large piece of foil. Wrap the courgettes (zucchini) in the foil and bake them for 30 minutes. When they are cooked, cut the courgettes (zucchini) in half lengthwise and scoop out the centres, leaving only thin shells. Lay the shells on a lightly-oiled ovenproof dish. Chop the vegetable flesh and put it into a bowl. Mix in the cheese, fresh crumbs and herbs and pile the mixture into the shells. Scatter the browned crumbs over the top and put the stuffed vegetables into the oven for a further 10 minutes.

Cooking time: 50 minutes

Parsnips Julienne

All varieties of root vegetables can be diced or cut into julienne sticks and baked in foil parcels. Parsnips are particularly good.

METRIC/IMPERIAL	AMERICAN
675g (1½lb) parsnips	1½lb parsnips
15g (½oz) butter	1tbls butter
30ml (2tbls) chopped parsley	2tbls chopped parsley
sea salt	sea salt
freshly ground black pepper	freshly ground black pepper

Heat the oven to gas mark 6 / 200°C (400°F). Cut the parsnips in half lengthwise and remove the cores. Cut the rest into julienne sticks of matchstick size. Thickly grease a large piece of foil with the butter. Put the parsnips on the foil, scatter them with the parsley and season lightly. Bring the edges of the foil together and fold them over several times to seal them. Lay the foil parcel on a baking sheet and put it into the oven for 45 minutes. Turn out the parsnips onto a warm serving dish.

Cooking time: 1 hour.

† Use chopped sage and thyme instead of parsley.
† Use parsnips with potatoes or carrots.
† Use a mixture of parsnips, carrots and swede (rutabaga).

Turnips Braised with Mustard and Lemon

Mustard and lemon really complement and lighten the flavour of turnips. This dish is good with plainly-roasted meat.

METRIC/IMPERIAL	AMERICAN
450g (1lb) small white turnips	1lb young turnips
15g (½oz) butter	1tbls butter
5ml (1tsp) mustard powder	1tsp dry mustard
150ml (¼ pt) stock	⅔ cup stock or broth
30ml (2tbls) chopped parsley	2tbls chopped parsley
juice of ½ lemon	juice of ½ lemon

Heat the oven to gas mark 4 / 180°C (350°F). Scrub the turnips and cut them into thin crosswise slices about 3mm (⅛in) thick. Melt the butter in a flameproof casserole or dutch oven on a low heat. Stir in the turnips, cover them and let them sweat for 10 minutes. Sprinkle in the mustard, fold it into the turnips and let everything cook gently for 1 minute. Pour in the stock and bring it to the boil. Add the parsley and lemon juice. Cover the pan and put it into the oven for 45 minutes.

Cooking time: 1 hour 5 minutes

Potato, Chives and Mustard Salad

Potato salads are always popular in the summer, especially if they are made from tiny, waxy-textured new potatoes. This one has a creamy-textured, mustard-flavoured dressing.

METRIC/IMPERIAL	AMERICAN
900g (2lb) small new potatoes	2lb small new potatoes
1 sprig mint	1 sprig mint
1 egg yolk	1 egg yolk
2.5ml (½tsp) made mustard	½tsp prepared mustard
pinch sea salt	pinch sea salt
60ml (4tbls) olive oil	4tbls olive oil
60ml (4tbls) natural yogurt	4tbls plain yogurt
60ml (4tbls) chopped chives	4tbls chopped chives

Put the potatoes on to boil with the mint sprig. Put the egg yolk into a bowl and beat in the mustard and salt. Gradually beat in the oil and then add the yogurt in a steady stream. Drain the potatoes and let them steam dry. Peel them as soon as they are cool enough to handle and cut them into 6mm (¼in) slices. Fold them into the dressing and let them cool completely. Put them into a serving bowl and scatter the chopped chives over the top.

Cooking time: 1 hour (allowing for time to cool)

† A mixture of chopped parsley and mint can be used instead of or as well as the chives.
† Spring onions (scallions) and sage make another good alternative.

Stir-fried Beans and Peppers

Stir-frying is the best way of preserving all the flavour of runner (snap) beans. They have a good, crunchy texture and glossy colour.

METRIC/IMPERIAL	AMERICAN
450g (1lb) runner beans	1lb green or snap beans
2 medium-sized green peppers	2 medium-sized green peppers
1 clove garlic	1 clove garlic
45ml (3tbls) oil	3tbls oil
30ml (2tbls) tamari sauce	2tbls Shoyu sauce

String and slice the beans. Remove stalks and seeds from the peppers and cut the peppers into pieces 5 x 3cm (¼ x 1in). Finely chop the garlic. Put the oil and garlic into a large frying-pan or wok and set them on a high heat. When the garlic begins to sizzle, put in the beans and (bell) peppers and stir them around for 1½ minutes. Add the tamari sauce and stir the vegetables around quickly. Take the pan from the heat and serve the vegetables as soon as possible.

Cooking time : 20 minutes

Spinach and Tomato Quiche

This moist and tasty quiche can be served hot with cooked vegetables and baked potatoes or cold with a salad.

METRIC/IMPERIAL	AMERICAN
shortcrust pastry made with 225g (½lb) wholemeal flour to line 23cm (9in) flan tin	1-crust pastry made with ½lb (2 cups) whole grain flour to line 9in quiche pan
700g (1½lb) spinach	1½lb spinach
5ml (1tsp) chopped rosemary	1tsp chopped rosemary
4 tomatoes	4 tomatoes
3 eggs	3 eggs
3 egg yolks	3 egg yolks
425ml (¾pt) milk	2 cups milk
sea salt	sea salt
freshly ground black pepper	freshly ground black pepper
50g (2oz) grated Gruyère cheese	½ cup grated Gruyère (Swiss) cheese
30ml (2tbls) chopped chives	2tbls chopped chives
30ml (2tbls) chopped parsley	2tbls chopped parsley

Heat the oven to gas mark 6 / 200°C (400°F). Line the flan tin (quiche pan) with the pastry. Break the stems from the spinach. Put the spinach into a saucepan with the rosemary and only the water that clings to it after washing. Cover it and set it over a low heat for 10 minutes, turning it over once. Drain the spinach well, put it onto a board and chop it finely. Scald, skin and chop the tomatoes. Beat the eggs, yolks and milk together and fold in the spinach, tomatoes, cheese, chives and parsley. Pour this filling into the pastry case and bake the quiche for 40 minutes so the filling is set and golden brown.

Cooking time : 1 hour 20 minutes

Spinach and tomatoes make a substantial filling for this quiche, which has a succulent cheese topping.

Pulses or Legumes

The large family of legumes produce beans, peas and lentils that can be preserved by drying and then reconstituted by soaking and cooking. The name pulse, which comes from the Latin 'puls' meaning porridge, is used to describe all these dried seeds. Man has been eating pulses for thousands of years, but it is only recently, as more is known about protein, that they have started to become really popular as an alternative to animal protein.

Not too long ago the only pulses (dried legumes) readily available were haricot (navy) beans, butter (or lima) beans, split peas and split red lentils. But now there are as many as 25 different varieties available—and even supermarkets are expanding their ranges. Every health food shop seems to sell different kinds. There are kidney-shaped beans: white haricot (navy) beans, red and brown kidney beans, glossy black beans, pale green and also white flageolets and the smaller, ivory beans with a black spot called black-eyed peas. Large dark-brown broad beans may be called fava beans, while creamy-coloured, large butter or lima beans are also available. Chick-peas or garbanzos are round with a slight point at one end and usually cream-coloured, though red and black are also found. The two smallest varieties are the pinky-red aduki (or adzuki or azuki) beans and the green mung (Mung or moong) beans.

Of the more unusual kinds you may find round, shiny field beans the colour of horse-chestnuts or speckly grey-pink kidney-shaped pinto peas, also called Mexican beans. Of course, there is also the superior bean of all, the soya bean, which is ivory-coloured, small and round, but becomes peanut-shaped after soaking. Every bean, as well as being a different size and shape, has also its own particular texture and flavour. Among them all, combined with all the herbs and spices you can use for flavouring, there is a wide choice of bean meals.

There are other kinds of lentils, apart from the commonly found split red type, and these are sold whole. The most commonly available are the tiny brown Chinese lentils, grey-coloured ones called puy, slightly larger, grey-green Egyptian lentils and white lentils which are sometimes used in Indian cooking. Beside these there are the split yellow and green peas.

All pulses have a high protein content. The quality of this protein can be enhanced by combining pulses with cereals products or whole grains, as their patterns of amino acids complement each other (see page 10). Therefore beans on toast or with brown rice, buckwheat or millet, or with wholemeal pasta or pancakes will provide you with an excellent protein dish.

Most beans and lentils are fairly high in carbohydrates, but soya beans contain very little. On the other hand, where the others have only a trace of fat, soya beans contain 18-22%. This fat consists mainly of polyunsaturated fats and it is also of a type which is quickly utilised by the body instead of being stored.

Minerals & Vitamins

All beans, soya beans and lentils contain the B group vitamins thiamin, riboflavin and niacin and contain significant amounts of iron, potassium and calcium.

Buying pulses

You can buy pulses in supermarkets and in health food shops and delicatessens or Indian and Middle Eastern shops where these are available. Find a shop which has a wide variety and also a quick turnover, as beans left on the shelf for too long may become tough. With this last point in mind, only buy a few weeks' supply at a time and throw any away after a year. Store all pulses in airtight containers, preferably in a cool, dark cupboard.

Cooking pulses

A dry weight of 225g ($\frac{1}{2}$lb) or $1\frac{1}{4}$ cups beans should make a very satisfying meal for four people. This may not look like very much when dry but, after soaking and cooking, they will more than double in bulk and with additional vegetables and flavourings be quite filling. Use 225-350g (8-12oz) or $1\frac{1}{4}$-2 cups lentils and split peas for four. If you are unsure of how much your family is likely to eat, try the smaller amount first and alter the amounts according to their needs the next time.

Pulses vary in the time that they need to soak and cook in order to become soft and tasty, not only between different varieties but also between batches, so it is really best to think ahead a little when you are planning a bean meal and have your main ingredient ready cooked and softened in advance. It is worth remembering that slightly over-cooked beans can be extremely palatable, but if they are under-cooked they can easily spoil a dish, no matter how carefully you otherwise prepare it. It is also a good idea to cook more beans than you need at any one time and store them in the refrigerator, so you can prepare a quick meal on another day. In a covered container they should keep for up to five days.

From the top, clockwise, are shown black-eyed peas, flageolet beans, black beans, broad or fava beans, small haricot or navy beans and speckled pinto or Mexican beans. From the bottom up are lima beans, butter beans, soya beans and red kidney beans.

A variety of pulses or dried legumes.

SOAKING AND COOKING TIMES FOR PULSES OR DRIED LEGUMES

Type	Soaking	Cooking
Aduki beans	1 hr.	30-60 mins.
Black-eyed peas	1 hr.	30-60 mins.
Black beans	3 hrs.	2 hrs.
Butter or lima beans	overnight in Thermos	3 hrs.
Chick-peas or garbanzos	overnight in Thermos	3 hrs.
Field peas	2½ hrs.	1½ hrs.
Flageolet beans	2 hrs.	2 hrs.
Haricot (navy) beans	2 hrs.	2 hrs.
Kidney beans, red	2-3 hrs.	2 hrs.
brown	2-3 hrs.	1 hr.
Lentils, red split	none	20-30 mins.
Chinese, Egyptian	none	45-60 mins.
Mung beans	1 hr.	30-45 mins.
Peas, whole dried	overnight in Thermos	3 hrs.
split yellow and green	none	45 mins.
Pinto pigeon peas	2 hrs.	1½ hrs.
Soya beans	overnight in Thermos	3 hrs.

Beans can be cooked on top of the stove, in the oven or in a presssure cooker. It all depends on your facilities. Lentils and split peas need no soaking at all and few of the beans need a long, overnight soaking. The best method is to put the beans into a saucepan and cover them with water. Cover the pan, bring them gently to the boil and simmer them for two minutes. Take the pan from the heat and leave the beans to soak. Then bring them back to the boil again and either put them into a low oven or simmer them until they are tender.

The soaking time can be speeded up by transferring the beans and the water to a wide-necked Thermos flask instead of leaving them in a saucepan. A pressure cooker will help speed the cooking time. Soak the beans first and put them into the pressure cooker with water and 30ml (2tbls) oil (this prevents foaming). The pressure cooker should be one-third to one-half full to allow for the expansion of the beans during cooking.

The cooking process for soya can be cut down by freezing the soaked beans together with their liquid. This has the added advantage of your having part-prepared beans in the freezer if there is no time to soak them overnight. Unlike the other types of beans, soya beans will always maintain a slight crispness, as they are the hardest of all.

Always cook beans in their soaking water, as this will contain some of their valuable vitamins and minerals. Use as little water as possible and keep adding extra if you feel the beans will boil dry. This ensures that very few vitamins are thrown away at the end. Any liquid left may be used in your final dish. The liquid from white (navy) beans may be added to vegetable stocks and soups, but that from brown or coloured beans will probably be too bitter. A tablespoon (15ml) of oil added when the beans are cooking will give them a richer flavour and will cut down on the foam in the pan. Never add baking soda to beans; it will speed up the cooking time but destroy vitamins. Salt and seasonings should be omitted as well, as they tend to toughen the beans. It is best to cook the beans first and add vegetables, herbs, spices and seasonings as a final stage in cooking.

Long, slow cooking makes for soft and tasty beans. The oven should be at gas mark 3/170°C (325°F), or the top of the stove turned down to a simmer. Use a heavy saucepan that will not allow the beans to cook too fast or boil dry.

Split red lentils and split peas should be cooked to a purée. To make it fairly stiff you will need 575ml (1pt) or 2½ cups water to 225g (½lb) or 1¼ cups lentils or peas. For one that is less stiff, use 725ml (1¼pt) or 3 cups liquid. You can use either stock or water for cooking lentils and split peas and, unlike beans, they benefit from being well-seasoned during cooking. A bayleaf added to the liquid also helps to improve their flavour.

The brown, grey and green whole lentils will not cook to a purée, but they soften very quickly. Use 575ml (1pt) or 2½ cups water or stock to 225g (½lb) or 1¼ cups lentils, season them and add a bayleaf. Bring them to the boil and simmer them gently for 1 hour by which time all the liquid will be absorbed and the lentils will be completely tender.

Adding flavourings

When your beans are cooked, you can add all the flavourings and vegetables that will turn them into a satisfying dish. Soften a large, sliced onion in a saucepan in 60ml (4tbls) oil, stir in the beans, spices such as paprika and cinnamon and some chopped herbs. Cover and simmer for about 15 minutes. Diced vegetables such as carrots or celery can be softened with the onion; Worcestershire or tamari (Shoyu) sauce can be added for extra flavour and so can lemon or orange juice or tomato purée or paste. A few chopped pickles will lighten the flavour of a bean dish. These can be capers, gherkins, dill pickles or green or black olives. Soya beans are best made into a casserole in a similar way to meat and cooked in the oven. All beans can be folded into a vinaigrette dressing to make a salad for a first or a main course.

Whole lentils can be flavoured in the same ways as beans. Stiff purées of red lentils or split peas can be made into patties and croquettes with finely-diced vegetables and flavourings such as curry powder or cayenne pepper. You can also beat in 90ml (6tbls) vinaigrette dressing to 225g (½lb) or 1¼ cups weight (before cooking) lentils or chick-peas to make a pleasant, light-tasting salad, which can be flavoured with chopped herbs and eaten cold with diced tomatoes and a green salad.

Serving beans

Beans can be served simply with wholemeal (whole grain) bread, pasta or brown rice, or they can be made into more substantial dishes. Put them into pies or pasties, roll them in wholemeal (whole grain) or buckwheat pancakes or make them into shepherd's pies with a thick layer of creamed potatoes on top. Puréed lentils or split peas can be mixed with a juicy vegetable such as tomatoes and made into open quiches.

If you have any beans left over, they can be pressed through a strainer or blended with stock to make tasty soups or puréed and mixed with a little lemon juice, wine vinegar or chopped pickles to make a sandwich spread.

Beans do not have to be cooked alone. Used half and half with meat they can make delicious, thick casseroles and stews.

Sprouting beans

Dried beans contain no vitamin C at all, but if they are sprouted they will yield jars full of nutritional sprouts high in vitamin C and other vitamins and also far lower in carbohydrates than the original beans. Sprouted beans and seeds can be used in salads and the larger ones can be stir-fried and used in oriental-style dishes. Most varieties of beans and whole lentils can be sprouted, but the most popular for this process are the tiny green mung beans which produce the familiar bean sprouts used by the Chinese. Special types of seed such as alfalfa and fenugreek are also sold for sprouting and the method is the same.

You can buy special sprouting jars and containers but these are not essential. All you need is a jam jar or honeypot (a 900g (2lb) jar is best for beans), a piece of cheesecloth to cover the top, a rubber band, a shallow china or earthenware dish and a large, brown paper bag.

Put 30ml (2tbls) beans into the jar, cover the top with cheesecloth and secure it with the band. Fill the jar with warm water, rinse the beans and drain them. Cover them with warm water again and leave them to soak for 24 hours. Drain them and rinse again and pour off all the rinsing water. Put the jar on its side in the dish and put the dish into the paper bag. Leave the sprouts in a warm place and rinse them every morning and evening. They will take between five days and a week to grow, depending on the type of bean.

The beans will make thicker, sturdier sprouts than lentils. Mung beans will grow to between 4-6cm (1½-2½in) long, soya beans and kidney beans to about 3cm (1in), chick-peas to about 2cm (¾in) and lentils to about 3cm (1in).

Soya beans

Soya beans (soy) form the base for many products which are invaluable in vegetarian and vegan (non-dairy) diets and which find a place in the kitchen of the meat-eating wholefood eater as well.

Soy sauce is probably the best-known soya product. It is common on Chinese restaurant tables and can be used with great effect as a flavouring in a great many dishes. Many of the commercial soya sauces that are available are made from soya bean extract and caramel.

Tamari (Shoyu) sauce, which is available from most health food shops is the original, Japanese type of soya sauce. It is made from whole fermented soya beans and sea salt and has a much rounder, fuller flavour than the other kind. Even if you do not always cook in a wholefood way, you will find that tamari sauce is far superior. Tamari, is from whole soya beans, and 30ml (2tbls) added to any dish will raise the protein level, as well as improving the flavour. It is particularly good with all kinds of beans and also with rice and nuts. A very little added to a basic vinaigrette will make a tasty and nutritious salad dressing.

Miso is another product made from whole, fermented soya beans, sea salt and, in some kinds, whole grains such as barley or brown rice. It is a concentrated thick paste, high in protein and containing B vitamins with a flavour similar in many ways to beef extract.

There are several types of miso, but hacho miso, which is thick and dark and made only from soya beans is the one most readily available. Mugi miso, from soya beans and barley is a lighter colour and slightly less salty in flavour. Kome is made from soya beans and white rice and is very salty. Genmai is from soya beans and brown rice and is slightly sweet. Hacho and mugi are recommended for a first trial of the product. Americans can use Dr Bronner's balanced soya mineral bouillon.

Miso is generally sold in small plastic bags, so you can cut off the corner and squeeze out the contents. Store it in a cool, dry place. Miso is very concentrated and so only a very little added to a vegetable soup or a vegetable or bean casserole will improve the flavour and add to the protein content. To obtain the maximum goodness, cook the dish first and add the miso only at the last minute.

Textured Vegetable Protein (TVP) is an extremely processed product of the soya bean, extensively used as a meat extender or substitute. It often contains artificial colouring and flavouring and deserves no place in a natural food diet. Its texture and flavour are not very pleasant either, to lovers of good food.

Soya flour is made from ground, dried soya beans. It is a creamy yellow colour with a nutty flavour. It does not possess the rising properties of whole grain flours but up to 25% soya (soy) flour can be used in bread and other dough and pastry recipes with great success. The flavour is hardly changed but the bread will contain a significant amount of protein. Add slightly more salt to the recipe and bake the bread at a slightly lower temperature, as soya flour has a tendency to burn after a short time. For those on a vegan diet, or even just for a change in any natural food diet, soya flour can be made into thick sauces without milk, eggs or dairy products.

Tofu or soy bean curd: if you look around a Chinese shop you are likely to find squares of a white, cheese-like substance which is referred to as tofu or 'the meat without bones'. This is soya (soy) bean curd or soya cheese. It has a fairly bland flavour eaten just as it is, but if it is mixed into stir-fried dishes with tamari and other flavourings, it can be made into a very tasty, high protein dish. You may also find thin sheets of bean curd skin which is the dried bean curd. It is used mainly in Chinese recipes.

Soya milk: for a vegan (one who eats no dairy produce) or for anyone allergic to cow's milk, a soya milk is also available. It is sold in cans, is almost indistinguishable from real milk and can be used in exactly the same ways. The flavour, like the flour, is slightly nutty.

Soya bean oil: the valuable oils of the soya beans are extracted and can be bought from wholefood shops. If it is unrefined it has a deep, amber colour. It is high in polyunsaturated fats, but it has a slightly fishy flavour and is definitely an acquired taste. In America, soya butter is also available. It is made from soya (soy) flour and is a light, golden spread which is used in the same way as peanut butter.

Soya grits or soya splits are made from cooked, cracked soya beans and save you the trouble of soaking and cooking the bean. Soya splits are larger than the grits and can be used instead of white beans in a recipe. They need no soaking and cook in 45 minutes. Soya grits have been ground into granules and, when cooked, become light and fluffy. They are excellent for making patties and croquettes. Cook 225g (½lb) or 1¼ cups soya grits for 45 minutes in 575ml (1pt) or 2½ cups stock, either on top of the stove or in a low oven.

RECIPES

Black Bean Soup

This soup is thick and dark and suitable for a main course. The rum and sour cream give a rich flavour, but for family meals the rum (or both) could be omitted.

METRIC/IMPERIAL	AMERICAN
225g (½lb) black beans	½lb black beans
up to 1.1L (2pt) stock	up to 4¾ cups stock or broth
225g (½lb) carrots	½lb carrots
4 sticks celery	4 sticks celery
2 large onions	2 large onions
1 bayleaf	1 bayleaf
30ml (2tbls) tomato purée	2tbls tomato paste
1 clove garlic, crushed with a pinch sea salt	1 clove garlic, crushed with a pinch of sea salt
60ml (4tbls) dark rum	4tbls dark rum
150ml (¼pt) soured cream	⅔ cup dairy sour cream

Put the beans into a saucepan with 575ml (1pt) or 2½ cups water and bring to the boil. Cover them and simmer them for 2 minutes. Turn off the heat and leave them for 2 hours.

Strain the beans and measure the bean liquid. Make it up to 1.4L (2½pt) or 6¼ cups with stock. Finely chop the carrots, celery and onion. Put them into a large saucepan with the beans, liquid, bayleaf and bouquet garni. Stir in the tomato paste and garlic. Bring the soup to the boil, cover and simmer for 2 hours or until the beans are completely tender.

Remove the bayleaf and bouquet garni. Blend half the soup or press it through a strainer. Then stir it into the remaining soup with the garlic, rum and sour cream. Reheat to serve but do not boil.

Cooking time : 4 hours 15 minutes

Add rum and sour cream to black beans to make soup.

Light Lentil Soup

Recipes using pulses or dried beans do not have to be thick and heavy. This lentil soup has a light texture and light, spicy flavour and is ideal to begin a meal.

METRIC/IMPERIAL	AMERICAN
125g (¼lb) red lentils	¾ cup red lentils
1 large onion	1 large onion
45ml (3tbls) oil	3tbls oil
5ml (1tsp) ground cumin	1tsp ground cumin
6 cloves	6 cloves
850ml (1½pt) stock	3¾ cups stock or broth
1 clove garlic, crushed with a pinch sea salt	1 clove garlic, crushed with a pinch sea salt
1 bayleaf tied with 2 thinly pared strips lemon rind	1 bayleaf tied with 2 thinly pared strips lemon rind
4 slices lemon	4 slices lemon

Finely chop the onion. Heat the oil in a saucepan on a low heat. Mix in the onion, cumin and cloves and cook them until the onion is golden. Stir in the lentils and cook them for 1 minute. Pour in the stock and bring it to the boil. Add the garlic, bayleaf and lemon rind and simmer, covered, for 45 minutes. Discard the bayleaf and lemon rind. Pour the soup into bowls and float a slice of lemon on top of each one.

Cooking time : 1 hour 5 minutes

Haricot Bean or Flageolet and Gherkin Salad

Haricot beans or flageolets make a delicately-flavoured salad to be served as the beginning of a meal.

METRIC/IMPERIAL	AMERICAN
225g (½lb) haricot beans, cooked	1¼ cups flageolets, cooked
2 large pickled Hungarian gherkins	2 large dill pickles
30ml (2tbls) sunflower oil	2tbls sunflower oil
15ml (1tbls) white wine vinegar	1tbls white wine vinegar
50g (2oz) grated Farmhouse Cheddar cheese	½ cup grated, aged Cheddar cheese
1 clove garlic, crushed with a pinch sea salt	1 clove garlic, crushed with a pinch of sea salt
freshly ground black pepper	freshly ground black pepper
1 small lettuce	1 small lettuce
4 tomatoes	4 tomatoes

Finely chop the gherkins and put them into a bowl with the beans. Beat the oil, vinegar, cheese, garlic and pepper together and fold them into the beans. Arrange a bed of lettuce leaves on 4 small plates and pile the beans on top. Garnish them with the tomatoes, cut into quarters.

Cooking time : 15 minutes

† The cheese can be omitted and 15ml (1tbls) tamari (Shoyu) sauce added to the dressing instead.

Stir-fried Cucumbers and Soya Bean Curd

METRIC/IMPERIAL	AMERICAN
350g (¾lb) tofu	about 1 cup tofu (soya bean curd)
½ medium-sized cucumber	½ cucumber
1 medium-sized onion	1 medium-sized onion
1 clove garlic	1 clove garlic
30ml (2tbls) oil	2tbls oil
5ml (1tsp) ground ginger	1tsp ground ginger
60ml (4tbls) sherry	4tbls sherry
30ml (2tbls) tamari sauce	2tbls tamari (Shoyu) sauce

Cut the tofu (beancurd) and cucumber into 1cm (½in) dice. Finely chop the onion and garlic. Heat the oil and garlic in a frying-pan on a high heat. When the garlic begins to sizzle, put in the onion and stir-fry it for 1 minute. Mix in the cucumber and cook for 1 minute more. Mix in the tofu and ginger and lower the heat. Add the sherry and tamari (Shoyu) sauce and cook gently for 1½ minutes. Serve as soon as possible.

Cooking time : 15 minutes

Brown Lentils and Mushrooms in Red Wine

Brown lentils are good with wholewheat pasta as they are very small and easily take the place of a Bolognese sauce. The olives, herbs and red wine complete the Italian flavour.

METRIC/IMPERIAL	AMERICAN
225g (½lb) brown Chinese or Puy lentils	1¼ cups brown Chinese lentils
225g (½lb) mushrooms	½lb mushrooms
2 medium-sized onions	2 medium-sized onions
1 clove garlic	1 clove garlic
10 green olives	10 green olives
45ml (3tbls) oil	3tbls oil
150ml (¼pt) dry red wine	⅔ cup dry red wine
30ml (2tbls) chopped thyme	2tbls chopped thyme
30ml (2tbls) chopped marjoram	2tbls chopped marjoram
30ml (2tbls) chopped parsley	2tbls chopped parsley
sea salt	sea salt
freshly ground black pepper	freshly ground black pepper

Simmer the lentils in lightly-salted water for 45 minutes and drain them. Finely chop the mushrooms, onions and garlic. Stone and quarter the olives.
Heat the oil in a saucepan on a low heat. Stir in the onions and garlic and cook them until they are soft. Raise the heat, stir in the mushrooms and cook them for 2 minutes. Lower the heat again and stir in the lentils, olives and herbs. Pour in the wine and bring it to the boil. Cover and simmer gently for 5 minutes.

Cooking time : 1 hour

Hummus is a chick-pea dip.

Hummus

Hummus is a Middle Eastern speciality made from puréed chick-peas, tahini (sesame seed paste), olive oil and lemon juice. These ingredients are used in varying amounts according to taste but the combination gives a light flavour and texture. Serve it as a dip with wholemeal (whole grain) bread or with a burghul (bulgar) salad. It can also be used as a spread for sandwiches and in smaller quantities, garnished with tomatoes as a first course.

METRIC/IMPERIAL	AMERICAN
225g (½lb) chick-peas, cooked until soft	1½ cups chick-peas, cooked until soft
150ml (¼pt) cooking liquid	⅔ cup cooking liquid
juice 2 lemons	juice 2 lemons
90ml (6tbls) tahini	6tbls tahini
30ml (2tbls) olive oil	2tbls olive oil
2 cloves garlic, crushed with a pinch sea salt	2 cloves garlic, crushed with a pinch of sea salt
freshly ground black pepper	freshly ground black pepper
30ml (2tbls) chopped parsley	2tbls chopped parsley
5ml (1tsp) paprika	1tsp paprika

Pass the chick-peas through a food mill and beat in the cooking liquid. Gradually beat in the lemon juice, tahini, oil, garlic and pepper. Spoon the hummus into a serving dish or bowl and chill it. Just before serving sprinkle the parsley and paprika over the top.

Cooking time : 30 minutes plus extra for chilling.

† To give a nutty flavour and interesting texture to hummus, toast 25g (1oz) or 1 tablespoon sesame seeds in an open pan until they brown. Cool them and mix them into the chick-peas purée.

Miso and Vegetable Soup

Serve this miso soup in large bowls and accompany it with wholemeal (whole grain) bread and a light salad. It is very tasty and full of nutritious, lightly-cooked vegetables and contains all the necessary protein.

METRIC/IMPERIAL	AMERICAN
350g (¾lb) carrots	¾lb carrots
6 sticks celery	6 stalks celery
2 large onions	2 large onions
½ medium-sized green cabbage	½ medium-sized green cabbage
60ml (4tbls) oil	4tbls oil
30ml (2tbls) wholemeal flour	2tbls whole grain flour
30ml (2tbls) tomato purée	2tbls tomato paste
1.4L (2½pt) stock	6¼ cups stock or broth
1 clove garlic	1 clove garlic
bouquet garni	bouquet garni
30ml (2tbls) hacho miso	2tbls hacho miso
30ml (2tbls) chopped parsley	2tbls chopped parsley

Finely dice the carrots, celery and onions and shred the cabbage. Heat the oil in a large saucepan on a low heat. Stir in the carrots, celery and onions, cover them and cook them gently for 10 minutes. Stir in the flour and cook it for 1 minute. Stir in the tomato paste. Stir in the stock and bring it to the boil. Crush the garlic without salt and add it to the soup with the bouquet garni. Simmer, uncovered for 10 minutes. Put in the cabbage and simmer for five minutes more. Remove the bouquet garni.

Put the miso into a bowl and gradually work in 120ml (8tbls) of the soup, so you have a smooth paste. Take the soup from the heat and stir in the miso paste and parsley. Serve in large bowls, immediately.

Cooking time: 35 minutes

Black-eyed Peas and Red (Bell) Peppers

This quickly-prepared dish of black-eyed peas is based on the stir-frying method of cooking. It is excellent with brown rice.

METRIC/IMPERIAL	AMERICAN
225g (½lb) black-eyed peas, cooked until soft	1¼ cups black-eyed peas, cooked until soft
2 medium-sized red peppers	2 medium-sized red bell peppers
2 medium-sized onions	2 medium-sized onions
1 large clove garlic	1 large clove garlic
45ml (3tbls) white wine vinegar	3tbls white wine vinegar
30ml (2tbls) tomato purée	2tbls tomato paste
5ml (1tsp) Barbados sugar	1tsp brown or Barbados sugar
45ml (3tbls) oil	3tbls oil
5ml (1tsp) paprika	1tsp paprika

Remove the stalks and seeds and finely chop the (bell) peppers. Finely chop the onions and garlic. Mix the wine vinegar, tomato paste and sugar together.

Heat the oil and garlic in a frying-pan on a high heat. When the garlic sizzles, put in the peppers and onions. Stir them around on the heat for 2 minutes. Mix in the beans and paprika and cook them for 2 minutes more. Pour in the vinegar mixture, mix it in well and let it bubble. Take the pan from the heat.

Cooking time: 15 minutes

† Cooked brown or red kidney beans also work well on this recipe.

Red Lentil and Tomato Quiche

Red lentils and fresh tomatoes make a moist filling for a quiche. The basil is essential for flavouring, so if no fresh basil is available use half the amount of dried.
The baked cheese topping gives the quiche an attractive appearance and also lends an element of surprise. When cut, the interior is a long way from the conventional custard filling!

METRIC/IMPERIAL	AMERICAN
shortcrust pastry made with 100g (¼lb) wholemeal flour	pie pastry for a single-crust 8in pie, made with whole grain flour
225g (½lb) split red lentils	1¼ cups split red lentils
1 large onion	1 large onion
1 clove garlic	1 clove garlic
45ml (3tbls) oil	3tbls oil
575ml (1pt) stock	2½ cups stock or broth
1 bayleaf	1 bayleaf
sea salt	sea salt
freshly ground black pepper	freshly ground black pepper
225g (½lb) tomatoes	½lb tomatoes
30ml (2 tbls) chopped basil	2tbls chopped basil
15ml (1tbls) chopped thyme	1tbls chopped thyme
15ml (1tbls) chopped parsley	1tbls chopped parsley
50g (2oz) Cheddar or Gruyère cheese, grated	½ cup grated Cheddar or Swiss (Gruyère) cheese

Quarter and thinly slice the onion and finely chop the garlic. Heat the oil in a saucepan on a low heat. Mix in the onions and garlic and cook them until they are golden. Stir in the lentils and cook them for 1 minute. Pour in the stock and bring it to the boil. Add the bayleaf and season well. Cover and simmer gently for 45 minutes so the lentils cook to a thick purée.
Scald, skin and roughly chop the tomatoes. Put them into a saucepan with the herbs, cover them and set them on a low heat. Cook them for 15 minutes so they are soft and pulpy. Gradually beat the tomatoes into the cooked lentils.
Heat the oven to gas mark 6/200°C (400°F). Roll out the pastry and line a 20cm (8in) diameter flan ring (quiche pan), and bake it lined with foil and beans for 10 minutes and for a further 10 minutes without the lining. Put the lentil mixture into the pastry shell and scatter the cheese on top. Return the quiche to the oven for 20 minutes.

Cooking time: 1 hour 10 minutes

Spiced Chick-peas

This spicy dish of chick-peas can be served as a main course with brown rice or with chapattis made from wholemeal (whole grain) flour. An Indian mango chutney and a yogurt seasoned with a little ground paprika are the best accompaniments. It is equally good served in small bowls, either hot or cold and with yogurt spooned over the top, to start a meal.

METRIC/IMPERIAL	AMERICAN
225g (½lb) chick-peas, cooked until soft	1¼ cups chick-peas, cooked until soft
2 medium-sized onions	2 medium-sized onions
2 cloves garlic	2 cloves garlic
60ml (4tbls) oil	4tbls oil
10ml (2tsp) cumin seeds	2tsp cumin seeds
10ml (2tsp) ground coriander	2tsp ground coriander
5ml (1tsp) ground turmeric	1tsp ground turmeric
10ml (2tsp) ground paprika	2tsp ground paprika
1.5ml (¼tsp) cayenne pepper	¼tsp cayenne pepper
150ml (¼pt) cooking liquid	⅔ cup cooking liquid
15ml (1tbls) tomato purée	1tbls tomato paste
30ml (2tbls) chopped mint	2tbls chopped mint
150ml (¼pt) natural yogurt	⅔ cup plain yogurt

Finely chop the onions and garlic. Heat the oil in a saucepan on a low heat. Stir in the onions, garlic and spices and cook them until the onions are soft. Stir in the chick-peas and tomato paste. Pour in the cooking liquid and bring it to the boil. Cover and simmer gently for 30 minutes. Serve with the chopped mint scattered over the top accompanied by a bowl of yogurt.

Cooking time : 45 minutes

Chick-peas eaten with a whole grain food as such chappatis, make a balanced protein meal.

Soya and lentil patties.

Soya and Lentil Patties

Soya grits and lentils make patties with a light and fluffy texture. Serve them with a green salad and baked potatoes for a light lunch or an evening meal.

METRIC/IMPERIAL	AMERICAN
4 large celery sticks	4 large stalks celery
2 medium-sized onions	2 medium-sized onions
1 clove garlic	1 clove garlic
60ml (4tbls) oil	4tbls oil
125g (¼lb) soya grits	½ cup soya grits
125g (¼lb) split red lentils	½ cup split red lentils
575ml (1pt) stock	2½ cups stock or broth
bouquet garni	bouquet garni
5ml (1tsp) curry powder	1tsp curry powder
sea salt	sea salt
freshly ground black pepper	freshly ground black pepper
60ml (4tbls) chopped mixed herbs	4tbls chopped mixed herbs
1 egg, beaten	1 egg, beaten
about 50g (2oz) dried whole-meal breadcrumbs	about ¾ cup dry, whole grain bread crumbs
oil for shallow frying	oil for shallow frying

Finely chop the vegetables and garlic. Heat the oil in a saucepan on a low heat. Stir in the vegetables and garlic, cover and cook gently for 10 minutes. Stir in the soya grits and lentils and cook, stirring, for 2 minutes. Add the stock, bouquet garni and curry powder and season well. Bring the stock to the boil, cover and simmer gently for 45 minutes until all the liquid is absorbed and you have a light, fluffy purée containing distinguishable pieces of chopped vegetable. Take the pan from the heat, beat in the herbs and let the mixture cool.

Form the mixture into 12 patties about 2cm (¾in) thick. Coat them in beaten egg and then in breadcrumbs. Heat the oil in a frying-pan on a moderate heat. Put in the patties and fry them until they are golden brown on both sides.

Cooking time : 1 hour 30 minutes

Creamy Lima or Butter Bean Salad

With a light, creamy dressing, lima or butter beans can be made into a delicate-flavoured salad. These quantities will make a main course, but they can all be halved for a smaller portion to start a meal.

METRIC/IMPERIAL	AMERICAN
225g (½lb) butter beans, cooked until soft	1¼ cups dried lima or butter beans, cooked until soft
2 hard-boiled eggs	2 hard-cooked eggs
30ml (2tbls) olive oil	2tbls olive oil
10ml (2tsp) Dijon mustard	2tsp Dijon-style mustard
30ml (2tbls) tarragon vinegar	2tbls tarragon vinegar
sea salt	sea salt
freshly ground black pepper	freshly ground black pepper
150ml (¼pt) double cream	⅔ cup heavy cream
grated rind ½ lemon	grated rind ½ lemon
30ml (2tbls) chopped parsley	2tbls chopped parsley

Peel the eggs, rub the yolks through a sieve and finely chop the whites. Gradually work the oil into the yolks, drop by drop as though you were making mayonnaise. Beat in the mustard and then the vinegar, 10ml (2tsp) at a time. Season lightly and gradually beat in the cream and lemon rind. Fold the beans into the dressing and leave them for 30 minutes for the flavours to combine. Fold in the egg whites and scatter the parsley over the top just before serving.

Preparation time : 50 minutes

† Extra hard-boiled eggs can be added for garnish and the salad can be served on a bed of lettuce, surrounded by tomatoes, cucumber and cooked beetroot (beets).
† The dressing may also be used for haricot or flageolet beans and chick-peas.

Green Pea Salad

Although split peas are usually made into thick soups and stews, a change of ingredients and method can make them into a light salad. This one, set in a ring mould, is decorative and appealing. Its appearance can also be varied from occasion to occasion by changing the filling.

METRIC/IMPERIAL	AMERICAN
225g (½lb) split green peas	½lb (1¼ cups) split green peas
575ml (1pt) water	2½ cups water
60ml (4tbls) olive oil plus a little for greasing	4tbls olive oil, plus a little for greasing
60ml (4tbls) white wine vinegar	4tbls white wine vinegar
8 large spring onions, chopped	8 large scallions, chopped
60ml (4tbls) chopped mint	4tbls chopped mint
30ml (2tbls) chopped parsley	2tbls chopped parsley
1 clove garlic crushed with a pinch sea salt	1 clove garlic, crushed with a pinch sea salt
freshly ground black pepper	freshly ground black pepper
mint sprigs or sliced tomatoes for serving	mint sprigs or sliced tomatoes for garnish

Put the split peas into a saucepan with the water and bring them to the boil. Cover them and simmer them for 45 minutes or until you can beat them to a smooth purée.
Cool the peas completely and beat in the oil, vinegar, onions, herbs, garlic and pepper. Press the mixture into a lightly-oiled, 18 or 20cm (7 or 8in) ring or savarin mould and turn it onto a flat plate. Fill the centre with a bunch of mint or, for a contrast in colour, some sliced tomatoes.

Cooking time : 1 hour 10 minutes

Aduki Bean Pie

Wholemeal (whole grain) pastry and beans cooked together will provide you with well-balanced protein. This pie contains delicate-flavoured aduki beans with cinnamon, ginger, herbs and tamari (Shoyu) sauce.

METRIC/IMPERIAL	AMERICAN
225g (½lb) aduki beans, cooked until soft	1¼ cups aduki beans, cooked until soft
2 medium-sized onions	2 medium-sized onions
1 clove garlic	1 clove garlic
4 large sticks celery	4 large stalks celery
30ml (2tbls) oil	2tbls oil
2.5ml (½tsp) ground ginger	½tsp ground ginger
5ml (1tsp) ground cinnamon	1tsp cinnamon
juice 1 lemon	juice 1 lemon
30ml (2tbls) tamari sauce	2tbls tamari (Shoyu) sauce
6 chopped sage leaves	6 chopped sage leaves
15ml (1tbls) chopped thyme	1tbls chopped thyme
30ml (2tbls) chopped parsley	2tbls chopped parsley
shortcrust pastry made with 175g (6oz) wholemeal flour	pie pastry for double-crust (8in) pie made with whole grain flour
beaten egg or milk for glaze	beaten egg or milk for glaze

Heat the oven to gas mark 6/200°C (400°F). Finely chop the onions, garlic and celery. Heat the oil in a saucepan on a low heat. Stir in the vegetables and garlic, cover them and let them sweat for 10 minutes. Stir in the ginger and cinnamon and cook, stirring for 1 minute. Stir in the beans, lemon juice, tamari and herbs. Cover and simmer for 2 minutes.
Roll out two-thirds of the pastry and line a 20cm (8in) flan ring (quiche or tart pan) or pie plate. Put in the beans and cover the top with the remaining pastry. Brush with beaten egg or milk and bake the pie for 40 minutes.

Cooking time : 1 hour 40 minutes

Shrimp Fu Yung

Bean sprouts are often used with eggs in Chinese cookery to make a dish called a Fu Yung. With prawns or shrimp as well they make a deliciously light main dish.

METRIC/IMPERIAL	AMERICAN
225g (1pt) boiled prawns, unshelled	½lb boiled shrimp, unshelled
8 eggs	8 eggs
30ml (2tbls) tamari sauce	2tbls Shoyu sauce
2 medium-sized onions	2 medium-sized onions
1 clove garlic	1 clove garlic
45ml (3tbls) oil	3tbls oil
½ x 900g (2lb) jar sprouted mung beans	½ x 2lb jar sprouted mung beans

Shell and clean the prawns (shrimp). Beat the eggs with the tamari (Shoyu) sauce. Finely chop the onions and garlic. Heat the oil in a large frying-pan on a high heat. Mix in the onions, garlic and bean sprouts and stir-fry them for 1 minute. Add the prawns (shrimp) and stir in the eggs and cook, folding the mixture continuously, until the eggs are set. Serve as soon as possible with a savoury rice.

Cooking time : 15 minutes

Minced (Ground) Beef and Red Beans

Red kidney beans, minced (ground) beef and red bell peppers are used here to make a dish similar to the Mexican chili con carne.

METRIC/IMPERIAL	AMERICAN
125g (¼lb) red kidney beans, cooked until soft	½ cup red kidney beans, cooked until soft
reserved cooking liquid	reserved cooking liquid
up to 275ml (½pt) stock	up to 1¼ cups stock or broth
2 medium-sized red peppers	2 medium-sized red bell peppers
2 medium-sized onions	2 medium-sized onions
1 large clove garlic	1 large clove garlic
450g (1lb) minced beef	1lb ground beef or hamburger
10ml (2tsp) paprika	2tsp paprika
2.5ml (½tsp) cayenne pepper	½tsp cayenne pepper
juice ½ lemon	juice of ½ lemon
30ml (2tbls) chopped coriander or parsley	2tbls chopped coriander or parsley

Measure the cooking liquid from the beans and make it up if necessary with stock to 275ml (½pt) or 1¼ cups. Remove the stalks and seeds and finely chop the peppers. Finely chop the onions and garlic.

Heat the oil in a large saucepan or large frying-pan on a low heat. Mix in the onions and garlic and cook them until they are soft. Raise the heat to high and mix in the beef. Break it up well with a wooden spoon and stir it about until it browns. Mix in the paprika, cayenne pepper, beans, red peppers and lemon juice. Pour in the stock and bring it to the boil. Cover the pan, lower the heat and simmer for 45 minutes. Serve with a savoury rice or pasta.

Cooking time: 1 hour 15 minutes

Below: a steaming casserole of beef and red beans.

Chick-peas add extra protein to this beef casserole.

Beef and Chick-pea Casserole

Beef and chick-peas make a thick, colourful and hearty stew that is deliciously lightened in flavour by the lemon juice.

METRIC/IMPERIAL	AMERICAN
125g (¼lb) chick-peas, soaked and cooked for 1 hour	¾ cup chick-peas, soaked and cooked for 1 hour
450g (1lb) shin of beef	1lb boneless beef (chuck, round, shoulder, arm)
1 large onion	
1 clove garlic	1 large onion
350g (¾lb) tomatoes	1 clove garlic
30ml (2tbls) oil	¾lb tomatoes
5ml (1tsp) paprika	2tbls oil
5ml (1tsp) ground cinnamon	1tsp paprika
10ml (2tsp) wholemeal flour	1tsp cinnamon
15ml (1tbls) tomato purée	2tsp whole grain flour
275ml (½pt) stock	1tbls tomato paste
juice 1 lemon	1¼ cups stock or broth
15ml (1tbls) chopped savory	juice 1 lemon
15ml (1tbls) chopped thyme	1tbls chopped savory
sea salt	1tbls chopped thyme
freshly ground black pepper	sea salt
	freshly ground black pepper

Heat the oven to gas mark 3/170°C (325°F). Cut the beef into 3cm (1in) cubes. Quarter and thinly slice the onion and finely chop the garlic. Scald, skin and roughly chop the tomatoes.

Heat the oil in a large, flameproof casserole or dutch oven on a high heat. Put in the pieces of beef, brown them well and remove them. Lower the heat, mix in the onions and garlic and cook them until they are soft. Stir in the spices and flour and cook them for ½ minute. Stir in the tomato paste and then the stock. Bring the stock to the boil and add the lemon juice and herbs. Add the beef, chick-peas and tomatoes. Bring everything to the boil again, cover the pan and put it into the oven for 2 hours: the dish will keep for ½ hour.

Cooking time: 2 hours 20 minutes

Soya Bean and Eggplant Casserole

With aubergines (eggplants), tomatoes and a green bell pepper, soya beans make a delicious and colourful casserole that is best cooked in an oven-to-table dish.

METRIC/IMPERIAL	AMERICAN
225g (½lb) soya beans, soaked and simmered for 3 hours	1¼ cups soya beans, soaked and simmered for 3 hours
450g (1lb) aubergines	1 large egg plant
10ml (2 tsp) sea salt	2tsp sea salt
225g (½lb) tomatoes	½lb tomatoes
1 medium-sized green pepper	1 medium-sized green bell pepper
2 medium-sized onions	
1 clove garlic	2 medium-sized onions
5ml (1tsp) turmeric	1 clove garlic
45ml (3tsp) boiling water	1tsp turmeric
60ml (4tbls) oil	3tbls boiling water
juice 1 lemon	4tbls oil
	juice 1 lemon

Heat the oven to gas mark 4 / 180°C (350°F). Cut the aubergines into 1cm (¾in) slices and layer them in a colander with the salt. Leave them for 30 minutes to drain. Scald, skin and roughly chop the tomatoes. Core, seed and dice the pepper. Thinly slice the onions and finely chop the garlic. Put the turmeric into the boiling water and leave to infuse.

Rinse and dry the aubergines (eggplants). Heat 30ml (2tbls) of the oil in a frying-pan on a moderate heat. Put in the aubergine (eggplant) slices, brown them quickly and remove them. Lower the heat and add the remaining oil. Put in the pepper, onion and garlic and cook them until they are soft. Mix in the beans, tomatoes, turmeric and lemon juice. Transfer the mixture to a casserole and arrange the aubergine (eggplant) slices on top. Put the casserole into the oven for 20 minutes.

Cooking time : 1 hour

Soya Bread

Soya and wholemeal (whole grain) flours together make a moist, slightly sweet, close-textured loaf with a predominantly wheaty flavour. Keep it in a very dry place as it has a tendency to become mouldy quickly under adverse conditions.

METRIC/IMPERIAL	AMERICAN
25g (1oz) fresh or 15g (½oz) dried yeast	1oz cake compressed yeast or 2tbls dry yeast granules
15ml (1tbls) honey	1tbls honey
350ml (12floz) warm water	1½ cups warm water
450g (1lb) wholemeal flour	1lb whole grain flour
100g (¼lb) soya flour	1 cup soya flour
15ml (1 tbls) sea salt	1tbls sea salt
30ml (2 tbls) soya or another good-quality oil	2tbls soya or another good-quality oil

If you are using fresh yeast, put it into a bowl and

cream it with the honey and water and use within 5 minutes. If using dried yeast, dissolve the honey in the water and sprinkle the yeast on top. Leave the yeast in a warm place until frothy, about 10 minutes. Mix the wholemeal and soya flours and salt in a bowl and make a well in the centre. Pour in the yeast and oil and mix everything well. Turn the dough onto a floured worktop and knead it until it is smooth. Return it to the bowl. Either cover the bowl with a clean cloth or put it into a large plastic bag. Put it into a warm place for 1 hour or until the dough doubles in bulk.

Heat the oven to gas mark 4 / 180°C (350°F). Knead the dough again and divide it between two 450g (1lb) loaf tins (3-cup pans). Put the loaves on top of the oven to rise for 15-30 minutes or until the dough rises 1cm (½in) above the edge of the tin (pan). Bake the loaves for 50 minutes and turn them onto a wire rack to cool.

Cooking time : 2 hours 30 minutes

† For a darker bread, substitute 15ml (1tbls) treacle or molasses for the honey.

Soya Brown Sauce

This sauce will transform lightly-steamed vegetables into a cheap and quickly-prepared main dish, to be served with brown rice or pasta. The amounts given here are for 450g (1lb) vegetables.

METRIC/IMPERIAL	AMERICAN
45ml (3tbls) oil	3tbls oil
15ml (1tbls) wholemeal flour	1tbls whole grain flour
45ml (1tbls) soya flour	1tbls soya flour
275ml (½pt) vegetable or meat stock	1¼ cups vegetable or meat stock or bouillon
60ml (4tbls) tamari sauce	4tbls Shoyu sauce
sea salt	sea salt
freshly ground black pepper	freshly ground black pepper

Heat the oil in a saucepan on a moderate heat. Stir in the wholemeal (whole grain) and soya flour and cook them, stirring, for 5 minutes or until they are a rich brown. Bring the stock to the boil and stir it quickly into the roux in the saucepan. Simmer gently, stirring for 5 minutes. Stir in the tamari (Shoyu) sauce and season to taste.

Cooking time : 15 minutes

† This sauce is the basic recipe. Flavourings that can be added include: juice ½ lemon; 30ml (2tbls) Worcestershire sauce; 15ml (1tbls) tomato purée or paste.
† Add 2.5ml (½tsp) ground ginger just before adding the stock.
† Cook 1 crushed garlic before adding the flour and then continue with any of the variations.
† To make a main dish, lightly steam 450g (1lb) or 2½-3 cups cooked vegetables, either of one kind or mixed, and coat them in the sauce.

Wheat & Rice

Wheat and rice are the two main staples of the world's diet, wheat in the West and rice in the East. Both, in their most natural form, contain B vitamins, protein and iron and have an outer coating which can provide much of the essential fibre in our diet. However, both wheat and rice undergo vast changes in their journey from the field to the shop counter. Instead of whole grains that are full of flavour, we can be offered soggy white bread and rice that cooks quickly; both offer less good value in terms of nutrition.

Wheat

Although a wheat grain is very tiny, it is full of goodness. Round the outside is the husk or skin, which we call bran and this provides the fibre. Inside the husk are the endosperm and the germ. The endosperm makes up 90% of the grain. It is white and consists mainly of starch. The tiniest portion of the wheat grain, amounting to only 2% of the whole kernel, is the germ which contains all the important vitamins and minerals and is therefore the most valuable part.

Contained in the germ are most of the vitamins in the B group, a large amount of vitamin E, essential mineral salts such as calcium, potassium, iron, copper, and magnesium and a little fat. There is also far more protein than there is in the endosperm.

A wheat grain, however tiny, is a complete and balanced food in itself. It contains starch for energy, vitamins and minerals in the right proportion to help us utilize that starch correctly and also bran to help it pass through our digestive systems. If anything is taken away or anything added then the whole balance is upset and we will not be able to obtain the maximum goodness. It is obvious wholewheat products are better for us, they are easy to use and, what is more, they taste far better than any of the white flour products.

Flours: unfortunately, only a small percentage of the world's wheat is ground to make what is called wholemeal, wholewheat or whole grain flour. The rest is ground on large roller mills. First the bran is extracted and is either used as animal food or is sold back to us again as an expensive 'health' product. The germ of

the wheat is also removed. This is mostly for economic reasons as the fat, as soon as the wheat is ground, starts to go rancid. The miller, the retailer, and the housewife as well require what is known as 'shelf life', that is, a product which will not go off quickly. Inevitably, any parts likely to decay are removed so that flour can be stored for long periods.

Freshly-milled flour containing no bran or germ is not the pure white that we expect, but a light, creamy colour. In order to achieve the marketable whiteness it has to be bleached. The main bleaching agent used today is chlorine dioxide which is added to the flour in a sealed gas chamber and destroys any remaining vitamin E as well as bleaching. No chemical is left in the flour at the end of the process, but the remaining product is reduced in nutritional value. The germ is meanwhile sold again as an expensive health food product.

In order to try and regain the nutritional balance, certain things have, by law in most countries, to be added back to the flour. Two B vitamins, thiamin and nicotinic acid, are replaced, but it is questionable how effective they are in the absence of the rest. Iron is added, in a form that is not easily absorbed; the other additive is powdered chalk. This was thought to help the absorption of iron but it alters the calcium: phosphorus ratio—in wholemeal (whole grain) flour it is 1:10 and in white 1:0.5. How much simpler it would be if everyone ate wholemeal (whole grain) flour!

The choice of flours and breads on the market can be quite bewildering. The names wholemeal, whole-wheat and whole grain are usually interchangeable. They refer to flour made from the whole of the wheat grain. Stone-ground means that the flour was milled in the old-fashioned way between two mill-stones, a

process which is said to retain more nutritional goodness. This is called graham flour in the US, and is of either whole grain or U.S. whole wheat (85%) type. Organically-grown flour has been milled from wheat that was grown without chemicals. The types of wheat in Great Britain generally have a lower gluten content than those grown in the U.S. or Canada. High gluten is thought to be essential for making bread rise well, so in Britain you will find special types of flour, often called 'strong' flour, sold for bread-making, and these may contain imported wheat. In the United States all-purpose or plain flours are used for bread-making.

Wholemeal (whole grain) flour can be used with great success to make bread, scones (biscuits), cakes and pastry, but if a lighter effect is required you can obtain 81% or 85% wheatmeal flours which contain all the germ of the wheat but from which the coarse bran has been removed. If you have never used wholemeal flour before, these wheatmeal types are ideal to start experimenting with and you can gradually progress to the 100% flours. Always remember when you buy wholemeal (whole grain) or wheatmeal (whole wheat) flours that the vitamin E may start to go rancid after about four weeks. It is best, therefore, to buy little and often, rather than in bulk.

Strong, unbleached bread flour is flour milled from high gluten wheat which has had the bran and germ removed but which has not been bleached. It has a far better flavour than ordinary white flour, but should not really be regarded as a health food product.

Bread flour, bread mixes and breads labelled simply 'brown' are not 100% wholemeal (whole grain). At best they are the 81% or 85% wheatmeal types and at worst they are white flours and bread which have been coloured.

Bran-enriched and germ-enriched breads are breads

to which bran or wheatgerm has been added during baking. They may or may not have been made from wholemeal flour—the best are. The worst are made from white flour which may or may not have been coloured and which has the other ingredients added. Far better for you are the wholemeal (whole grain) flours and loaves which have all the ingredients naturally in the right proportions.

Granary flour, although it can look quite coarse, is made from wheatmeal flour and added to it are whole grains of wheat and rye which have been malted, that is first sprouted then toasted. It makes a very tasty bread. Provided that you obtain enough fibre from other sources, it is a very good occasional purchase on the natural food shopping list. This is difficult to obtain in America, though there is a wheat germ flour that is slightly toasted.

Wheat bran: if you eat 150g (5oz) wholemeal bread a day you will be getting the right amount of fibre in your diet. If you think that you need more fibre, then you can buy bags of bran from health food shops, supermarkets, small grocers or delicatessens and chemists (drug stores). You can add a few large spoonfuls to your bread or soda bread recipe, sprinkle it over cereals, mix it into nut and meat loaves and into crumble (crumb) toppings. You can even mix it into fruit juice and drink it.

Wheatgerm: the other part of the wheat grain, the germ, is also sold separately. It is packed full of protein, B vitamins, vitamin E and minerals and when fresh it has a sweet, nutty flavour. Buy a small amount and keep it in an airtight jar in a cool place to make sure you always get the maximum goodness. You can also buy 'stabilised' wheatgerm under specific brand names. It is not quite such a natural product, but it will be far better than untreated germ which has been allowed to go rancid. Like bran, wheatgerm can be spooned over breakfast cereals. If you add it to bread and cake mixes it gives a delicious sweet flavour as well as extra goodness. It is also good stirred into yogurt and sprinkled over a compote of dried fruits and you can mix it into crushed crumbs for a cheesecake base, into crumble (crumb) toppings and over gratin dishes.

Whole wheat grains: you will probably find that your whole or health food shop will also sell whole wheat grains. If you have a grain mill, either electrically or hand-operated, then you will be able to grind these to produce your own flour. Used directly after it is ground, the flour will retain the maximum amount of vitamin E and the bread will have a delicious moist texture and nutty flavour.

Wheat grains can also be cooked and used as an accompaniment to the main meal. Better still, use them for a sweet dish such as the old English frumenty, because they have such a sweet flavour. They are exceptionally hard and should be cooked in water very slowly overnight. When cooked, they will be round and plump. For a savoury dish, add some chopped herbs and a softened onion to the cooked grains.

Wheat sprouts: you can also produce highly nutritious sprouts from wheat grains in exactly the same ways that are used for sprouting beans and seeds (see Pulses or Legumes). The wheat will retain its vitamins and minerals but the carbohydrate count will be less. Wheat sprouts will also contain vitamin C, one vitamin absent from the original grain. Wheat sprouts should not be left to grow long, but are at their most nutritious when the sprout is the same length as the grain.

Sprouted wheat can be used, like rice or potatoes, as the accompaniment to the main meal. It can also be mixed into salads, form the base of a nutritious main dish or mixed into biscuit (cookie) and bread recipes. You can also make your own granary-type flour from malted wheat. Spread a 450g (1lb) jar of sprouted wheat on a baking sheet and toast it in a moderate oven for 20 minutes. Let the wheat cool completely and store it

Wholemeal macaroni and pasta shapes are shown here with a variety of natural foods for balanced meals.

in an airtight jar. When you make bread, add 45ml (3tbls) of this malted wheat to 450g (1lb) flour. You can also use a mixture of wheat and rye grains.

Cracked wheat or kibbled wheat is also available from whole or health food shops. It consists simply of the whole wheat grain coarsely ground into large coarse pieces. The grains can be soaked and cooked to be served as an accompaniment or a few spoonfuls can be added to bread doughs to make a loaf with a bulky texture. Kibbled or cracked wheat is most often used as a decorative topping for wholemeal (whole grain) loaves and rolls.

Burghul or bulgar wheat, also called bulgur or tabbouleh, is used mainly in Middle Eastern countries. It is made by soaking wheat grains and then toasting them until they crack. Burghul (bulgar) wheat, therefore, needs little or no cooking. One of the most popular, and one of the most delicious, ways of serving it is in a salad. The wheat must be soaked first in cold water for 20-30 minutes and then drained and squeezed dry. It is then mixed with a vinaigrette or lemon salad dressing and preferably left for another 15 minutes or longer. The salad can be served as an accompaniment in place of rice or potatoes. Alternatively add chopped vegetables to it and serve the dish on its own. With the addition of diced meat or some grated cheese, it will make a complete light meal. Burghul (bulgar) wheat can also be cooked in a casserole to make a hot dish.

Wholemeal pasta: not too long ago, wholefood lovers of pasta had either to make their own, use the white kinds once in a while, or go without completely. Now the situation has changed considerably. You can buy not only whole wheat spaghetti, but also pasta rings, macaroni and lasagne. All of these cook just as quickly as the white kinds and can be used in exactly the same ways. Pasta is made from a special hard, high protein wheat called **durum wheat** which is grown mainly on the plains of the United States and Canada.

Wholemeal semolina: durum wheat is also the only wheat suitable for making semolina, which is a coarsely-ground flour. Wholemeal semolina is also available. It makes delicious milk puddings, that are far more flavoursome than those made from white semolina. It can also be used for salads in a similar way to burghul (bulgar) wheat. For salads the semolina is best not soaked first, but mixed with the dressing and left to stand for about 30 minutes before any further ingredients are added.

Rice

Brown rice is really the rice equivalent of whole wheat —it retains its germ and bran husk. Like wheat, it contains a considerable amount of protein, a little fat, most of the B vitamins but in particular thiamin and nicotinic acid, large amounts of phosphorus, potassium and iron and some calcium. White rice is made by polishing the rice grains to remove the outer husk, and as in the production of white flour, much of the goodness is lost. Polishing does away with up to half the mineral content, a little protein, some fat and nearly all the B vitamins, together with most of the fibre.

In the United States white rice, like white flour, is in some cases 'enriched': that is thiamin is put back artificially. But again, as the B vitamins work together, it is questionable how good this is. Obviously the rice would be far better if it was not polished in the first place.

Whereas white rice can be tasteless if it is not served with spicy meat dishes, brown rice has a definite flavour of its own. It also has a firmer, more chewy, texture and there is less chance of it becoming soggy and sticking together in a mass through careless cooking.

There are two types of brown rice available, long-grain and short-grain. Long-grain rice is usually only used to make soups, casseroles and main dishes, but short-grain rice can be used in sweet dishes too. There is little difference in flavour and texture, but on the whole, short-grain rice has a lighter flavour and the grains tend to remain more separate, even if they are cooked for a long time. In terms of buying and storing, it is probably most convenient to buy short-grain rice and use it for all your rice dishes. Both kinds of brown rice will keep for up to six months without losing their nutritive value, so you can safely buy it in bulk and store it in a dry container. Either kind of rice can be used in all the savoury dishes below.

The other distinction between the types of brown rice is whether or not it has been organically grown. Some whole or health food shops sell only organic rice and others will offer you a choice. In general, the organically grown is slightly more expensive.

Cooking rice: both long- and short-grain types of rice are easy to cook, although they take longer than polished white rice. If you are boiling rice, bring a pan of lightly-salted water to the boil, scatter in the rice— 225g (½lb) or 1 cup for 4 people. Stir the rice, cover and simmer for around 45 minutes. Some types need only 35-40 minutes, so bite a piece at this stage to see if it is done. When cooked, it should be soft but still slightly chewy. After boiling, the rice should be drained and immediately rinsed with cold water to stop the cooking process. It can then be tossed in butter or oil, mixed with chopped herbs or a softened onion or fried.

To make a richer dish, to which you can add flavours as it cooks, the rice can be steamed. Melt 30ml (2tbls) butter or heat 60ml (4tbls) oil in a saucepan on a low heat. Stir in the rice and cook it for 1 minute. Pour in 575ml (1pt) or 2½ cups water or stock, season and bring it to the boil. Cover the rice and simmer it very gently for 45 minutes without uncovering the pan. Turn off the heat and let the rice stand for 10 minutes. All the liquid will have been absorbed, the rice will cook in its own steam and be moist and glossy. An onion can be softened in the butter before you add the rice. You can also add chopped herbs, spices such as paprika and turmeric or Worcestershire or tamari (Shoyu) sauce.

If more convenient, brown rice started off by frying can also be transferred to a moderate oven after the liquid has come to the boil. Cover it, bake it for 45 minutes and then leave it standing for 10 minutes. Flaked almonds and dried fruits are excellent additions to baked rice. The baked dish will be slightly richer in flavour than if it were cooked on top of the stove.

RECIPES

Tomato Burghul (Bulgar)

This recipe can be served either on its own for a light lunch, or a prelude to a meal or to accompany cold meats and egg dishes.

METRIC/IMPERIAL	AMERICAN
225g (½lb) burghul wheat	about 2 cups bulgar wheat
10 spring onions	10 scallions
60ml (4tbls) chopped parsley	4tbls chopped parsley
60ml (4tbls) chopped mint	4tbls chopped mint
90ml (6tbls) olive oil	6tbls olive oil
juice ½ lemon	juice ½ lemon
1 clove garlic, crushed with a pinch sea salt	1 clove garlic, crushed with a pinch sea salt
freshly ground black pepper	freshly ground black pepper
450g (1lb) tomatoes, plus 4 extra for garnish if required	1lb tomatoes, plus 4 extra for garnishing if desired
1 small lettuce (optional)	1 small head lettuce (optional)

Soak the wheat in cold water for 30 minutes. Drain it, squeeze it dry and put it into a bowl. Chop the onions and mix them into the wheat with the parsley and mint. Beat the oil, lemon juice, garlic and pepper together and fold them into the wheat. Leave the wheat for 30 minutes to pick the flavour.

Roughly chop the 450g (1lb) tomatoes and fold them into the wheat just before serving. Either serve the salad directly from the bowl or pile it onto a bed of lettuce leaves and surround it with the remaining tomatoes, cut into quarters.

Cooking time : 1 hour 20 minutes

Tomatoes are combined with burghul (bulgar) wheat to make this colourful and substantial salad.

Sprouted Wheat with Green Peppers

Sprouted wheat dishes are full of goodness which need no lengthy cooking process which could destroy it. This dish can be served hot or cold, depending on the main dish.

METRIC/IMPERIAL	AMERICAN
175g (6oz) sprouted wheat	1-1½ cups sprouted wheat
2 medium-sized green peppers	2 medium-sized green bell peppers
1 large onion	1 large onion
60ml (4tbls) olive oil	4tbls olive oil
30ml (2tbls) white wine vinegar	2tbls white wine vinegar
1 clove garlic, crushed with a pinch sea salt	1 clove garlic, crushed with a pinch sea salt
freshly ground black pepper	freshly ground black pepper

Rinse and drain the wheat. Core, seed and finely chop the (bell) peppers. Quarter and thinly slice the onion. Heat the oil in a saucepan on a low heat. Mix in the onion and cook it until it is beginning to look transparent. Mix in the peppers, cover and cook for 5 minutes. Mix the vinegar with the garlic and pepper. Fold the wheat into the saucepan, cover and let it heat through for 1 minute. Pour in the vinegar mixture, let it bubble and take the pan from the heat.
Either serve immediately or let the wheat cool completely.

Cooking time: 20 minutes

Pasta and Mushroom Salad

Pasta shapes can make very cheap and tasty first courses. This salad contains succulent raw mushrooms, flavoured with Parmesan cheese and a selection of herbs.

METRIC/IMPERIAL	AMERICAN
125g (¼lb) wholemeal pasta shapes	¼lb wholewheat pasta shapes
125g (¼lb) button mushrooms	¼lb (about 1 cup) small mushrooms
8 green olives	8 green olives
15ml (1tbls) chopped thyme	1tbls chopped thyme
15ml (1tbls) chopped marjoram	1tbls chopped marjoram
30ml (2tbls) olive oil	2tbls olive oil
15ml (1tbls) white wine vinegar	1tbls white wine vinegar
1 clove garlic, crushed with a pinch sea salt	1 clove garlic, crushed with a pinch sea salt
freshly ground black pepper	freshly ground black pepper
30ml (2tbls) grated Parmesan cheese	2tbls grated Parmesan cheese

Simmer the pasta shapes in lightly-salted water until they are tender—up to 10 minutes. Drain them and run cold water through them. Leave them until they are completely cold.
Thinly slice the mushrooms. Stone (pit) and quarter the olives. Mix the mushrooms, olives and herbs with the pasta. Beat the oil, vinegar, garlic and pepper together and fold it into the salad. Fold in the cheese and let the salad stand for 30 minutes before serving so the mushrooms will absorb a little of the dressing.

Cooking time: 1 hour (including marinating)

Mushroom Pizza

This pizza comes out of the oven large and bubbling. The moist mushroom and tomato filling sinks deliciously into the dough.

METRIC/IMPERIAL	AMERICAN
For the pizza base:	**For the pizza base:**
15g (½oz) fresh yeast or 10g (¼oz) dried yeast	½oz compressed yeast or 2tsp dried yeast granules
2.5ml (½tsp) Barbados sugar	½tsp brown or Barbados sugar
90ml (6tbls) warm water	6tbls warm water
225g (½lb) wholemeal flour	½lb (2 cups) whole grain flour
5ml (1tsp) sea salt	1tsp sea salt
1 egg, beaten	1 egg, beaten
For the topping:	**For the topping:**
30ml (2tbls) olive oil	2tbls olive oil
175g (6oz) flat mushrooms	6oz flat mushrooms
50g (2oz) button mushrooms	2oz button mushrooms
225g (½lb) tomatoes	½lb tomatoes
12 green olives	12 green olives
6 anchovy fillets	6 anchovy fillets
15ml (1tbls) chopped basil	1tbls chopped basil
15ml (1tbls) chopped thyme	1tbls chopped thyme
sea salt	sea salt
freshly ground black pepper	freshly ground black pepper
175g (6oz) Mozzarella cheese	6oz Mozzarella cheese
1 medium-sized green pepper	1 medium-sized green bell pepper
15ml (1tbls) chopped savory	1tbls chopped parsley
1 clove garlic	1 clove garlic 1 onion
1 onion	

If you are using fresh (compressed) yeast, crumble it into a bowl and cream it with the sugar and half the water. If using dried yeast, dissolve the sugar in half the water and sprinkle the yeast on top; put the yeast in a warm place to froth for about 10 minutes.
Put the flour and salt into a bowl and make a well in the centre. Pour in the yeast mixture and the remaining water and mix everything together with a flat-bladed knife. Turn the dough onto a well-floured work surface and knead it until it is smooth. Put it into a large plastic bag and leave in a warm place for 1 hour to rise. Finely chop the flat mushrooms and thinly slice the button mushrooms, keeping them separate. Finely chop the onion and garlic. Scald, skin and finely chop the tomatoes. Stone (pit) and chop the olives. Finely chop the anchovies. Heat the oil in a frying-pan over low heat. Mix in the onion and garlic and cook them until they are soft. Raise the heat to moderate, add the chopped, flat mushrooms and cook them, stirring, for 2 minutes. Mix the mushrooms and onions with the tomatoes, olives, anchovies and herbs. Season lightly. Thinly slice the Mozzarella. Remove the stalks and seeds and cut the peppers into rings.

Heat the oven to gas mark 6 / 200°C (400°F). Knead the dough again and roll it out to a large circle about 6mm (¼in) thick. Lay it on a large baking sheet and fold over about 1cm (½in) all around to make a thick edge. Spread the mushroom and tomato mixture over the dough. Lay the cheese on top and decorate it with the sliced button mushrooms and the rings of pepper. Scatter the parsley over the top.

Put the pizza on top of the stove for 10 minutes to rest, then bake it for 30 minutes. Serve it hot.

Cooking time : 1 hour 45 minutes

Wholemeal (whole grain) flour makes an unusual base for this decorative **mushroom, pepper and Mozzarella pizza.**

Brown Rice with Vegetable Mould

This substantial rice salad will make a meal in itself for four people or it can accompany a cold meat or egg dish and be enough for six.

METRIC/IMPERIAL	AMERICAN
225g (½lb) long-grain brown rice	1¼ cups long-grain brown rice
1 medium-sized aubergine weighing around 225g (½lb)	1 medium-sized eggplant weighing around ½lb
10ml (2tsp) sea salt	2tsp sea salt
1 large red pepper	1 large red bell pepper
2 large sticks celery	2 large stalks celery
4 firm tomatoes	4 tomatoes
1 large onion	1 large onion
1 large clove garlic	1 large clove garlic
60ml (4tbls) olive oil	4tbls olive oil
5ml (1tsp) paprika	1tsp paprika
oil for greasing	oil for greasing
8 flat mushrooms	8 flat mushrooms
15ml (1tbls) dry white wine	1tbls dry white wine
For the cabbage salad:	**For the cabbage salad:**
½ medium-sized green cabbage	½ medium-sized green cabbage
2 sticks celery	2 stalks celery
30ml (2tbls) olive oil	2tbls olive oil
15ml (1tbls) white wine vinegar	1tbls white wine vinegar
1 clove garlic, crushed with a pinch sea salt	1 clove garlic, crushed with a pinch sea salt
freshly ground black pepper	freshly ground black pepper

Simmer the rice in lightly salted water for 45 minutes. Drain it, refresh it with cold water and drain it again. Put it into a bowl.

Cut the aubergine (eggplant) into 1cm (½in) dice and put it into a colander. Sprinkle it with the salt and leave it for 30 minutes to drain. Rinse it through with cold water and pat it dry with absorbent paper.

Remove the stalk and seeds and cut the pepper into strips 6mm x 3cm (¼ x 1in). Chop the celery into 1cm (½in) dice. Scald, skin and chop the tomatoes and finely chop the onion and garlic.

Heat 45ml (3tbls) of the oil in a frying-pan on a low heat. Mix in the celery, onion and garlic and cook them until the onion is soft but not coloured. Mix in the aubergine (eggplant), pepper and paprika, cover and cook for a further 10 minutes. Mix in the tomatoes, cover again and cook for 5 minutes. Take the pan from the heat and mix all the contents into the rice. Fry the mushrooms on a high heat in the remaining oil for 1 minute. Add the wine and immediately take the pan from the heat.

Lightly oil an 18cm (7in) diameter soufflé dish. Arrange the mushrooms in an attractive pattern in the bottom black side down. Put the rice mixture on top and press it down evenly. Chill the mould for at least 6 hours and turn it onto a flat plate.

To make the cabbage salad, finely shred the cabbage and chop the celery. Put them together in a bowl. Beat the remaining ingredients together to make the dressing and fold it into the cabbage and celery. Put a little of the salad around the rice mould and serve the rest separately.

Left: brown rice and vegetable mould is served in a ring of cabbage salad.

Cooking time: 1¼ hours plus 6 hours for chilling

Steamed Rice with Tamari (Shoyu)

Tamari sauce adds protein and extra flavour to a glossy dish of steamed brown rice.

METRIC/IMPERIAL	AMERICAN
225g (½lb) brown rice	1¼ cups brown rice
1 small onion	1 small onion
1 clove garlic	1 clove garlic
575ml (1pt) stock	2½ cups stock or broth
60ml (4tbls) tamari sauce	4tbls Shoyu sauce
pinch sea salt	pinch sea salt

Halve and thinly slice the onion. Finely chop the garlic. Heat the oil in a saucepan on a low heat. Mix in the onion and garlic and cook them until they are just beginning to soften. Stir in the rice and cook it for 1 minute. Pour in the stock and bring it to the boil. Add the tamari (Shoyu) and salt. Cover and simmer for 45 minutes. Turn off the heat and let the rice rest for a further 10 minutes.

Cooking time: 1 hour 5 minutes

Sprouted Wheat Kedgeree

Cooked quickly with hard-boiled eggs, sprouted wheat becomes a main meal. This is an original variation of kedgeree, of Anglo-Indian origin, which is usually a dish of rice and hard-boiled eggs.

METRIC/IMPERIAL	AMERICAN
450g (1lb) jar sprouted wheat	1lb jar sprouted wheat
1 bunch watercress	1 bunch watercress
225g (½lb) tomatoes	½lb tomatoes
8 hard-boiled eggs	8 hard-cooked eggs
30ml (2tbls) white wine vinegar	2tbls white wine vinegar
5ml (1tsp) Dijon mustard	1tsp Dijon-style mustard
25g (1oz) butter	2tbls butter
50g (2oz) currants	⅓ cup currants or raisins

Rinse and drain the wheat. Chop the watercress. Cut the tomatoes in half lengthwise and thinly slice them. Chop the eggs fairly coarsely. Mix the vinegar and mustard together.

Heat the butter in a large frying-pan or paella pan on a moderate heat. Put in the wheat and stir it for 1 minute. Mix in the watercress, tomatoes, eggs and currants or raisins and heat them through for about ½ minute, so the watercress does not wilt too much and the tomatoes stay firm. Pour in the vinegar mixture, let it bubble and mix everything together well. Serve immediately.

Cooking time: 15 minutes

Rice and Peanut Casserole

This all-in-one rice dish is excellent for a family main meal. All you need to go with it is a large, mixed salad.

METRIC/IMPERIAL	AMERICAN
225g (½lb) brown rice	1¼ cups brown rice
225g (½lb) carrots	½lb carrots
1 large onion	1 large onion
60ml (4tbls) oil	4tbls oil
575ml (1 pt) stock	2½ cups stock or broth
sea salt	sea salt
freshly ground black pepper	freshly ground black pepper
30ml (2tbls) chopped parsley	2tbls chopped parsley
15ml (1tbls) chopped marjoram	1tbls chopped marjoram
15ml (1tbls) chopped thyme	1tbls chopped thyme
30ml (2tbls) Worcestershire sauce	2tbls Worcestershire sauce
grated rind and juice 1 lemon	grated rind and juice 1 lemon
125g (¼lb) grated Farmhouse Cheddar cheese	1 cup grated aged Cheddar cheese
175g (6oz) unroasted peanuts	about ¾ cup fresh peanuts

Heat the oven to gas mark 4/180°C (350°F). Finely chop the carrots and onion. Heat the oil in a flameproof casserole or dutch oven on a low heat. Stir in the carrots and onion, cover them and let them sweat for 10 minutes. Stir in the rice. Pour in the stock and bring it to the boil. Season and add the herbs, Worcestershire sauce and lemon juice. Cover the pan and put it into the oven for 45 minutes.

Take the rice from the oven and fork in the cheese. Mix in the peanuts, cover the rice again and set aside for 10 minutes.

Cooking time: 1 hour 5 minutes

Mung Bean Biriani

Pulses (dried legumes) and brown rice are the perfect protein combination to give you an authentic Indian-style meal every bit as nutritious as a meat one.

METRIC/IMPERIAL	AMERICAN
225g (½lb) mung beans	½lb mung beans
2 medium-sized onions	2 medium-sized onions
4 cloves garlic	4 cloves garlic
1 large potato	1 large potato
4 tomatoes	4 tomatoes
60ml (4tbls) oil	4tbls oil
5ml (1tsp) ground turmeric	1tsp turmeric
2.5ml (½tsp) cayenne pepper	½tsp cayenne pepper
5ml (1tsp) ground cumin	1tsp ground cumin
5ml (1tsp) ground coriander	1tsp ground coriander
225g (½lb) brown rice	1¼ cups brown rice
soaking water from the beans, made up to 850ml (1½pt) with stock	water from soaking the beans, made up to 3¾ cups with stock or broth
pinch sea salt	pinch sea salt
juice 1 lemon	juice 1 lemon
extra tomatoes for garnish	extra tomatoes for garnishing

Put the mung beans into a saucepan with 575ml (1pt) or 2½ cups water. Cover them, bring them to the boil and simmer them for 2 minutes. Turn off the heat and soak the beans for 1 hour.

Finely chop the onion and garlic. Scrub the potato and cut it into 1cm (½in) dice. Scald, skin and roughly chop the tomatoes.

Heat the oil in a saucepan on a low heat. Stir in the onions and garlic and cook them until they look transparent. Stir in the spices and cook them until the onions are soft. Drain the beans and stir them into the pan with the rice, potatoes and tomatoes. Stir them over the heat for 5 minutes. Make the cooking liquid up with stock, pour it into the pan and bring it to the boil. Cover and simmer gently for 40 minutes.

for a filling dish to go with it. Burghul (bulgar) salad also makes a first course salad.

METRIC/IMPERIAL	AMERICAN
225g (½lb) burghul wheat	about 2 cups bulgar wheat
60ml (4tbls) olive oil	4tbls olive oil
juice 1 lemon	juice 1 lemon
1 clove garlic, crushed with a pinch sea salt	1 clove garlic, crushed with a pinch sea salt
freshly ground black pepper	freshly ground black pepper
16 black olives plus extra for decoration	16 black olives, plus extra for decoration
60ml (4tbls) chopped parsley	4tbls chopped parsley
heart 1 small lettuce	heart of 1 small lettuce
2 tomatoes	2 tomatoes
1 cucumber	1 cucumber

Soak the wheat in cold water for 30 minutes. Drain it and squeeze it dry. Beat the oil, lemon juice, garlic and pepper together. Fold the dressing into the wheat and leave for 30 minutes. Stone (pit) and quarter the olives and add them to the wheat with the chopped parsley. Shred the lettuce and thinly slice the tomatoes and cucumber. Put the burghul (bulgar) onto a large plate and surround it with the lettuce, tomatoes and cucumber. Garnish with more olives if desired.

Cooking time : 1 hour 15 minutes

Brown Rice with Mushrooms, Lemon and Cress

Slightly sharp ingredients, added before serving, can often greatly enhance the flavour of brown rice. Lemon, mushrooms and cress make this into a delicious accompanying dish.

METRIC/IMPERIAL	AMERICAN
225g (½lb) brown rice	1¼ cups brown rice
100g (¼lb) mushrooms	¼lb (1 cup) mushrooms
1 lemon	1 lemon
1 large onion	1 large onion
1 clove garlic	1 clove garlic
25g (1oz) butter or 60ml (4tbls) oil	2tbls butter or 4tbls oil
	1 jar sprouted alfalfa seeds
2 boxes salad cress	

Simmer the rice in lightly-salted water for 40 minutes. Drain it, refresh it with cold water and drain it again. Thinly slice the mushrooms. Cut away the rind and white fibre or pith from the lemon and chop the flesh very finely. Finely chop the onion and garlic. Melt the butter in a frying-pan on a low heat. Put in the onion and cook it until it is soft. Mix in the mushrooms and continue cooking until the onion is brown. Raise the heat to high and fork in the rice. When it has heated through, mix in the lemon and cut in the cress or watercress. Allow them to just heat through, then serve immediately.

Cooking time : 1 hour

Mung beans and brown rice make an unusual biriani.

Turn off the heat and quickly stir in the salt and lemon juice. Cover again and leave the pan standing for 15 minutes.
Serve with a tomato salad and garnish with extra tomato slices if desired.

Cooking time : 2 hours

Burghul (Bulgar) Salad with Olives

With olives and herbs, burghul makes a plain dish, best served as an accompaniment to cold meats and quiches. As it is quite substantial, there is no need

Steamed Rice with Onions

In this recipe the onion used to flavour the rice is chopped and softened in stock, instead of oil. This simple change gives a more pronounced flavour.

METRIC/IMPERIAL	AMERICAN
1 medium-sized onion	1 medium-sized onion
575ml (1pt) stock	2½ cups stock or broth
225g (½lb) brown rice	1¼ cups brown rice
pinch sea salt	pinch sea salt
freshly ground black pepper	freshly ground black pepper

Finely chop the onion. Put a quarter of the stock into a saucepan and bring it to the boil. Add the onion, cover and simmer for 10 minutes. Stir in the rice and stir it for 1 minute. Pour in the remaining stock and bring it to the boil. Season, cover and simmer for 45 minutes. Turn off the heat and let the rice rest for a further 10 minutes.

Cooking time: 1 hour 10 minutes

Lamb and Tomato Burghul (Bulgar)

Burghul (bulgar) wheat can be cooked as well as being simply soaked. It goes particularly well with rich meats such as lamb.

METRIC/IMPERIAL	AMERICAN
575-675g (1¼-1½lb) lean, boneless shoulder of lamb	1¼-1½lb lean, boneless shoulder of lamb
350g (¾lb) tomatoes	¾lb tomatoes
2 large onions	2 large onions
1 large clove garlic	1 large clove garlic
120ml (8tbls) oil	8tbls oil
5ml (1tsp) ground cumin	1tsp cumin
30ml (2tbls) tomato purée	2tbls tomato paste
425ml (¾pt) stock	2 cups stock or broth
juice ½ lemon	juice ½ lemon
225g (½lb) burghul wheat	1¼ cups bulgar wheat
30ml (2tbls) chopped mint	2tbls chopped mint

Cut the lamb into 2cm (¾in) cubes. Scald and skin the tomatoes and cut them into wedges. Finely chop the onions and garlic.
Heat 60ml (4tbls) of the oil in a large saucepan on a high heat. Put in the meat, in two batches if necessary, brown it then remove it. Add the onions and garlic to the pan, and cook them until they are just beginning to soften. Stir in the cumin and cook for 1 minute more. Stir in the tomato paste. Pour in the stock and bring it to the boil. Add the meat and lemon juice. Cover and simmer for 1 hour.
While the meat is cooking, heat the rest of the oil in a large pan on a low heat. Mix in the burghul (bulgar) and stir it on the heat for 10 minutes. Add the wheat, tomatoes and mint to the lamb. Cover and cook on the lowest heat for 30 minutes.

Cooking time: 2 hours

Cheese, Walnut and Wheatgerm Casserole

Wheatgerm adds a sweet, nutty flavour and extra protein and vitamin E to a delicious, creamy casserole of summer vegetables.

METRIC/IMPERIAL	AMERICAN
900g (2lb) peas (unshelled)	2lb peas (unshelled)
350g (¾lb) carrots	¾lb carrots
1 large onion	1 large onion
25g (1oz) butter	2tbls butter
15ml (1tbls) wholemeal flour	1tbls whole grain flour
275ml (½pt) milk	1¼ cups milk
30ml (2tbls) chopped parsley	2tbls chopped parsley
15ml (1tbls) chopped thyme	1tbls chopped thyme
125g (¼lb) grated Gruyère of Farmhouse Cheddar cheese	1 cup grated Gruyère or aged Cheddar cheese

60ml (4tbls) wheatgerm | 4tbls wheatgerm
125g (¼lb) chopped walnuts | 1 cup chopped walnuts

Shell the peas and finely chop the carrots and onion. Melt the butter in a large pan on a low heat. Stir in the vegetables, cover them and let them sweat for 10 minutes. Stir in the flour and cook it for 1 minute. Stir in the milk and bring it gently to the boil. Cover and simmer very gently, without boiling for 15 minutes. Preheat the grill (broiler) to high. Take the pan from the heat and stir in three-quarters of the cheese, 30ml (2tbls) of the wheatgerm and all the walnuts. Transfer the mixture to a heatproof serving dish and scatter over the remaining wheatgerm and then the remaining cheese. Put the dish under the grill (broiler) about 10cm (4in) away from the heat. Cook until the cheese has melted and the wheatgerm is beginning to brown.

Cooking time: 55 minutes

Chicken and Shrimp Paella

Paella is a traditional Spanish dish and its ingredients vary tremendously from region to region. This is a very simple one containing only chicken and prawns or shrimp. The rice used in a paella is usually white, but it works equally well and is more tasty with brown, providing the cooking time is lengthened and more liquid used.

METRIC/IMPERIAL	AMERICAN
1.1-1.3g (2½-3lb) roasting chicken	2½-3lb chicken pieces
450g (1lb) boiled prawns, in their shells	1lb boiled shrimp (unshelled)
2 large onions	2 large onions
2 cloves garlic	2 cloves garlic
450g (1lb) tomatoes	1lb tomatoes
2 large red peppers	2 large red bell peppers
12 green olives	12 green olives
1.5ml (¼tsp) saffron	¼tsp saffron
30ml (2tbls) boiling water	2tbls boiling water
45ml (3tbls) olive oil	3tbls olive oil
225g (½lb) brown rice	1¼ cups brown rice
10ml (2tsp) paprika	2tsp paprika
275ml (½pt) stock	1¼ cups stock or broth
sea salt	sea salt
freshly ground black pepper	freshly ground black pepper

Cut the chicken into small serving pieces. Shell and clean all but 8 of the prawns (shrimp). Quarter and thinly slice the onions and finely chop the garlic. Scald, skin and roughly chop the tomatoes. Core and seed the (bell) peppers and cut them into 3cm (1in) strips. Stone (pit) and quarter the olives. Add the saffron into the spoonfuls of boiling water in a cup and leave to infuse.

Heat the oil in a large paella pan (or skillet) on a moderate heat. Put in the chicken pieces and fry them until they are brown all over. Remove them, lower the heat and mix in the onions and garlic. Cook them until they are soft. Mix in the rice and paprika and cook, stirring for 1 minute. Pour in the stock and bring it to the boil. Season and mix in the tomatoes, chicken pieces and infused saffron. Cover the pan with a large pan lid or with foil and simmer for 30 minutes. Mix in the shelled prawns (shrimp) and put the unshelled ones on top. Cover again and simmer for a further 20 minutes. If, by this time, there is still too much liquid in the pan, remove the cover and simmer until it has been absorbed. The rice should be moist but not too wet. Either serve directly from the pan or in a large serving dish with the unshelled prawns on top for decoration.

Cooking time: 1 hour 50 minutes

A few spoonfuls of wheatgerm, added to a casserole, add to the protein content and give an individual note to the dish. Cheese, walnut and wheatgerm casserole, shown here with ears of wheat, also contains summer peas and carrots.

Quick Bran and Wheatgerm Bread

This bread is quicker to make than the usual yeasted bread because it only requires a little kneading and one short rising time. It is moist, chewy and full of flavour and goes very well with cheese.

METRIC/IMPERIAL	AMERICAN
450g (1lb) wholemeal flour	1lb (4 cups) whole grain flour
50g (2oz) bran	½ cup bran
50g (2oz) wheatgerm	½ cup wheat germ
25g (1oz) fresh or 15g (½oz) dried yeast	1oz cake compressed yeast or 2tbls dried yeast granules
5ml (1tsp) Barbados sugar	1tsp brown or Barbados sugar
425ml (16floz) warm water	2 cups warm water
10ml (2tsp) sea salt	2tsp sea salt
oil or butter for greasing two 450g (1lb) loaf tins	oil or butter for greasing two 3-cup bread pans

Heat the oven to gas mark 6 / 200°C (400°F). Toss the flour, bran and wheatgerm together in a bowl. If you are using fresh yeast, cream it with the sugar and 150ml (¼pt) or ½ cup water; use it within 5 minutes. If using dried yeast dissolve the sugar in 150ml (¼pt) or ½ cup water and sprinkle the dried yeast on top. Leave the yeast in a warm place until it is frothy, about 10 minutes. Dissolve the salt in the remaining water. Grease two 450g (1lb) loaf tins (3-cup bread pans). Make a well in the centre of the flour and pour in the yeast mixture and salt water. Mix everything to a dough and knead it in the bowl, lifting the sides and bringing them to the centre.

Divide the dough between the two prepared tins (pans) and press it down lightly. Put the loaves on top of the stove, cover them with a clean cloth and leave them for 30 minutes or until the dough has risen to 1.5cm (½in) above the edge of the tins (pans). Bake the loaves for 40 minutes and turn them onto wire racks to cool.

Cooking time : 1 hour 25 minutes

Wholewheat Semolina Pudding

Wholewheat semolina can be made into a creamy, golden, sweet pudding.

METRIC/IMPERIAL	AMERICAN
125g (¼lb) wholemeal semolina	about 1 cup wholewheat
5ml (1tsp) ground cinnamon	semolina
pinch sea salt	1tsp ground cinnamon
575ml (1pt) gold top milk	pinch sea salt
50g (2oz) raisins	2½ cups whole milk
50g (2oz) sultanas	⅓ cup raisins
2 eggs, beaten	⅓ cup white raisins (muscats)
little butter for greasing	2 eggs, beaten
	little butter for greasing

Heat the oven to gas mark 4 / 180°C (350°F). Put the semolina into a saucepan with the cinnamon and salt. Stir in the milk and add the raisins and sultanas. Put the saucepan on a moderate heat and bring the mixture to the boil, stirring all the time. Simmer, still stirring, for 3 minutes. Take the pan from the heat and let the mixture cool. Beat in the eggs.

Pour the mixture into a buttered pie dish and bake it for 25 minutes or until the top is risen and a good, golden brown.

Cooking time : 40 minutes

† For a plainer pudding, omit the dried fruit, sweeten with 50g (2oz) or 4 tablespoons Barbados sugar or honey to taste and add the grated rind ½ lemon.
† To make semolina for breakfast, cook the semolina as above with milk, milk and water, or plain water in the same way. Leave out the eggs and serve straight from the saucepan.

Quick bran and wheatgerm bread.

Brown Rice Pudding

When brown rice is made into a sweet milk pudding it does not turn out as fluffy as white rice does, but it has a far richer flavour, particularly with Barbados, (raw) sugar, molasses or honey. You still get a delicious brown skin on the top!

METRIC/IMPERIAL	AMERICAN
50g (2oz) short-grain brown rice	¼ cup short-grain brown rice
575ml (1pt) gold top milk	2½ cups whole milk
50g (2oz) Barbados sugar or	¼ cup Barbados or molasses
30ml (2tbls) clear honey	sugar or 2tbls honey
little freshly grated nutmeg	little freshly grated nutmeg
25g (1oz) butter	2tbls butter

Heat the oven to gas mark 1 / 140°C (275°F). Mix the rice with the milk, sugar or honey and nutmeg. Pour the mixture into a pie dish and add the butter, cut into small pieces. Bake the pudding for 3 hours, stirring well after the first hour.

Cooking time : 3 hours 10 minutes

† 2.5ml (½tsp) ground cinnamon can be added as well as the nutmeg to make the pudding spicier.

Frumenty

Frumenty is an old English dish served either for breakfast or as a dessert at Christmas and on other festive occasions. The flavour and texture really do make it rather a special dish. Without the brandy it can be very economical and excellent for everyday breakfasts in the winter. These amounts will be enough for about 10 servings, as it is uneconomical to make it in smaller portions. It keeps and reheats well and is also good served cold. (Serves 10).

METRIC/IMPERIAL	AMERICAN
225g (½lb) wheat grains	1¼ cups wheat grains or
275ml (½pt) milk	groats
30ml (2tbls) honey	1¼ cups milk
75g (3oz) sultanas	2tbls honey
75g (3oz) raisins	½ cup white raisins (muscats)
5ml (1tsp) ground cinnamon	½ cup raisins
⅛ nutmeg, grated	1tsp ground cinnamon
pinch ground mace	⅛ whole nutmeg, grated
60ml (4tbls) brandy (optional)	pinch ground mace
	4tbls brandy (optional)

Heat the oven to gas mark ½ / 100°C (200°F). Put the wheat into a large casserole dish and fill the pan to the top with water. Cover the wheat and put it into the oven for 8 hours, so the grain swells but does not burst. Take out the wheat and drain it. Put it into a saucepan with all the rest of the ingredients apart from the brandy. Bring them gently to the boil and simmer for 45 minutes, uncovered and stirring frequently. Add the brandy just before serving.

Cooking time : 9 hours

More Unusual Grains

Wheat and rice are the most common types of grains that find a place in the wholefood or health food cupboard but there are other, less-familiar ones that can be just as useful and equally good to eat. The most popular is probably oats and then there are rye, barley and millet. There is also a newly-developed cereal called triticale. Buckwheat is technically a seed but because it is used in a similar way to grains, it is included here.

Whole oats
Whole oats contain more protein and more thiamine than any other grain. They also contain a little fat and valuable amounts of important minerals such as iron, and potassium.

The first thing many people think of when oats are mentioned is a steaming bowl of breakfast porridge. When you consider their nutritional value it is no wonder that oats have for so long been considered one of the best ways to start the day. But porridge is not the only dish you can make with oats. In fact, whole oats are marketed in a variety of forms, each with its own different use.

Oat groats are the whole oat grain. 'Groats' can also refer to whole wheat grains. They can be cooked in a similar way to rice, either by steaming or baking to make an accompaniment or a substantial grain-based main dish. They will keep for up to six months in an airtight jar.

Oatmeal: whole oats are ground to make oatmeal of varying textures. Once ground, however, they may quickly become bitter, so only buy a small quantity at a time. It is also worth remembering that they tend to pick up the flavour of whatever they are stored in, so use glass jars instead of plastic or metal containers.

Pin-head oats (short oats) are the coarsest oats. They are used mainly for making porridge because they need far too long to cook to be suitable for breads or any other form of baking. They should be soaked over night and cooked very gently the next morning to

make a really traditional Scottish porridge.

Medium oatmeal makes crunchy, griddle-cooked oatcakes and bannocks, and the fine variety can be added to bread recipes. Oatmeal by itself does not have sufficient gluten to make successful bread, but it will provide flavour and extra goodness in a wheat loaf if you use three-quarters wheat flour to one-quarter fine oatmeal.

Rolled oats (oatmeal) or oat flakes are the type that are used as a base for muesli. They are produced from either whole oats or the pin-head (short oats) type which are first softened by steam and then flattened on a roller, cooled and dried. Those produced from whole oats are larger and are sometimes called jumbo oats. As well as muesli, rolled oats can be used in biscuits (cookies) and cakes such as the children's favourite flapjacks. They can also be used in crumble (crumb) toppings.

Quick porridge oats have been rolled and then partially cooked before being cooled and dried. Instant oats are made from a mixture of oatflakes and oat flour. These are not generally considered a natural food.

Rye

Rye is normally sold in the form of whole grains, flour (or rye meal in the United States, which is a coarsely ground rye flour) or rye flakes. It has a similar

From left: whole oats in sack (with ears of oats behind), oatmeal, rolled oats and pearl barley in front; pot barley behind, with malt extract and barley flour; millet in tub; buckwheat and whole grain rye in sacks; ears of barley centre and rye flour in front.

fat and thiamin content to whole wheat with more riboflavin and less protein and nicotinic acid. The whole grains are not suitable for cooking, but they can be sprouted in a similar way to wheat. They can be mixed with wheat, sprouted and used to make your own granary flour (see wheat). Rye flour is a very dark colour and makes a very tasty and slightly chewy loaf. It has a lower gluten content than wheat, so the bread will tend to be on the heavy side unless rye flour is used with an equal portion of wheat flour. Rye flakes are seldom used alone, but are mixed with oats and barley—and sometimes wheat flakes—to make a base for muesli (granola).

Barley

There are various types of barley. The whole grain is called pot barley in Britain and it contains protein and thiamin. It takes a similar amount of time to cook as brown rice and can be used in exactly the same ways. Pot barley can also be added to slow-cooking meat casseroles to thicken and enrich them. Pearl barley is the polished grain and, like white rice, is not really

59

considered a natural food. Barley flour is light-coloured and, used half and half with wholewheat (whole grain) flour, it makes a loaf with a delicious, slightly sweet flavour and soft texture. Rolled or flaked barley can be used with rolled oats to make a muesli base or flapjack type biscuits (large, crumbly cookies).

Malt extract: the other product of barley that can be bought in wholefood shops is the delicious, slightly bitter-sweet, dark brown and syrupy malt or malt extract. It contains a significant amount of protein, B vitamins and the minerals iron, calcium and potassium. Its sugar count is high.

Malt extract (malt) is useful in yeast cookery. Yeast thrives particularly well on the enzymes which it contains and so is excellent both for brewing your own beer and for making a delicious, moist malt loaf. Add 45ml (3tbls) malt or malt extract (or in the US powdered malt) to 450g (1lb) or 4 cups wholemeal (whole grain) flour when you add the liquid and knead in 175g (6oz) or 1 cup mixed sultanas (white raisins) and raisins and make the bread up as normal. When you are making a plain loaf, 5ml (1tsp) malt extract can also be used to raise the yeast.

Mixed grains

Many types of muesli base are made with a mixture of rolled oats, rye, barley and wheat. The commercially-made mueslis tend to be rather sweet, so it is a good idea to buy this base and add nuts, dried or fresh fruits and brown sugar to your own taste. Some wholefood shops sell each rolled cereal separately so that you can really start from the beginning. The best mixture is 450g (1lb) or 4 cups oats to 350g (¾lb) each wheat (whole grain), rye and barley.

Triticale

Triticale (pronounced trit-i-carly) is a new cereal derived from many patient crossings of wheat and rye. It is high in protein and the protein quality is excellent as it contains more of the amino acid lysine, which tends to be low in other cereals. The flour, sold at present in the US, has a low gluten content and so it must be mixed with a large proportion of wholewheat (whole grain) flour. In Britain, triticale grains are sold for sprouting. Triticale sprouts are more tender and sweet than wheat sprouts and take less time to grow.

Millet

Millet takes the form of a fine, pale yellow grain, high in protein, calcium and iron and the B vitamins thiamin, riboflavin and nicotinic acid. It is very quickly cooked and should be served as an accompanying dish with a main protein meal. It has a light grain flavour and a delicious fluffy texture. The best method is to stir it first into oil and then simmer it with 850ml (1½pts) or 3¾ cups water to every 225g (½lb) or 2 cups of the uncooked grain.

Buckwheat

Buckwheat resembles tiny, brown heart-shaped seeds which are difficult to remove from their sheath-like husk, which makes them expensive compared with other grains. It is high in protein, phosphorus and potassium and contains most of the B vitamins. Buckwheat is most often cooked to make the dish called kasha which has a strong, almost pungent, nutty flavour. The seeds are first toasted in an open pan then simmered in water or stock to make them fluffy and soft. Diced vegetables, such as onions or mushrooms, can also be added for extra flavour.

Buckwheat flour is grey-coloured and very fine. It contains no gluten and should not really be used for yeasted loaves. However, for someone on a gluten-free diet it can be valuable. Make a loaf using a normal plain bread recipe. It will not rise very high and will look as heavy as a stone, but the texture will be silky and surprisingly crumbly. The best use for buckwheat flour is for making buckwheat pancakes. Made with yeast and water, they will be thin and crisp with a characteristic kasha flavour.

Buckwheat flour is made into a delicious spaghetti which is the only whole grain pasta which does not contain eggs. It cooks remarkably quickly (in about 10 minutes) and does not have the strong flavour normally associated with buckwheat. It can be used in all recipes that require ordinary wholewheat spaghetti.

Wild rice

Wild rice is the seed of an aquatic grass that grows in the northern part of the U.S. Because of the problems of harvesting it, it is very expensive and so is usually served with brown rice. Use them in the proportion of one-eighth wild rice with seven-eighths brown rice.

RECIPES

Savoury Muesli Salad

Muesli base need not only be used for a sweet breakfast. Here it is mixed with chopped and grated vegetables and a yogurt dressing for a salad to start a meal.

METRIC/IMPERIAL	AMERICAN
125g (¼lb) muesli base	about 1 cup muesli base
125g (¼lb) carrots	¼lb carrots
1 small green pepper	1 small green bell pepper
50g (2oz) chopped walnuts	½ cup chopped walnuts
30ml (2tbls) sesame seeds	2tbls sesame seeds
25g (1oz) raisins	2tbls raisins
150ml (¼pt) natural yogurt	⅔ cup plain yogurt
1 clove garlic, crushed with a pinch sea salt	1 clove garlic, crushed with a pinch sea salt
freshly ground black pepper	freshly ground black pepper
4 thin slices lemon	4 thin slices lemon

Put the muesli base into a bowl. Grate the carrots and core, seed and finely chop the (bell) pepper. Mix them into the muesli with the walnuts, sesame seeds and raisins. Beat the yogurt with the garlic and pepper and fold it into the salad.
Divide the salad between four small bowls and garnish the top with a twist of lemon.

Cooking time: 15 minutes

Barley Bake

Pot barley can be used instead of potatoes, rice or other grains to accompany the main dish. It is best baked in the oven with stock and flavourings.

METRIC/IMPERIAL	AMERICAN
225g (½lb) pot barley	about 2 cups barley grains
225g (½lb) mushrooms	½lb mushrooms
2 medium-sized onions	2 medium-sized onions
1 clove garlic	1 clove garlic
25g (1oz) butter	2tbls butter
5ml (1tsp) paprika	1tsp paprika
1.5ml (¼tsp) cayenne pepper	¼tsp cayenne pepper
350ml (12floz) stock	1½ cups stock or broth
sea salt	sea salt
30ml (2tbls) chopped parsley	2tbls chopped parsley

Heat the oven to gas mark 3/170°C (325°F). Thinly slice the mushrooms. Finely chop the onions and garlic. Melt the butter in a heavy-bottomed heatproof casserole or dutch oven on a low heat. Stir in the onions and garlic and cook them until they are soft. Stir in the mushrooms and cook them for 2 minutes. Stir in the barley, paprika and cayenne. Pour in the stock and bring it to the boil. Season with the salt. Cover the pan and put it into the oven for 40 minutes.

Cooking time: 1 hour

Barley and mushrooms are casseroled together for a substantial dish. Garnish with parsley if liked.

Rye and caraway bread.

Rye and Caraway Bread

Rye flour makes a dark and chewy loaf that is superb with cheese.

METRIC/IMPERIAL	AMERICAN
25g (1oz) fresh or 15g (½oz) dried yeast	1oz cake compressed yeast or 2tbls dried yeast granules
5ml (1tsp) Barbados sugar	1tsp brown or Barbados sugar
150ml (¼pt) warm water	⅝ cup warm water
225g (½lb) rye flour	½lb (2 cups) rye flour
225g (½lb) wholemeal flour	½lb (2 cups) whole grain flour
10ml (2tsp) sea salt	2tsp sea salt
15ml (1tbls) caraway seeds	1tbls caraway seeds
40g (1½oz) butter	3tbls butter
150ml (¼pt) warm milk	⅔ cup warm milk
1 egg, beaten	1 egg beaten

If you are using fresh yeast, cream it in a bowl with the sugar and water; use within 5 minutes. If using dried yeast, dissolve the sugar in the water and crumble the yeast on top. Put the yeast into a warm place to froth— about ten minutes.
Put the rye and wholemeal (whole grain) flours into a bowl with the salt and 10ml (2tsp) of the caraway seeds and rub in the butter. Make a well in the centre and pour in the yeast mixture and milk. Mix everything to a dough. Turn it onto a well-floured work surface and knead it well. Return the dough to the bowl. Either cover the bowl with a clean cloth or put it into a large plastic bag. Leave it in a warm place for 1 hour for the dough to double in bulk.
Heat the oven to gas mark 6/200°C (400°F). Knead the dough again and form it into one round loaf. Put it

onto a greased baking sheet, brush it with the beaten egg and sprinkle the remaining caraway seeds over the top. Put the loaf on top of the stove, cover it with a cloth and leave it for 20 minutes to rise for the second time. Bake the loaf for 50 minutes and lift it onto a wire rack to cool.

Cooking time: 2 hours 20 minutes

Millet

This is the basic recipe for millet. Once you have made it this way you can experiment with other additions and flavourings.

METRIC/IMPERIAL	AMERICAN
225g (½lb) millet	½lb (about 2 cups) millet
30ml (2tbls) oil	2tbls oil
850ml (1½pt) boiling water	3¾ cups boiling water
2.5ml (½tsp) sea salt	½tsp sea salt

Heat the oil in a heavy frying-pan on a moderate heat. Stir in the millet then stir it around for 4 minutes. Pour in the water. Lower the heat and add the salt. Cover and simmer very gently for 20 minutes. The millet should be light, soft and fluffy in texture and the separate seeds should still be distinguishable.

Cooking time: 25 minutes

† 1 medium-sized chopped onion can be added to the pan with the millet.
† Other vegetables, such as diced green (bell) pepper, carrots or celery, can also be added.
† For extra flavour, add some fresh chopped herbs or 30ml (2tbls) tamari (Shoyu) sauce.
† To make millet croquettes, let the cooked millet cool. Form it into balls about as big as golf balls, coat them in egg and breadcrumbs and deep-fry them.
† For a complete light meal fork 125g (¼lb) or 1 cup grated strong cheese into the cooked millet. Put it into a dish, scatter 50g (2oz) or ½ cup more cheese on top and put the dish under the grill (broiler) for the cheese to melt.

Toasted Cereal

This nutty, golden cereal is ideal for breakfast with or without milk or yogurt. You can also use it to garnish hot and cold sweets.

METRIC/IMPERIAL	AMERICAN
350g (¾lb) rolled oats	¾lb (3 cups) oatmeal
125g (¼lb) wheatgerm	¼lb (1 cup) wheatgerm
50g (2oz) sunflower seeds	¼ cup sunflower seeds
50g (2oz) chopped almonds	⅓ cup chopped almonds
50g (2oz) desiccated coconut	½ cup shredded coconut
90ml (6tbls) sunflower oil	6tbls sunflower oil
5ml (1tsp) sea salt	1tsp sea salt
175g (6oz) raisins	1 cup raisins

Heat the oven to gas mark 4/180°C (350°F). Put all the ingredients into a bowl and mix them well, making sure that the oil is evenly distributed. Spread the mixture onto a large baking tray and put it into the oven for 45 minutes turning it several times during cooking. It should be crisp and golden when it is done. Pour the cereal onto a flat dish and let it cool completely. Mix in the raisins. Store the cereal in an airtight container.

Cooking time : 1 hour

Parkin

Medium oatmeal is also an ingredient of this chewy parkin which was traditionally served in the north of England on Guy Fawkes night which is on November 5th.

METRIC/IMPERIAL	AMERICAN
350g (¾lb) medium oatmeal	3 cups regular oatmeal
100g (¼lb) wholemeal flour	1 cup whole grain flour
5ml (1tsp) ground ginger	1tsp ground ginger
2.5ml (½tsp) ground cinnamon	½tsp ground cinnamon
little freshly grated nutmeg	little freshly grated nutmeg
5ml (1tsp) bicarbonate of soda	1tsp baking soda
5ml (1tsp) sea salt	1tsp sea salt
50g (2oz) lard	4tbls shortening
50g (2oz) butter (or use all butter or vegetable margarine)	4tbls butter (or use all butter or vegetable margarine)
125g (¼lb) Barbados sugar	½ cup brown or Barbados sugar
225g (½lb) molasses	¾ cup molasses
60ml (4tbls) milk	4tbls milk
little butter for greasing a 6cm (2in) deep, square tin	butter for greasing a 2in deep, square cake pan

Heat the oven to gas mark 4/180°C (350°F). Grease a 6cm (2in) deep square cake tin (pan). Put the oatmeal and flour into a mixing bowl and toss in the ginger, cinnamon, nutmeg, soda and salt. Put the lard, butter, sugar and molasses into a saucepan and melt them together on a low heat. Make a well in the oatmeal and flour and pour in the contents of the pan. Add the milk and mix everything well. Transfer the mixture to the tin (pan) and smooth the top. Bake the parkin for 45 minutes. Cut it into squares while it is still in the tin (pan) and turn it onto a wire rack to cool.

Cooking time : 1 hour 5 minutes

Rolled oats can be toasted with coconut and almonds to make a delicious breakfast cereal (granola) base. Mix in raisins and serve with milk and yogurt.

Oatmeal and honey are combined with butter and lemon juice to make a traditional flapjack (cookie).

Honey and Oatmeal Biscuits (Cookies)

These crunchy biscuits (cookies) made with medium oatmeal and lightly flavoured with honey and lemon.

METRIC/IMPERIAL	AMERICAN
125g (¼lb) medium oatmeal	1 cup regular oatmeal
125g (¼lb) wholemeal flour	1 cup whole grain flour
pinch sea salt	pinch sea salt
75g (3oz) butter	6tbls butter
30ml (2tbls) clear honey	2tbls honey
juice ½ lemon	juice ½ lemon
little butter for greasing	little butter for greasing
whole blanched almonds	whole blanched almonds

Heat the oven to gas mark 3/170°C (325°F). Put the oatmeal, flour and salt into a bowl. Put the butter, honey and lemon juice into a saucepan and melt them together on a low heat. Make a well in the flour and oatmeal and pour in the butter mixture. Mix everything thoroughly. Press the mixture into a 1cm (⅜in) thick square on a lightly-greased baking sheet and cut it into squares or rectangles. Press a blanched almond onto each biscuit. Bake the biscuits for 50 minutes, cool them for a short time on the baking sheet and lift them onto a cooling rack.

Cooking time: 1 hour 10 minutes

Oat Groats and Bacon

Serve this dish with light egg or cheese meals or with a salad as a meal in itself.

METRIC/IMPERIAL	AMERICAN
225g (½lb) oat groats	½lb (about 2 cups) oat groats
125g (¼lb) lean bacon	¼lb bacon strips
1 medium-sized onion	1 medium-sized onion
15ml (1tbls) oil	1tbls oil
450ml (¾pt) water	2 cups water
sea salt	sea salt
freshly ground black pepper	freshly ground black pepper
6 chopped sage leaves	6 chopped sage leaves

Finely chop the bacon and onion. Put the bacon into a heavy saucepan and set it on a low heat. When the fat begins to run, mix in the onion. Cook the bacon and onion and oatmeal until soft, adding the oil only if necessary. Pour in the stock and bring it to the boil. Season with more pepper than salt and add the sage leaves. Cover and simmer very gently for 1 hour or until all the water has been absorbed.

Cooking time: 1 hour 20 minutes

† To make a complete supper or lunch dish add 450g (1lb) lightly-cooked and finely-chopped spring greens, kale or cabbage after the oats are cooked.

Wholemeal Bannocks

A bannock is a traditional Scottish oatcake, cooked on a heavy iron griddle on top of the stove. In this recipe they are made with a slightly richer mixture than plain oatcakes. They are delicious eaten hot, straight from the griddle, with butter and honey. You can also let them get quite cold and eat them with cheese or peanut butter. (Makes about 16 oatcakes).

METRIC/IMPERIAL	AMERICAN
175g (6oz) fine or medium oatmeal	1½ cups fine or regular oatmeal
50g (2oz) wholemeal flour	½ cup whole grain flour
10ml (2tsp) baking powder	2tsp baking powder
5ml (1tsp) sea salt	1tsp sea salt
25g (1oz) butter	2tbls butter
150ml (¼pt) milk	⅔ cup milk
oil or butter for greasing griddle	oil or butter for greasing griddle

Put the oatmeal and flour into a mixing bowl with the baking powder and salt and rub in the butter. Make a well in the centre and pour in the milk. Mix everything to a dough and roll it out to about 6mm (¼in) thick. Stamp it into 6cm (2in) rounds with a biscuit cutter.

A traditional Scottish oatcake, bannocks are cooked on a girdle here : use a griddle or frying-pan at home.

Lightly grease a griddle or a fat, heavy frying-pan, and set it on a low to moderate heat. Cook the bannocks for about 10 minutes each side or until they are just beginning to brown and sound slightly hollow when you tap them lightly.

Cooking time : 30 minutes

Kasha

Kasha is good with highly-flavoured dishes and with rich meats. Stir in extra butter if desired.

METRIC/IMPERIAL	AMERICAN
225g (½lb) buckwheat groats	½lb (about 2 cups) buckwheat groats
725ml (1¼pt) boiling water	3 cups boiling water
2.5ml (½tsp) sea salt	½tsp sea salt

Heat a heavy frying-pan on a moderate heat with no fat. Put in the buckwheat and stir it around until it browns. Pour in the water and bring it to the boil. Lower the heat and add the salt. Cover and simmer for 20 minutes.

Cooking time : 30 minutes

Muesli Slices

Muesli base, a mixture of rolled oats, wheat, barley and rye, is used for these substantial biscuits (cookies). They are excellent for a packed lunch box as they are easy to carry and full of well-balanced goodness. (Makes 8-12 slices).

METRIC/IMPERIAL	AMERICAN
175g (6oz) muesli base	*1½ cups muesli base*
50g (2oz) raisins or sultanas	*½ cup raisins*
15ml (1tbls) sesame seeds	*1tbls sesame seeds*
50g (2oz) peanuts, chopped walnuts, sunflower seeds, chopped toasted hazelnuts or a mixture	*½ cup peanuts, chopped walnuts, sunflower seeds, chopped toasted hazelnuts or a mixture*
90ml (6tbls) corn oil (plus extra for greasing)	*6 tbls corn oil (plus extra for greasing)*
60ml (4tbls) honey	*4tbls honey*

Heat the oven to gas mark 5 / 190°C (375°F). Put the muesli base into a mixing bowl with the raisins or sultanas, sesame seeds and nuts. Put the oil and honey into a saucepan and stir them on a low heat until the honey has melted. Mix them into the muesli base. Press the mixture into a lightly-oiled 20cm (8in) diameter sponge tin (cake pan) and bake it for 30 minutes. Cut the round into 8 or 12 wedges, and leave them until they are completely cool before lifting them out.

Cooking time : 45 minutes

Yogurt Muesli with Almonds

The original muesli was made simply with oats, grated apple and chopped hazelnuts. Now, anything goes and you can experiment with all kinds of different nutritious ingredients.

METRIC/IMPERIAL	AMERICAN
175g (6oz) muesli base	*1½ cups muesli base*
575ml (1pt) natural yogurt	*2½ cups plain yogurt*
125g (¼lb) almonds	*¾ cup almonds*
4 sweet, crisp eating apples	*4 sweet, crisp eating apples*

The night before, put the muesli into a bowl and stir in the yogurt. Blanch and split the almonds and put them into a covered container.
The next morning, grate in the apples. Divide the muesli between four bowls and scatter the almonds over the top.

Cooking time : 30 minutes (plus standing overnight)

† Up to 125g (¼lb) or ¾ cup dried fruits such as sultanas or (white or dark) raisins or soaked apricots or prunes can be added with the apples. These give extra sweetness and flavour.
† Use chopped toasted hazelnuts or chopped walnuts and brazil nuts instead of almonds.
† Natural orange juice or apple juice can be used to moisten the muesli instead of the yogurt.
† For extra sweetness stir in 15-30ml (1-2tbls) honey or brown sugar.

Oatmeal Porridge

Pin-head oatmeal (short oats) makes a far tastier and better-textured porridge than porridge oats or instant breakfast oats (oatmeal). It is very easy to make, provided you remember to soak the oatmeal the night

Yogurt muesli with almonds.

before. You can eat it plain or with dried fruits, yogurt, honey or molasses.

METRIC/IMPERIAL	AMERICAN
225g (½lb) pin-head oatmeal	2 cups short oats
1.1L (2pt) water	5 cups water
pinch salt	pinch salt

The night before, put the oatmeal into a heavy saucepan and pour in the water. Leave the oatmeal to soak. When you come down next morning, add the salt. Set the pan on a moderate heat on top of the stove and bring the porridge to the boil, stirring. Turn the heat right down and simmer for 20 minutes, stirring frequently. Pour the porridge into warm bowls.

Cooking time: 25 minutes plus overnight soaking.

† Add 100g (¼lb) or 1¼ cup mixed sultanas and (white and dark) raisins before putting the porridge on the stove.
† Top each bowl with soaked dried prunes or apricots.
† Top each bowl with natural (plain) yogurt or 15-30ml (1-2tbls) honey or molasses.

Buckwheat Pancakes

Buckwheat flour can be made into crisp pancakes that have the characteristic kasha flavour. Serve them with fresh or stewed fruit and a bowl of dairy sour cream or natural yogurt. (This mixture makes 8-10 pancakes).

Pancakes show off the flavour of buckwheat flour. Serve them with fresh fruit and sour cream.

METRIC/IMPERIAL	AMERICAN
15g (½oz) fresh or 10g (¼oz) dried yeast	½oz compressed cake yeast or 1tbls dried yeast granules
5ml (1tsp) honey	1tsp honey
275ml (½pt) warm water	1¼ cups warm water
125g (¼lb) buckwheat flour	1 cup buckwheat flour
pinch sea salt	pinch sea salt
1 egg, separated	1 egg, separated
30ml (2tbls) oil	2tbls oil
oil for frying	oil for frying

If you are using fresh yeast, crumble it into a bowl and cream it with the honey and half the water; leave for up to 5 minutes. If using dried yeast, dissolve the honey in half the water and sprinkle the yeast on top. Put the yeast in a warm place to froth—about 10 minutes.
Put the flour and salt into a bowl and make a well in the centre. Gradually beat in the egg, the remaining water, oil and yeast mixture. Cover the bowl with a clean cloth and leave it in a warm place for 1 hour to rise.
Heat 15ml (1tbls) oil in an omelet pan on a high heat. Spoon in 45ml (3tbls) of the batter and tip the pan to spread it evenly. Cook the pancake until it is golden brown on both sides, keep them hot on a plate over a pan of hot water, layered with greaseproof or waxed paper between, and cook the rest in the same way, adding more oil as and when necessary.

Cooking time: 1 hour 40 minutes

Fruit

Fruits are Nature's luxuries. They are attractive and full of goodness and, thanks to modern storage and transport, different kinds can be eaten all the year round. Fruits contain natural sugars fructose, glucose and sucrose. Fruit, both fresh and dried, can be included in the natural food diet every day and can even be eaten at every meal.

The constituents of dried fruits are very much more concentrated than those of fresh. Their sugar content is high but this is a natural sugar accompanied by other nutrients and as such is better for us than any form of refined sugar. The real value of dried fruits lies in their higher mineral content and ability to be stored. A handful of dried fruits a day in a salad or a sweet dish is a good idea and will supply valuable vitamins.

Shopping for dried fruit
The best dried fruit that you can buy is sold loose in health food shops. It looks duller and stickier than that found in supermarkets in see-through packs but this means that it has not been coated with mineral oil wax to prevent it from sticking together, a substance which has been considered harmful. If you do buy dried fruit in this form, then wash it in warm water before adding it to your recipe.

In many modern methods of drying many of the paler kinds of fruit such as apricots, peaches, apples, pears and sultanas (white raisins or muscats) have sulphur added to them to keep the pale, translucent yellow colour and also to make the fruit porous to facilitate drying. It is thought that too much sulphur tends to put a strain on the kidneys and inhibits the growth of red blood cells and in the state of New Hampshire it is actually banned. If you eat only a little

Minerals & Vitamins

The vitamin that is associated with fresh fruit is vitamin C, and most fruit does contain significant amounts. Blackcurrants are at the head of the list for their vitamin C content and others with large amounts are strawberries, citrus fruit, red currants and gooseberries. The amount is far greater when the fruit is fresh. Cooking can destroy 50% or more and freezing destroys 20%. The less-known vitamin K is also present in some fresh fruit and is at its highest in the pith or white fibre of citrus fruit. Though it looks attractive to cut this away for special-occasion meals, if you are making a citrus fruit salad for the family, simply peel the oranges and pull them into segments, without removing the membrane. Carotene, converted to vitamin A, is found in yellow-coloured fruit, such as fresh apricots (which have the highest count), mangos, peaches and yellow melons. There is also a little vitamin A in blackcurrants and gooseberries.

All dried fruit except peaches and apricots provide significant amounts of vitamin B_1 (thiamin). Most fresh fruits contain a little thiamin, citrus fruits, pineapple, plums, melon and bananas are the best sources. Both fresh and dried fruits contain small amounts of riboflavin, nicotinic acid, pyridoxine, pantothenic acid and folic acid and some fruits contain a little biotin.

Dried apricots and peaches contain large amounts of vitamin A, prunes contain a little, but other dried fruits contain little or no vitamin A. Boiling destroys a large percentage of some B vitamins, in particular thiamin. However, losses due to leaching into the cooking liquid are more significant, so this should always be used.

dried fruit, then this will probably do you no harm, but if your family eats it regularly then look out for the unsulphured varieties of these fruits. They will be darker in colour and more chewy and they will also have a better flavour and will improve any recipe that is made with them.

Do not buy more than about one month's supply of dried fruit at a time or it may become dry looking and slightly sugary. It will still be fine for cakes and other cooked dishes but it may not be quite so effective in compotes and for serving unsoaked.

Serving dried fruit
Dried fruit can be eaten or used just as it is, for example in salads or for baking, or it can be reconstituted. The simplest way of doing this is to cover it with a liquid and leave it for about 8 hours, by which time it will have soaked up most of the liquid and will be soft and plump. The fruit can then be eaten as it is or it can be simmered for a short time. Water is perfectly effective for soaking dried fruit, but you can make it more delicious with natural orange or apple juice or, for special occasions, grape juice, cider or red or white wine. Always use the soaking liquid.

Fruit through the day
Both fresh and dried fruits can be eaten in different ways right through the day. They are so sweet and delicious that it probably will not be too difficult to encourage the children to eat them instead of sweets. Keep a well-stocked fruit bowl within easy reach so they can help themselves whenever they like, instead of reaching for a bar of chocolate or asking for an

ice-cream. A bite on an apple will be far better for you, too, instead of a mid-morning snack. You can also keep out a small bowl of mixed peanuts and raisins.

A beautiful, refreshing start to the morning is a bowl full of chopped seasonal fruits, topped with a cup of plain yogurt. In the winter you can slice apples, pears and oranges; in the summer there are strawberries, raspberries, peaches, apricots and perhaps blueberries and in the autumn there are blackberries and plums. You can mix soaked, dried fruit with your fresh fruit for breakfast or have fresh fruit alone. Other fruit ideas for breakfast are muesli (mixed cereal grains and nuts) to which you can add grated apples or other finely chopped fresh fruits, along with raisins and sultanas; or eat hot oat porridge, to which raisins can be added as it cooks. You can also top porridge with soaked fruits such as apricots or prunes.

At lunch time fruit can be mixed into vegetable salads. It adds to the flavour and goodness and makes them really attractive. Experiment with unusual combinations such as grapefruit and watercress or with sliced cauliflower, oranges with tomatoes, lettuce and olives; pomegranate seeds with red cabbage; and in the summer raspberries with a salad of lettuce and cucumber with plenty of chopped fresh herbs and spring onions (scallions); or plums with finely chopped celery. Lemon, orange, lime and grapefruit juices can also be made into salad dressings instead of vinegar. Currants, sultanas (white raisins), raisins and chopped dried apricots and dates can be added in fairly small amounts to vegetable salads to give delicious occasional contrasting sweetness, as well as adding tremendously to their mineral content.

Small, attractive salads based on fruit are an excellent way in which to start the main meal of the day and, when it comes to making the main dish, fruit can be incorporated in that as well. If fruit is cooked or served in some way with meat, its acids tend to break down the fats in the meat, so making it more digestible. Fruit juices used as marinades will also tenderize and flavour most meats. Apples and gooseberries can be made into sauces for pork and fresh red currants can be mixed into sauces for chicken and game. You can make meat and fruit kebabs, use a small amount of chopped fruit in stuffings for meat or simply squeeze a small amount of lemon or orange juice into the sauce. Not only meat, but oily fish such as mackerel or herrings, and rich nut roasts also benefit from the flavour of a slightly sharp fruit. Dried fruits must be used very carefully in main course dishes or you may find them too sweet. They are best used with a sharper fruit such as lemon or orange.

Fruits have been more traditionally used as the sweet finish to the meal. The simplest way of all is just to place the fruit bowl on the table and let everyone help themselves. Then there are fruit salads or compotes, and you can make these with endless combinations of available fruits from the more ordinary apples, pears and oranges to the exotic tropical fruit salads containing mangos, pawpaws, lychees and Chinese gooseberries or kiwi fruit. It is not at all necessary to pour a sweet syrup made from refined white sugar over the fruit. Many fruits are sweet enough to be eaten absolutely plain, but if you find them slightly sharp, then spoon over a little honey or brown or raw sugar. It is also a good idea to use dried fruits as a natural sweetener. Soak them first in fruit juice and then add them to the fresh fruits before you serve them. You can also save the dried fruits for another purpose and just mix their soaking liquids into the fruit mixture.

Soft fruits such as strawberries, raspberries and peaches can be made into uncooked fruit purées which can be spooned over other fruits or mixed into plain yogurt. They can also be folded into stiffly whipped egg whites to make a fruit snow.

Cooked fruit

The harder fruits can be made into cooked fruit purées and used in the same ways. Use a little honey or brown or raw sugar to sweeten them or try stewing them with dried fruits such as raisins or sultanas to see if you can cut down on the extra sweeteners altogether. You can also sweeten tart fruits by cooking them with the chopped leaves of angelica or sweet cicely. Cook them first and then taste to see how little honey or sugar you need.

If you are poaching fruit or making a fresh fruit compote, you can again do it quite successfully without a sugar syrup. Try using natural orange juice as the poaching liquid, or concentrated apple juice diluted with a little water. Delicious fruit compotes can also be made with dried fruits. Soak them first with a stick of cinnamon, a vanilla pod (bean) or a thinly-pared strip of lemon or orange peel for flavour. Then simmer them gently for a few minutes and serve them hot or cold.

Grilling (broiling) is a very simple and effective way of cooking many kinds of fresh fruit. They can be sliced and laid on a lightly-greased dish, or for a more impressive effect, threaded onto kebab skewers. Before putting the fruit under the grill (broiler) spoon over a little liquid such as fruit juice with honey added, or brush them with a little concentrated apple juice. Spices such as cinnamon, nutmeg or ginger can be lightly sprinkled over the top.

Another good way of cooking fruit is to bake it. Apples can simply be cored and baked whole. They can be baked plainly with honey spooned over them, filled with brown sugar or stuffed with dried fruits. Bananas can be baked in their skins and then peeled open and coated with honey or warmed concentrated apple juice. Peeled whole pears can be baked in a casserole in red wine or cider; halve peaches and apricots and bake in a dish with a little orange juice. Fruit can also be sliced and baked individually wrapped in foil packages. They can be sprinkled with brown or raw sugar and spices; or raisins or chopped dates can be used instead.

Dried fruits are commonly used in baking to give a natural sweetness to cakes, breads and buns or rolls, while occasionally fresh fruits such as apples can be added to cake mixtures to make them moist and tasty. Fresh fruits can be made into pies or topped with crumb toppings or with sponge-cake batter.

If you make your own jam then it can easily be made with fresh fruits and brown sugar. You may have a little difficulty obtaining a good set with Barbados (brown) or molasses sugar, but real Demerara raw sugar (see baking chapter) works perfectly. Your jams, jellies and marmalades will be a darker colour but there will be no significant difference in the flavour and you will be sure you have a good, natural product.

The freshly-squeezed juices of citrus fruits can be used to make refreshing drinks, both hot and cold.

Freshly-squeezed orange juice makes a good start to the day, and to finish the day on the right note, drink lemon juice and honey topped up with hot water.

RECIPES

Melon filled with Grapes and Tahini

Sweet, refreshing melon and thick, nutty tahini complement one another superbly in this attractive first course.

METRIC/IMPERIAL	AMERICAN
1 large honeydew melon	1 large honeydew melon
16 black grapes	16 Concord grapes
2 large pieces preserved stem ginger	2 large pieces preserved stem ginger
40ml (8 tsp) tahini	8tsp tahini
20ml (4tsp) sesame seeds	4tsp sesame seeds

Cut the melon into quarters and scoop out the seeds. Put the melon quarters into dishes. Halve and seed the grapes and place them on top of the pieces of melon. Cut each piece of ginger in half lengthwise. Finely chop each piece and scatter them over the grapes. Spoon the tahini on top and scatter the sesame seeds over that.

Preparation time: 15 minutes

Grapefruit and Tomato Mayonnaise

A tomato-flavoured mayonnaise makes a creamy dressing for this unusual salad to start a meal.

METRIC/IMPERIAL	AMERICAN
2 grapefruit	2 grapefruit
4 large tomatoes	4 large tomatoes
60ml (4tbls) mayonnaise (homemade if possible)	4tbls mayonnaise (homemade if possible)
15ml (1tbls) tomato purée	1tbls tomato paste
2.5ml (½tsp) Tabasco sauce	½tsp Tabasco sauce
30ml (2tbls) chopped parsley	2tbls chopped parsley
1 small lettuce	1 small lettuce

Peel the grapefruit, divide them into segments and chop each segment into 3 or 4 pieces, depending on their size. Chop the tomatoes into equal-sized pieces and put them into a bowl with the grapefruit. Mix the mayonnaise with the tomato paste and Tabasco sauce and fold the resulting dressing into the tomatoes and grapefruit. Arrange a bed of lettuce on 4 small plates and pile the salad on top. Scatter the parsley over the salad.

Preparation time: 30 minutes

Pineapple with Savoury Coconut

Pineapple rings with an unusual savoury coconut topping make a light first course.

METRIC/IMPERIAL	AMERICAN
4 thick slices fresh pineapple	4 thick slices fresh pineapple
50g (2oz) desiccated coconut	½ cup shredded coconut
150ml (¼pt) natural yogurt	⅔ cup plain yogurt
1 clove garlic, crushed with a	1 clove garlic, crushed with a
pinch sea salt	pinch sea salt
freshly ground black pepper	freshly ground black pepper
grated rind 1 lemon	grated rind 1 lemon

Mix the coconut and yogurt together and leave them for 30 minutes. Mix in the garlic and pepper. Put a slice of pineapple onto each of four small plates. Top it with the coconut mixture and scatter the lemon rind over the top.

Preparation time : 45 minutes

Pineapple rings make a fresh salad for a first course with yogurt and coconut topping.

A Delicate White Wine Salad

Grapes and white wine are included in this pretty winter salad.

METRIC/IMPERIAL	AMERICAN
125g (¼lb) seedless green grapes	⅔ cup Thompson seedless green grapes
1 small, firm, Drumhead cabbage	1 small, firm head cabbage
2 medium-sized carrots	2 medium-sized carrots
5ml (1tsp) English vineyard mustard	1tsp wine-based prepared granular mustard
30ml (2tbls) dry white wine	2tbls dry white wine
60ml (4tbls) olive oil	4tbls olive oil

Halve and seed the grapes. Shred the cabbage very finely and coarsely grate the carrots. Put them all into a salad bowl. Put the mustard into a small bowl and gradually beat in the wine and then the oil. Fold the dressing into the salad. If possible, let the salad stand for 10 minutes before serving.

Preparation time : 30 minutes

Pear and Anchovy Salad

Pears, anchovies and natural yogurt make an attractive and light salad to start a meal.

METRIC/IMPERIAL	AMERICAN
4 firm Conference pears	4 firm Bartlett, d'Anjou or Bosc pears
8 anchovy fillets	8 anchovy fillets
150ml (¼pt) natural yogurt	⅔ cup plain yogurt
30ml (2tbls) cider vinegar	2tbls cider vinegar
2 boxes salad cress or ½ x 450g (1lb) jar sprouted alfalfa	½ x lb jar of sprouted alfalfa

Peel, quarter, core and chop the pears. Pound 4 of the anchovy fillets to a paste with a pestle and mortar and mix them with the yogurt and vinegar. Mix in the pears and the cress or sprouted alfalfa. Divide the salad between 4 small dishes. Cut the remaining anchovy fillets in half lengthwise and arrange them in crosses on the tops of the salads.

Preparation time : 30 minutes

Cabbage makes a delicate salad with grapes, grated carrots and a white wine and mustard dressing.

Watercress and Orange Salad

This refreshing side salad goes well with bean dishes and also with lamb and chicken.

METRIC/IMPERIAL	AMERICAN
2 bunches watercress	2 bunches watercress
2 medium-sized oranges	2 medium-sized oranges
8 black olives	8 black olives
60ml (4tbls) olive oil	4tbls olive oil
15ml (1tbls) white wine vinegar	1tbls white wine vinegar
15ml (1tbls) freshly squeezed orange juice	1tbls freshly squeezed orange juice
5ml (1tsp) Dijon mustard	1tsp Dijon-style mustard
1 clove garlic, crushed with a pinch sea salt	1 clove garlic, crushed with a pinch sea salt
freshly ground black pepper	freshly ground black pepper

Break the watercress into small sprigs. Peel away the rind and white fibres or pith from the oranges. Pull or cut them into segments and, if desired, cut away the skin. Stone (pit) and quarter the olives. Beat the remaining ingredients together to make the dressing. Arrange the watercress and orange segments on a flat dish and scatter the olives over the oranges. Spoon the dressing over both the oranges and watercress.

Cooking time: 20 minutes

Tomato and Currant Salad

Tomatoes, onions and currants make a salad with a Middle Eastern flavour. It is excellent with hummus and a burghul (bulgar) salad.

METRIC/IMPERIAL	AMERICAN
450g (1lb) tomatoes	1lb tomatoes
1 small onion	1 small onion
50g (2oz) currants	⅓ cup currants or raisins
30ml (2tbls) chopped basil or parsley	2tbls chopped basil or parsley
	3tbls olive oil
45ml (3tbls) olive oil	1tbls white wine vinegar
15ml (1tbls) white wine vinegar	freshly ground black pepper
freshly ground black pepper	

Thinly slice the tomatoes and finely chop the onion. Put them into a bowl with the currants and basil (or parsley). Beat the rest of the ingredients together to make the dressing and fold it into the salad. Tomato salads are best served as soon as they are made.

Preparation time: 15 minutes

Spring Greens and Orange

METRIC/IMPERIAL	AMERICAN
450g (1lb) spring greens	1lb mixed greens
25g (1oz) butter	2tbls butter
juice 1 large orange	juice 1 large orange
90ml (6tbls) stock or water	6tbls stock, broth or water
15ml (1tbls) chopped thyme	1tbls chopped thyme

Wash and finely chop the spring greens. Melt the butter in a saucepan on a moderate heat. Stir in the greens and add the orange juice, stock and thyme. Cover and cook on a moderate heat for 15 minutes.

Cooking time: 25 minutes

New Potatoes and Red Currants

Red currants add a light flavour to small, new potatoes and colour them pinky red. Serve them with plainly-cooked lamb or pork, with white fish or a nut roast.

METRIC/IMPERIAL	AMERICAN
675g (1½lb) new baby potatoes	1½lb tiny new potatoes
25g (1oz) butter	2tbls butter
60ml (4tbls) dry red wine	4tbls dry red wine
175g (6oz) red currants, stalkless	1 cup red currants, stalkless
30ml (2tbls) chopped mint	2tbls chopped mint

Boil the potatoes in their skins until they are just tender. Drain and peel them as soon as they are cool enough to handle. Melt the butter in a saucepan on a low heat. Add the wine and bring it to the boil. Let it reduce by about a quarter. Gently fold in the potatoes and add the red currants and mint. Cover and simmer gently for 3 minutes.

Cooking time: 30 minutes

Apple Rice

Slightly sharp flavours go well with brown rice, especially if it is to be served with rich meats or an oily fish such as mackerel or herrings.

METRIC/IMPERIAL	AMERICAN
225g (½lb) brown rice	½lb (1¼ cups) brown rice
1 small onion	1 small onion
30ml (2tbls) oil	2tbls oil
575ml (1pt) stock	2½ cups stock or broth
pinch of sea salt	pinch of sea salt
freshly ground black pepper	freshly ground black pepper
1 large cooking apple	1 large tart apple
15ml (1tbls) cider vinegar	1tbls cider vinegar

Finely chop the onion. Heat the oil in a saucepan on a low heat. Mix in the onion and cook it until it is soft. Mix in the rice and stir for 1 minute. Pour in the stock and bring it to the boil. Season, cover and cook gently for 45 minutes without uncovering. Peel, core and finely chop the apple. When the rice is done, mix in the vinegar and put the apple on top. Cover the rice again and leave it standing off the heat for 10 minutes. Mix in the apple before serving.

Cooking time: 1 hour 10 minutes

Fruit-stuffed Pork

This is an extremely attractive way of cooking pork tenderloin. Take the pork to the table before you carve it to show it off at its best. Each tenderloin is sandwiched together with yellow fruit.

METRIC/IMPERIAL	AMERICAN
2 pork fillets, weighing 700g (1½lb) together	2 pork tenderloin, weighing 1½lb together
175g (6oz) green gooseberries	1 cup yellow plums
1 medium-sized onion	1 medium-sized onion
25g (1oz) butter	2tbls butter
75g (3oz) wholemeal breadcrumbs	about 3 cups whole grain bread crumbs
15ml (1tbls) mixed chopped thyme, marjoram and parsley	1tbls mixed, chopped thyme, marjoram and parsley
4 chopped sage leaves	4 chopped sage leaves
275ml (½pt) plus 30ml (2tbls) stock	1¼ cups plus 2tbls stock or broth
30ml (2tbls) clear honey	2tbls honey

Heat the oven to gas mark 6/200°C (400°F). Cut the tenderloins across into two pieces, lengthwise. Top and tail the gooseberries (or pit the plums) and finely chop two-thirds of them. Finely chop the onion.

Melt the butter in a frying-pan on a low heat. Mix in the onion and cook it until it is beginning to look transparent. Mix in the chopped fruit and continue cooking until the onion is completely soft. Take the pan from the heat and mix in the breadcrumbs and herbs and the 30ml (2tbls) stock. Lay the stuffing on two pieces of tenderloin. Top with the other pieces and tie them round with fine cotton string. Lay the pieces on a rack in a roasting tin (pan). Put them into the oven for 45 minutes.

Remove the rack and put the pork in the bottom of the pan. Spoon the honey over the top and decorate with the reserved fruit, cut in half lengthwise. Pour in the stock and put the pork back into the oven for 15 minutes. Remove the string and put them onto a warm serving dish.

Cooking time: 1 hour 30 minutes

Gingered Orange and Pineapple Salad

This simple fruit salad with a hint of ginger is superb after a rich meal.

METRIC/IMPERIAL	AMERICAN
2 medium-sized oranges	2 medium-sized oranges
1 medium-sized pineapple	1 medium-sized pineapple
30ml (2tbls) clear honey	2tbls honey
juice ½ lemon	juice ½ lemon
1.5ml (¼tsp) ground ginger	¼tsp ground ginger

Cut the rind and white fibre or pith from the oranges. Cut the flesh into lengthwise quarters and thinly slice it. Cut the husk from the pineapple and cut the flesh

into rings. Stamp out the cores and cut the rings into 2cm (¾in) pieces. Put the oranges and pineapple into a bowl. Put the honey, lemon juice and ginger into a saucepan and warm them on a low heat until the honey has melted. Pour the contents of the pan over the fruit and leave for 1 hour.

Preparation time: 1 hour 30 minutes

Strawberry Whip

This light, fluffy pink whip should be served as soon as it is made.

METRIC/IMPERIAL	AMERICAN
225g (½lb) strawberries	½lb (about 1½ cups) strawberries
2 egg whites	2 egg whites
60ml (4tbls) natural yogurt	4tbls plain yogurt

Rub the strawberries through a strainer. Stiffly whip the egg whites. Fold first the yogurt and then the egg whites into the strawberries. Pile the whip into chilled glasses and serve immediately.

Preparation time: 20 minutes

† The whip is excellent spooned over chopped peaches and apricots.

Lamb with Raisin and Orange Stuffing

The combination of fruit in this recipe contrasts with the richness of the meat. It is excellent with watercress and orange salad.

METRIC/IMPERIAL	AMERICAN
1.4-1.8kg (3-4lb) shoulder lamb	3-4lb square cut lamb shoulder
1 medium-sized onion	1 medium-sized onion
25g (1oz) butter	2tbls butter
50g (2oz) raisins	⅓ cup raisins
50g (2oz) wholemeal breadcrumbs	about 2 cups whole grain bread crumbs
15ml (1tbls) chopped parsley	1tbls chopped parsley
5ml (1tsp) chopped rosemary	1tsp chopped rosemary
grated rind and juice ½ medium-sized orange	grated rind and juice ½ medium-sized orange
For the sauce:	**For the sauce:**
275ml (½pt) stock	1¼ cups stock or broth
grated rind and juice ½ medium-sized orange	grated rind and juice ½ medium-sized orange

Heat the oven to gas mark 4/180°C (350°F). Bone the lamb and lay it out flat. Finely chop the onion. Melt the butter in a small frying-pan on a low heat. Mix in the onion and cook it until it is soft. Add the raisins and take the pan from the heat. Mix in the herbs and orange rind and juice. Lay the mixture on the cut surface of the meat. Roll up the meat and tie it with

Sliced pears are given an unusual spicy syrup, cooked with cardomon, brown sugar and apple juice.

fine cotton string or thread. Put the lamb on a rack in a roasting tin (pan) and put it into the oven for 2 hours. Take out the lamb, untie it and let it rest.

Pour all the fat from the roasting pan. Set the pan on top of the stove on a moderate heat. Pour in the stock and bring it to the boil, stirring in any residue from the bottom of the tin (pan). Add the orange rind and juice and let the sauce simmer while you carve the lamb. Serve it separately in a sauce boat.

Cooking time: 2 hours 30 minutes

Spiced Pears

Pear slices, gently spiced and baked in apple juice, can look very attractive served in stemmed goblets and topped with whipped cream or plain yogurt.

METRIC/IMPERIAL	AMERICAN
3 large, firm pears	3 large, firm pears
30ml (2tbls) Barbados sugar	2tbls brown or Barbados sugar
5ml (1tsp) ground cardamom	1tsp ground cardamom
pinch ground cloves	pinch ground cloves
150ml ($\frac{1}{4}$pt) natural apple juice	$\frac{2}{3}$ cup apple juice
natural yogurt or whipped cream for serving	plain yogurt or whipped cream for serving

Heat the oven to gas mark 4/180°C (350°F). Quarter the pears and cut away the cores. Cut them into 1cm ($\frac{3}{8}$in) lenthwise slices. Put the pears into an ovenproof dish, such as a pie dish, and sprinkle them with the sugar and spices. Pour in the apple juice and bake them for 40 minutes or until they are tender when pierced with a fine skewer. Take the dish from the oven and either serve the pears hot or let them cool completely. Serve them in goblets topped with natural yogurt or whipped cream.

Cooking time: 55 minutes plus extra for cooling

Peach and Apricot Kebabs

When peaches and apricots are heated quickly they stay firm but become even juicier than they are raw. These kebabs are a beautiful bright yellow and the concentrated apple juice gives a sugar-free sweetness.

METRIC/IMPERIAL	AMERICAN
4 large peaches	4 large peaches
8 ripe apricots	8 ripe apricots
60ml (4tbls) concentrated apple juice	4tbls concentrated apple juice

Halve and stone (pit) the peaches and cut them into quarters. Halve and stone the apricots. Thread the fruit onto four kebab skewers in the order of peach, apricot, 2 peaches, apricot etc, ending with one piece of peach. Lay the kebabs in a dish and baste them with the concentrated apple juice.

Preheat the grill (broiler) to high. Lay the kebabs on the hot rack about 8cm (3in) from the heat and cook them for 3 minutes, turning them once.

Cooking time : 20 minutes

Compote of Dried Fruit in Apple Juice

This compote of dried fruit is full of natural sweetness gently flavoured with cinnamon and lemon.

METRIC/IMPERIAL	AMERICAN
75g (3oz) dried, unsulphured apricots	½-⅔ cup dried apricots, unsulphured
75g (3oz) dried apples	½-⅔ cup dried apples
75g (3oz) dried prunes	½-⅔ cup dried prunes
40g (1½oz) sultanas	¼ cup white raisins (muscats)
40g (1½oz) raisins	¼ cup raisins
425ml (¾pt) natural apple juice	2 cups apple juice
6cm (2in) cinnamon stick	2in cinnamon stick
thinly pared rind 1 lemon	thinly pared rind 1 lemon

Put the fruit into a bowl and cover it with the apple juice. Put in the cinnamon stick and lemon rind and leave the fruit to soak for 12 hours. Remove the lemon rind and cut it into thin strips.

Put the fruit, cinnamon stick and lemon rind into a saucepan. Set them on a low heat and bring them gently to the boil. Simmer for 15 minutes. Remove the

Dried fruit compote.

Yogurt with honey, citrus fruits and nuts make a quickly-prepared creamy fruit dessert.

cinnamon stick. Either serve the compote hot or let it cool completely and serve it topped with natural yogurt or dairy sour cream.

Cooking time : 12 hours soaking, then 20 minutes

Orange and Lemon Whip

This easily-prepared fruit and yogurt sweet will make a refreshing end to any meal.

METRIC/IMPERIAL	AMERICAN
8 medium-sized oranges	8 medium-sized oranges
juice ½ lemon	juice ½ lemon
60ml (4tbls) clear honey	4tbls clear honey
575ml (1pt) natural yogurt	2½ cups plain yogurt
60ml (4tbls) chopped nuts (walnuts, hazelnuts or almonds)	4tbls chopped nuts (walnuts, hazelnuts or filberts or almonds)

Thinly pare 3 strips of the rind of one of the oranges and finely chop and reserve it. Cut all the peel and white fibre or pith from this and all the remaining oranges. Finely chop the flesh, removing all the seeds and put it into a blender with the lemon juice, honey and yogurt. Work them together so you have a smooth, thick purée. Pour the mixture into individual serving glasses and sprinkle each one with chopped nuts and the reserved orange rind.

Cooking time : 30 minutes

Orange and Lemon Cup

Orange and lemon juice whisked with honey make a refreshing starter to a meal or can wake you up at breakfast time. Lighten it with naturally sparkling mineral water.

METRIC/IMPERIAL	AMERICAN
juice of 8 oranges	juice of 8 oranges
juice of 4 lemons	juice of 4 lemons
60ml (4tbls) honey (or more to taste)	4tbls honey (or more to taste)
275ml (½pt) mineral water	1¼ cups mineral water
crushed ice if required	crushed ice if desired

Put the orange and lemon juices into a blender with the honey and work them until the honey has dissolved. Put them into a jug or pitcher, top them up with mineral water and stir. Add the crushed ice.

Preparation time: 30 minutes

†For a fizzy fruit cup, top the sweetened juices with soda water or an alternative.

Dried Fruit Mousse

Dried fruit can be made into a sweet, rich mousse without sugar or cream. Serve it plainly for family meals or garnished for special occasions.

METRIC/IMPERIAL	AMERICAN
125g (¼lb) dried prunes	⅔ cup dried prunes
125g (¼lb) dried apricots, unsulphured	⅔ cup dried apricots, unsulphured
275ml (½ pt) natural orange juice	1¼ cups orange juice
15g (½oz) gelatin	2tbls unflavoured gelatin
2 eggs, separated	2 eggs, separated
150ml (¼pt) natural yogurt	⅔ cups plain yogurt
For the garnish:	**For the garnish:**
either whipped cream	either whipped cream
or chopped, toasted hazelnuts	or chopped, toasted hazelnuts
or chopped walnuts	(filberts) or chopped walnuts
or blanched and split almonds	or blanched, slivered almonds

Put the prunes, apricots and orange juice into a bowl and leave them for 12 hours. Soak the gelatin in a small pan in 60ml (4tbls) of the orange juice. Stone (pit) the prunes. Put the prunes, apricots and remaining juice into a blender and blend them until you have a smooth purée. Put the purée into a saucepan and set it on a low heat. Melt the gelatin gently over a low heat, then quickly stir it into the fruit purée. Beat in the egg yolks and stir until the mixture is very thick and creamy, without letting it boil. Take the pan from the heat and let the mixture cool until on the point of setting.
Stiffly whip the egg whites. Fold first the yogurt and then the egg whites into the fruit. Pour the mousse either into individual serving dishes or into one glass bowl. Put it into the refrigerator to set and decorate the top with your chosen garnish.

Cooking time: 12 hours soaking, then 1½ hours plus setting.

Vegetarian Mincemeat

For wholefood Christmas mince pies, make the pastry with wholemeal (whole grain) flour and fill them with this delicious, moist suet-free mincemeat. It will keep for up to 6 months and fills about three 450g (1lb) jars.

METRIC/IMPERIAL	AMERICAN
350g (¾lb) fairly sharp eating apples	¾lb tart red apples
25g (1oz) whole candied peel	1tbls candied fruit
50g (2oz) almonds	2tbls almonds
125g (¼lb) green grapes	⅔ cup seedless grapes
225g (½lb) raisins	1½ cups raisins
225g (½lb) currants	1½ cups currants
125g (¼lb) sultanas	¾ cup white raisins (muscats)
grated rind and juice 1 lemon	grated rind and juice 1 lemon
2.5ml (½tsp) ground cinnamon	½tsp ground cinnamon
2.5ml (½tsp) ground allspice	½tsp ground allspice
little freshly grated nutmeg	little freshly grated nutmeg
125g (¼lb) Barbados sugar	½ cup brown or Barbados sugar
25g (1oz) melted butter	2tbls melted butter
120ml (8tbls) brandy	½ cup brandy

Peel, core and finely chop the apples. Finely chop the candied peel. Blanch and split the almonds and cut them into fine slivers. Halve and seed the grapes. Put them all into a large bowl and mix in the rest of the ingredients. Mix well and pack the mixture into sterilized jam jars.

Preparation time: 45 minutes

Raisin and Molasses Bread

This raisin bread is moist and chewy with a good, crisp top crust. The molasses makes it a rich, dark colour and not too sweet. You can eat it with or without butter and it also goes surprisingly well with cheese.

METRIC/IMPERIAL	AMERICAN
25g (1oz) fresh or 15g (½oz) dried yeast	1oz cake compressed yeast or 1tbls dried yeast granules
45ml (3tbls) plus 5ml (1tsp) molasses	3tbls plus 1tsp blackstrap molasses
150ml (¼pt) warm water	⅝ cup warm water
450g (1lb) wholemeal flour	1lb (4 cups) whole grain flour
10ml (2tsp) sea salt	2tsp sea salt
50g (2oz) butter	4tbls butter
175g (6oz) muscatel raisins	¾ cup seeded raisins
150ml (¼pt) milk	⅝ cup milk
little extra butter for greasing one 900g (2lb) loaf tin	little extra butter for greasing 1 x 5-cup bread pan

Raisins and molasses combine well with wholemeal (whole grain) flour to make this dark, chewy bread.

If you are using fresh (compressed) yeast, cream it with the 5ml (1tsp) molasses and water; leave it no more than 5 minutes. If using dried yeast, dissolve the molasses in the water and sprinkle the yeast on top. Leave the yeast in a warm place to froth for about 10 minutes.

Put the flour and salt into a bowl and rub in the butter. Toss in the raisins with your fingers and make a well in the centre. Put the molasses and milk into a saucepan and warm them gently together until the molasses has melted. Pour the yeast and the milk mixture into the flour and mix everything together to make a moist dough. Turn it out onto a floured worktop and knead it until it is smooth. Return the dough to the bowl and either cover the bowl with a clean cloth or put it onto a large plastic bag. Put the dough into a warm place for 1 hour to double in size.

Heat the oven to gas mark 6/200°C (400°F). Grease a 900g (2lb) loaf tin (5-cup bread pan). Knead the dough again and put it into the greased loaf tin (pan). Put it on top of the stove, cover it with a clean cloth and leave it for 15 minutes, or until it has risen 1.5cm (½in) over the edge of the tin. Bake the loaf for 50 minutes and turn it onto a wire rack to cool.

Cooking time: 2 hours 30 minutes

Nuts & Seeds

Nuts and seeds are included in many people's diets as between-meal snacks, as garnishes and toppings for breads, sweet dishes or main courses, as a small ingredient in a salad and possibly as a traditional ending to the Christmas dinner. You certainly do not have to be a vegetarian to enjoy them; but it is the vegetarians who take them most seriously, make best use of them and know how to plan meals so that nuts contribute the main protein.

'Nuts' said Dr J. H. Kellogg, the founder of Kelloggs breakfast cereals, 'are the quintessence of nutriment'. They certainly are full of very concentrated goodness. Nuts and seeds are richest in fats and protein, while the highest percentage of fats is polyunsaturated. The nuts richest in fats are brazil nuts, cashew nuts and peanuts.

The advertisement tells us that peanuts contain more protein than beef—and this is true. Pine (Indian) nuts, almonds, pistachio nuts, sunflower seeds and all other nuts and seeds are richer in protein than any of the pulses (dried legumes). Few of them contain the complete proteins found in meat and fish or dairy products, but if you eat a selection of nuts with other foods that contain protein, particularly the grains, they will then be a good substitute for meat.

Chestnuts are unusual as the only nut to contain significant carbohydrate. They are a good source of natural, unprocessed starch and should be combined with other protein foods or made into sweets.

Nuts are a very highly concentrated and, when eaten alone, a highly calorific food (due to the fat). If you eat a large amount of nuts on their own you will probably find them both fattening and expensive. If you eat them after a large meat meal, you may find them difficult to digest. To obtain the very best value and enjoyment from nuts, combine them in quite small amounts in dishes with other foods.

Planning meats with nuts

Nuts and seeds combined with vegetables and fruit and whole grains will provide you with the perfect meal, one that is highly nutritious, non-fattening, easy to digest and easy on the pocket. It is a good idea, too, to put several kinds of nuts and seeds together so you get a selection of all the different fats, proteins, vitamins and minerals that they provide. This will also give you a wide variety of delicious, new combinations of flavours.

Mix nuts and seeds into salads and cooked vegetables for side or main dishes; into stuffings for vegetables; into nut roasts with wholemeal (whole

Minerals & Vitamins

All nuts and seeds contain more minerals than meat. They are particularly high in phosphorus, which works with the B vitamins; in potassium, which aids in the regulation of blood pressure and in iron, though these may not be absorbed as well as from meat.

One mineral more often associated with dairy products than nuts is calcium. Hazelnuts (or filberts) are particularly high in calcium and, weight for weight, they contain more than dried milk. Sesame seeds are another good source of calcium.

Almonds, brazil nuts, pine kernels (Indian nuts) peanuts and pistachio nuts are high in the B group of vitamins. Vitamin E is found in chestnuts and C in cashews. Sunflower seeds contain vitamins D and E.

Types of nuts and seeds

There are many different kinds of nuts in the world, but those which most often find their way into European kitchens include almonds, brazil nuts, cashew nuts, chestnuts, cobs and hazels, coconuts, pecan nuts, peanuts, pine kernels and walnuts. In the United States are found almonds, brazil nuts, pecans, peanuts, macadamia and cashews, walnuts, pistachio nuts, pine or Indian nuts, hickory and beechnuts and also hazelnuts.

With the growing interest in cooking natural foods, different kinds of seeds are also becoming easier to buy. There are grey, creamy-tasting sunflower seeds, melon seeds and squash seeds with their slightly citrus-like, refreshing flavour, gently bitter sesame seeds and tiny black or white poppy seeds. If you are an ambitious gardener you can even grow your own pumpkin nuts.

All nuts and seeds are sold when they are ripe and fully mature and at the height of their nutritional value. After this peak has been reached, they may soon start to deteriorate, so it is best not to bulk-buy but to keep your supplies down to one month's supply at a time. Nuts will obviously be fresher if you buy them in their shells, but it can be very time-consuming if, every time you want a nutty meal, you have to get busy with the crackers first. Therefore it is best from the cook's

grain) breadcrumbs, or perhaps combine them in light dishes with a small amount of meat. Add them to the mixture when you are making bread, cakes or scones (biscuits) or scatter them over the top.

You can eat nuts at any meal and in any course of the meal. Have them with muesli for breakfast, in a salad or spread on bread in the form of a nut butter for a quick lunch. For a main meal they can make the basis of a soup or the main dish, or they can be added to the vegetable or salad accompaniment. Alternatively, you can wait until the end of the meal and scatter them over fresh or dried fruits.

Left to right, working diagonally: unshelled and shelled walnuts; unshelled and shelled pecans; sweet chestnuts, shelled cashews and pinky, shelled pistachios at the front; unshelled and shelled hazelnuts (filberts), with white pine kernels (Indian nuts or pignolias); unshelled and shelled brazil nuts; unshelled and shelled peanuts; coconuts; unshelled and shelled almonds.

point of view to buy them ready-shelled. Good health food shops are usually the best source of supply (the nuts there look fresher than those in supermarkets) and so, too, are Indian and Middle Eastern shops, where these exist. Shelled nuts should be bright and fresh in appearance. If they are dull and oily, then look elsewhere.

Some nuts, such as cashews and walnuts, are cheaper if they are broken instead of being in whole pieces. If they look fresh, then this is an ideal way to buy them, especially if they are going to be ground or chopped in your final dish. You can also buy chopped, toasted hazelnuts. These are very good sprinkled into muesli (granola) or used in other sweet dishes.

Do not, however, buy blanched and chopped or ground almonds. As soon as they are blanched they begin to lose their natural oils and also their flavour. It is better to buy them in their skins and blanch them yourself as you need them. Do this by putting them into a shallow pan of cold water and bringing them to the boil. Drain them immediately and squeeze them out of their skins. Other nuts can be used with their skins on and this will preserve their B vitamins. To grind any nuts, use a blender, coffee grinder or food processor. Failing this, chop them finely, put them between two pieces of greaseproof or waxed paper and crush them with a rolling pin. You can also crush them in a mortar with a pestle.

Coconuts and chestnuts differ from other nuts. Although desiccated (shredded or flaked) coconut is easy to use, freshly grated coconut that you have just taken from the shell is more moist and has more flavour and the difference, whether it is in curries or cakes, is tremendous. You can also buy coconut as a moist cream in either 200g (7oz) blocks, or small cans, depending on where you live. This cream can be used in curries and sweet dishes. If you whip it with warm water you can make an excellent real cream substitute (see recipe) that contains no cholesterol and is ideal in a vegan diet (one that excludes meat and dairy products).

Fresh chestnuts are always bought in their shells and they are usually only available during the winter months. At other times, you can buy cans of chestnut purée which you can use for soups or sweet dishes. Always buy the unsweetened kind and sweeten it yourself if necessary. You can also buy dried chestnuts. These can be reconstituted by soaking them in water for three hours and then simmering them in the soaking water for 30 minutes. They will be firm-textured and excellent in dishes where whole chestnuts are required.

Dried chestnuts just about double in weight when reconstituted. Allowing for the weight of the shells of fresh chestnuts and also that dried chestnuts taste richer and sweeter, use 175g (6oz) dried where a recipe calls for 450g (1lb) fresh chestnuts.

Storing nuts
At home, all shelled nuts and seeds should be stored in airtight containers and kept cool and dry. Only chop them as you need them. Chop with a heavy knife on a chopping board or with a curved chopper called a mezzaluna which fits into a wooden bowl and prevents your nuts from scattering all over your work surface.

Nut and seed butters
Nuts are made into nut butters, the most popular of which is peanut butter. These are excellent nutritionally because the digestibility of nuts increases by 10% when they are ground. The nature of the butter means that usually only a small amount is eaten, for example spread on bread or crisp-breads. However, as with many commercial products, you do have to be careful as to which type you buy. Many of the better-known brands contain nuts which have been roasted for too long or at too high a temperature, processes which destroy their B vitamins. Excess salt may have been added and also sugar, which is totally unnecessary and only put in to cater for the sweet taste of the consumer. Some peanut butters also contain a preservative. You can, however, buy some excellent peanut butter in wholefood shops which is made with gently roasted nuts and a little sea salt. The motto is to look at the label before buying. Mixed nut and seed butters are also quite widely sold. Hazelnut and sunflower seed is the most delicious of these. You can also very easily make your own butter with your favourite combinations (see recipe on page 86).

As well as spreading for bread nut butters can be mixed into cake, biscuit and bread recipes and used in stuffings, nut roasts and patties. Nut oils easily form an emulsion with water or other liquids, so nut butters can be mixed very effectively into salad dressings. The best proportion is 15ml (1tbls) nut butter, 45ml (3tbls) oil and 30ml (2tbls) vinegar.

The sesame seed equivalent of nut butter is tahini, a thick grey-coloured paste with a nutty, slightly bitter flavour. By itself, it can be a little too thick and rich to spread on bread but you can make a superb, savoury paste by mixing it with tamari (Shoyu) sauce. The basic mix is three parts tahini to one of tamari (Shoyu) sauce. It is delicious just as it is, but you could also add crushed garlic, chopped parsley or some grated organge or lemon for extra flavour. Tahini can also be used in baking and in other dishes like nut butters. With the same proportions of oil and vinegar makes a really delicious salad dressing. For a quick and easy first course, spoon a little over slices of pineapple or over melon. The two extremes will go together perfectly.

Nut and seed oils
Another product of nuts and seeds is oil which can be used for cooking and for salad dressings. Safflower seed oil is the highest in polyunsaturated fats; second to it, and cheaper and more readily available, is sunflower oil, which is excellent for sautéeing, stir-frying and for salads. Ground nut or peanut oil is another fairly common oil. It does not have such a good flavour as sunflower oil, but it is preferred by the Chinese for stir-fried dishes. The oil from sesame seeds is a deep amber colour and it has that characteristic bitter nutty flavour. It is absolutely delicious for salads and, if you can afford it, stir-frying. Another oil which should be kept for special occasion salads is walnut with a very round rich flavour of walnuts. It is best for salads. Almond oil is one that is less often used; again,

it is expensive but it can add its delicate flavour to salads and mayonnaise.

Seed salts

Sesame salt is made by separately roasting sesame seeds and sea salt and then grinding them together with a little more sea salt. Crush garlic with it for salads and you will have just a hint of sesame flavour without too pronounced a saltiness.

Sprouting seeds

Some seeds are specially sold for sprouting, perhaps the best-known being alfalfa. You can also buy sunflower seeds still in their stripe shells from pet shops and these produce thick, succulent sprouts with a slightly peppery flavour that are good in salads. Sprout them in jam jars in the same way as beans and you will have a constant supply of fresh salads all the year round.

RECIPES

Grapefruit and Sesame Salad

Rich sesame paste contrasts beautifully with fresh grapefruit in this first course and the sesame seeds supply a nutty topping.

METRIC/IMPERIAL	AMERICAN
1 small lettuce	1 small lettuce
2 large grapefruit	2 large grapefruit
60ml (4tbls) tahini	4tbls tahini
40ml (8tsp) sesame seeds	8tsp sesame seeds
1 box cress	½ x 1lb jar sprouted alfalfa seeds

Wash and dry the lettuce and refrigerate for 30 minutes to crisp it. Shred the lettuce and divide into 4 portions. Arrange on 4 small serving plates. Remove the rind and all fibre or pith from the grapefruit and segment the fruit. Arrange the slices, slightly overlapping, on top of the lettuce on the plates. Decorate with the cress or sprouting seeds. Spoon the tahini over the grapefruit and scatter the sesame seeds on top.

Preparation time : 40 minutes

Grapefruits and tahini make an original salad.

Sunflower Seeds Roasted with Tamari (Shoyu) sauce

Nuts or seeds combined with another protein food make an excellent substitute for meat or dairy products. This is one of the simplest combinations and also a very delicious one. These sunflower seeds with a dark coating of tamari (Shoyu) sauce are excellent in salads and mixed into bread and scone (biscuit) dough. They are also good as a before-dinner snack.

METRIC/IMPERIAL	AMERICAN
125g (¼lb) sunflower seeds	¼lb sunflower seeds
45ml (3tbls) tamari sauce	3tbls Shoyu sauce

Heat the oven to gas mark 4/180°C (350°F). Put the sunflower seeds into a bowl and mix in the tamari (Shoyu) sauce. Spread the seeds onto a baking sheet and put them into the oven for 20 minutes. Let the seeds cool on the baking sheet, then store them in an airtight container.

Cooking time : 25 minutes

Peanut Butter

Peanut butter is a great favourite with adults and children alike. Spread it on bread and top it with a smear of yeast extract or something sweet, like mashed banana. For the all-American snack, top it with cream cheese or a good preserve. You can also mix it into salad dressings in a similar way to tahini.

METRIC/IMPERIAL	AMERICAN
225g (½lb) unroasted peanuts	½lb unroasted peanuts
30ml (2tbls) sunflower or groundnut oil	2tbls sunflower or peanut oil
pinch fine sea salt if required	pinch fine sea salt if required

Heat the oven to gas mark ½/120°C (250°F). Spread the nuts out on a baking tray and put them into the oven for 20 minutes. Cool them a little and rub off all the skins.
Put the nuts into a blender or food processor and work them until they are finely ground, stopping and easing them from the sides whenever necessary. Add the oil and work again until you have a smooth paste. Add the salt if required. Put the butter in a screw-topped jar. This amount will fill a 450g (1lb) jar about three-quarters full.

Cooking time : 45 minutes

† Nut butters can be made with any combination of mixed nuts and you can experiment with your own mixture of flavours. Bags of mixed nuts are ideal. The method for mixed nut butters is the same as for pea-nuts, only it is not necessary to rub away the skins for other types.
† A combination of two nuts or seeds can also be used.

Creamy Coconut

This cream, made from creamed coconut, can be used to replace dairy cream in a vegan (dairy-free) diet.

METRIC/IMPERIAL	AMERICAN
75g (3oz) creamed coconut	1 cup canned moist coconut
150ml (¼pt) warm water	⅝ cup warm water

Cut the creamed moist coconut into small pieces. Put the water into a bowl. Add the coconut and beat until it melts and you have a smooth thick cream. Use it to garnish cakes and to top fresh and dried fruits and other desserts.

Preparation time : 15 minutes

Celery, Chestnut and Apple Soup

Chestnuts, being a starchy food, provide all the necessary thickening for this warming autumn (fall) soup. The slightly sharp apple complements their sweetness well, without masking the basic celery flavour.

METRIC/IMPERIAL	AMERICAN
125g (¼lb) fresh chestnuts or 40g (1½oz) dried chestnuts	¼lb fresh chestnuts or ⅛lb dried chestnuts
6 sticks celery	6 large stalks celery
1 large Bramley apple	1 large tart apple
1 medium-sized onion	1 medium-sized onion
25g (1oz) butter	2tbls butter
850ml (1½pt) stock	3¾ cups stock or broth
bouquet garni	bouquet garni
sea salt	sea salt
freshly ground black pepper	freshly ground black pepper

If using fresh chestnuts, cut a small portion from the tops of their shells and put them into a saucepan of cold water. Bring them to the boil and simmer for 5 minutes. Take the pan off the heat. As soon as the chestnuts are cool enough to handle, peel them, leaving them immersed until skinned.
If using dried chestnuts, pour hot water on them and leave them for 3 hours. Put the chestnuts and the chestnut liquid into a saucepan, bring them to the boil and simmer for 30 minutes. Drain them if necessary.
Finely chop the chestnuts and celery. Peel, core and finely chop the apple. Finely chop the onion. Melt the butter in a saucepan on a low heat. Mix in the celery, apple and onion, cover them and let them sweat for 10 minutes. Mix in the chestnuts. Pour in the stock and bring it to the boil. Add the bouquet garni, season and simmer, covered, for 20 minutes.
Remove the bouquet garni and either purée the soup in a blender or food processor until it is smooth, or press it through a vegetable mill. Return the soup to the saucepan and reheat before serving.

Cooking time : 50 minutes (plus 3½ hours for dried chestnuts)

Make tomato-flavoured nut roast (page 88) from ground brazil nuts, hazelnuts and sesame seeds.

Walnut-dressed Watercress Salad

For this first course salad, the walnuts are pounded with vinegar to make a nut-flavoured dressing.

METRIC/IMPERIAL	AMERICAN
1 large bunch watercress	1 large bunch watercress
350g (¾lb) firm tomatoes	¾lb firm tomatoes
75g (3oz) raisins	¾ cup raisins
75g (3oz) shelled walnuts	¾ cup chopped walnuts
30ml (2tbls) white wine vinegar	2tbls white wine vinegar
1 clove garlic, crushed with a pinch sea salt	1 clove garlic, crushed with a pinch sea salt

Break the watercress into small pieces and chop the tomatoes. Put them both into a bowl with the raisins. Finely chop the walnuts and crush them with a large pestle and mortar. Work in the vinegar and garlic to make a fairly smooth dressing. Fold the dressing into the salad and then divide it between four small dishes.

Preparation time : 20 minutes

Mixed Nut and Seed Roast

Nut roasts are a popular dish with both vegetarians and non-vegetarians. This one is very moist, with a good blend of different, nutty flavours. The tamari and herbs add the essential savouriness.

METRIC/IMPERIAL	AMERICAN
2oz (50g) brazil nuts	½ cup brazil nuts
2oz (50g) hazelnuts	½ cup hazelnuts (filberts)
2oz (50g) sesame seeds	¼ cup sesame seeds
100g (¼lb) sunflower seeds	¼lb (½ cup) sunflower seeds
3 large onions	3 large onions
1 clove garlic	1 clove garlic
125g (¼lb) fresh wholemeal breadcrumbs	3-4 cups soft whole grain bread crumbs
60ml (4tbls) oil	4tbls oil
120ml (8tbls) chicken or vegetable stock	8tbls chicken or vegetable stock
60ml (4tbls) tamari sauce	4tbls Shoyu sauce
90ml (6tbls) mixed chopped fresh herbs	6tbls mixed chopped fresh herbs
extra oil for greasing pie or soufflé dish	extra oil for greasing pie or soufflé dish

Heat the oven to gas mark 4/180°C (350°F). Put the brazil nuts and hazel nuts into a blender or food processor and work them until they are finely ground. Put the sesame seeds into a frying-pan with no fat and set them in a moderate heat until they brown, shaking the pan occasionally. Turn them onto a plate to cool. Mix the nuts, sesame and sunflower seeds together. Finely chop the onions and garlic.

Heat the oil in a large frying-pan (skillet) on a low heat. Mix in the onion and garlic and cook them until they are soft. Take the pan from the heat and mix in the nuts, breadcrumbs, stock, tamari (Shoyu) sauce and herbs. Press the mixture into a large, lightly-greased pie dish or soufflé dish and smooth the top. Bake in the oven for 45 minutes. Serve directly from the dish.

Cooking time : 1 hour 10 minutes

† To make a tomato-flavoured nut roast add 30ml (2tbls) tomato purée or paste to the mixture instead of the tamari (Shoyu). The roast can then be baked in a ring mould. To serve, turn it out onto a flat plate and fill the centre with steamed broccoli or steamed diced green beans.

Cheese, Nut and Cauliflower Quiche

Puréed cauliflower and onion in this recipe provide the base for an unusual nut-flavoured quiche. All the ingredients mix together to make a light and flavoursome, mushroom-coloured filling.

Cauliflower and cheese fill this nut-pastry quiche.

METRIC/IMPERIAL	AMERICAN
shortcrust pastry made with 175g (6oz) wholemeal flour	single-crust pie pastry using 1½ cups whole grain flour
1 small cauliflower	1 small cauliflower
1 small onion	1 small onion
bouquet garni	bouquet garni
150ml (¼pt) stock	⅝ cup stock or broth
50g (2oz) walnuts	½ cup walnuts
50g (2oz) hazelnuts	½ cup hazelnuts (filberts)
75g (3oz) Farmhouse Cheddar cheese	¾ cup grated aged Cheddar cheese
4 eggs	4 eggs
sea salt	sea salt
freshly ground black pepper	freshly ground black pepper
butter for greasing 23cm (9in) flan tin	butter for greasing 9in quiche pan

Heat the oven to gas mark 6/200°C (400°F). Line a greased flan tin or quiche pan with the pastry. Break the cauliflower into florets and thinly slice the onion. Put them into a saucepan with the bouquet garni and stock. Set them on a moderate heat for 10 minutes, so they are just tender and most of the stock is evaporated. Rub them through a vegetable mill or mash them to a purée with a potato masher.

Grind the nuts in a blender, food processor or nut mill. Grate the cheese and beat the eggs. Mix all the ingredients together and season. Pour them into the pastry shell and smooth the top. Bake the quiche for 40 minutes so the top is golden brown and risen. Serve the quiche hot with baked potatoes and a green vegetable or cold with a light salad.

Cooking time : 1 hour 20 minutes

Carrot, Watercress and Poppy Seed Salad

This is a lovely brightly-coloured side salad, enriched with the nutty flavour of poppy seeds. Black poppy seeds are best to use as they show up more than the white. Sherry vinegar gives a full-bodied flavour to the dressing, but if none is available use a good cider vinegar.

METRIC/IMPERIAL	AMERICAN
350g (¾lb) carrots	*¾lb carrots*
1 bunch watercress	*1 bunch watercress*
30ml (2tbls) black poppy seeds	*2tbls black poppy seeds*
60ml (4tbls) olive or sunflower oil	*4tbls olive or sunflower oil*
30ml (2tbls) sherry vinegar	*2tbls sherry vinegar*
1 clove garlic, crushed with a pinch sea salt	*1 clove garlic, crushed with a pinch sea salt*
freshly ground black pepper	*freshly ground black pepper*

Coarsely grate the carrots and chop the watercress. Put them into a salad bowl with the poppy seeds. Beat the oil, vinegar, garlic and pepper together to make the dressing and fold it into the salad.

Cooking time: 15 minutes

Stir-fried Chicken and Peanuts

Chicken is often mixed with nuts to make a Chinese-type stir-fried dish. Here it is combined with peanuts and green bell peppers in a dark spicy sauce to make a very robust and satisfying dish. A savoury rice is the best accompaniment.

METRIC/IMPERIAL	AMERICAN
½ x 1.3kg (3lb) roasting chicken	*½ x 4lb roasting chicken*
30ml (2tbls) cornflour	*2tbls cornstarch*
1 large onion	*1 large onion*
2 medium-sized green peppers	*2 medium-sized green bell peppers*
1 large clove garlic	*1 large clove garlic*
15ml (1tbls) tomato purée	*1tbls tomato paste*
30ml (2tbls) tamari sauce	*2tbls Shoyu sauce*
2.5ml (½tsp) ground ginger	*½tsp ground ginger*
1.5ml (¼tsp) cayenne pepper	*¼tsp cayenne pepper*
275ml (½pt) chicken stock	*1¼ cups chicken stock or broth*
60ml (4tbls) oil	*4tbls oil*
175g (6oz) peanuts	*1½ cups peanuts*

Remove the chicken meat from the bones and cut it into 2cm (¾in) pieces. Coat them with the cornflour (cornstarch). Chop the onion and peppers fairly coarsely and finely chop the garlic. Mix together the tomato paste, tamari (Shoyu) sauce, ginger, cayenne pepper and stock.
Heat the oil and garlic in a large frying-pan or skillet on a high heat until the garlic sizzles. Put in the chicken pieces and move them around on the heat until they brown. Lower the heat to moderate. Put in the onion, peppers, and peanuts and continue cooking in the same way for 2 minutes. Pour in the stock mixture and bring it to the boil. Simmer, uncovered, for 3 minutes or until the sauce is thick and has reduced by about half. Serve immediately.

Cooking time: 30 minutes

Mixed Nut and Seed Platter

Serve this colourful platter of salads for a special main meal which combines all sorts of goodness and freshness. It is composed of two different salads arranged and decorated separately on each person's plate, with cheese in the centre.

METRIC/IMPERIAL	AMERICAN
1 large ripe avocado	*1 large ripe avocado*
½ medium-sized pineapple	*½ medium-sized pineapple*
30ml (2tbls) olive oil	*2tbls olive oil*
15ml (1tbls) tarragon vinegar	*1tbls tarragon vinegar*
1 small clove garlic, crushed with a pinch sea salt	*1 small clove garlic, crushed with a pinch sea salt*
freshly ground black pepper	*freshly ground black pepper*
50g (2oz) melon seeds	*¼ cup melon seeds*
For the second salad:	**For the second salad:**
350g (¾lb) tomatoes	*¾lb tomatoes*
4 large sticks celery	*4 large stalks celery*
½ x 450g (1lb) jar sprouted alfalfa seeds (or two boxes salad cress)	*½ x 1lb jar sprouted alfalfa seeds (or 1 bunch watercress)*
25g (1oz) currants	*2tbls currants or raisins*
15ml (1tbls) chopped basil (or parsley)	*1tbls chopped basil (or parsley)*
30ml (2tbls) olive oil	*2tbls olive oil*
15ml (1tbls) white wine vinegar	*1tbls white wine vinegar*
1 clove garlic, crushed with a pinch sea salt	*1 clove garlic, crushed with a pinch sea salt*
freshly ground black pepper	*freshly ground black pepper*
50g (2oz) blanched and split almonds	*2tbls blanched and split almonds*
To serve:	**To serve:**
1 large lettuce	*1 large lettuce*
225g (½lb) curd or yogurt cheese	*1⅓ cups farmer's or cottage cheese or yogurt cheese*

Peel the avocado. Cut it into thin lengthwise slices and then into 2cm (¾in) pieces. Cut the pineapple into 2cm (¾in) chunks. Put the pineapple and avocado into a bowl. Beat the oil, vinegar, garlic and pepper together and fold them into the salad.
Finely chop the tomatoes and celery. Put them into a bowl with the alfalfa, currants and basil. Beat the oil, vinegar, garlic and pepper together and fold them into the salad.
Arrange a bed of lettuce leaves on 4 large meat plates. Put the pineapple salad on one side of the plates and the tomato salad on the other. Scatter the melon seeds over the pineapple salad and the almonds over the tomato. Put a portion of cheese in the centre of each plate.

Preparation time: 30 minutes

Chicory, Sesame and Walnut Salad

This is a very luxurious salad for a special occasion. It is refreshing and nutty at the same time. The sesame oil adds extra flavour, but if none is available, use olive, sunflower or safflower oil. Serve the salad at the beginning of a meal.

METRIC/IMPERIAL	AMERICAN
2 small or 1 large bulb chicory about 225g (½lb) in all	½lb French or Belgian endive (Witloof chicory)
30ml (2tbls) sesame seeds	2tbls sesame seeds
50g (2oz) chopped walnuts	½ cup chopped walnuts
100g (¼lb) black grapes	⅔ cup black Concord grapes
30ml (2tbls) sesame oil	2tbls sesame oil
60ml (4tbls) white wine vinegar	2tbls white wine vinegar
1 clove garlic crushed with a pinch sea salt	1 clove garlic crushed with a pinch sea salt
freshly ground black pepper	freshly ground black pepper

Chop the chicory (endive) and divide it between 4 small bowls. Put the sesame seeds into a heavy frying-pan without any fat and set them on a moderate heat until they brown, shaking the pan from time to time. Turn them out immediately and cool them.
Scatter the sesame seeds and walnuts over the chicory (endive). Halve and seed the grapes and put them around the edges of the bowls. Beat the oil, vinegar, garlic and pepper together to make the dressing and spoon it over the salads.

Preparation time: 20 minutes

Chestnuts with Cabbage and Bacon

Chestnuts and bacon make a good cold-weather dish with cabbage. The small amount of bacon makes a good contrast with the slightly sweet chestnuts. Vegetarians can use 30ml (2tbls) tamari (Shoyu) sauce instead.

METRIC/IMPERIAL	AMERICAN
450g (1lb) fresh chestnuts or 175g (6oz) dried chestnuts	1lb fresh chestnuts or 6oz dried chestnuts
225g (½lb) unsmoked lean bacon	½lb sliced bacon
1 large green cabbage	1 large head Savoy cabbage
1 large onion	1 large onion
60ml (4tbls) oil	4tbls oil
6 chopped sage leaves	6 chopped sage leaves
90ml (6tbls) cider vinegar	6tbls cider vinegar

If using fresh chestnuts, cut a small portion from the tops of their shells and put them into a saucepan of cold water. Bring to the boil and simmer for 5 minutes. Take the pan off the heat. As soon as the chestnuts are cool enough to handle, peel them, leaving them immersed until skinned.
If using dried chestnuts, pour hot water on them and leave them for 3 hours. Put the chestnuts and the soaking water into a saucepan, bring them to the boil and simmer for 30 minutes. Drain them if neccessary.

Dice the bacon, finely shred the cabbage and peel, quarter and thinly slice the onion. Heat the oil in a heavy saucepan on low heat. Put the onion and bacon and cook them until the onion is soft. Fold in the chestnuts, cabbage and sage. Add the vinegar and cover the pan tightly. Cook gently for 10 minutes.

Cooking time: 50 minutes (plus 3½ hours for dried chestnuts)

Cheese and Sunflower Salad

Serve this salad for a main course. It combines the goodness of both shelled and sprouted sunflower seeds with a small amount of cheese. It is a very soft and delicate salad in both colour and flavour.

METRIC/IMPERIAL	AMERICAN
450g (1lb) jar sprouted sunflower seeds	1lb jar sprouted sunflower seeds
225g (½lb) Caerphilly cheese	½lb Mozzarella or Scmorzel cheese
125g (¼lb) shelled sunflower seeds	¼lb shelled sunflower seeds
1 large, crisp eating apple	1 large crisp apple
4 sticks celery	4 stalks celery
50g (2oz) sultanas	⅓ cup white raisins (muscats)
60ml (4tbls) sunflower oil	4tbls sunflower oil
30ml (2tbls) cider vinegar	2tbls cider vinegar
1 clove garlic, crushed with a pinch sea salt	1 clove garlic, crushed with a pinch sea salt
freshly ground black pepper	freshly ground black pepper

Pick the sprouts from the husks and break off any coarse roots. Dice the cheese, quarter, core and chop the apples and chop the celery. Put them all into a salad bowl with the shelled sunflower seeds and sultanas or raisins. Beat the oil, vinegar, garlic and pepper together to make the dressing and fold it into the salad.

Preparation time: 20 minutes

Leeks with Pine Nuts

This is an example of how a small amount of nuts can combine very effectively with vegetables to make a cooked side dish. These leeks have a Middle Eastern flavour and they go very well with all egg dishes and with chicken.

METRIC/IMPERIAL	AMERICAN
450g (1lb) leeks (both green and white parts)	1lb leeks (both green and white parts)
25g (1oz) butter	2tbls butter
50g (2oz) pine nuts	½ cup pine (Indian) nuts
5ml (1tsp) ground cumin	1tsp ground cumin
juice 1 lemon	juice 1 lemon

Wash the leeks well and cut them into 1cm (⅜in) slices. Melt the butter in a saucepan on a moderate heat. Put

Green peppers are stuffed with walnuts, onions and tomatoes and topped with cheese for a summer supper.

in the pine nuts and stir them around until they are beginning to brown. Stir in the cumin and cook it for ½ minute. Stir in the leeks and pour in the lemon juice. Turn the heat down low, cover the pan and cook the leeks for 10 minutes.

Cooking time : 25 minutes

Green Peppers with Walnut Stuffing

This walnut and wheat filling for green peppers is very light in texture and flavour, which makes it an excellent dish for summer.

METRIC/IMPERIAL	AMERICAN
50g (2oz) burghul wheat	⅔ cup bulgar
4 medium-sized green peppers	4 medium-sized green bell peppers
100g (¼lb) walnuts	1 cup walnuts
2 small tomatoes	2 small tomatoes
1 medium-sized onion	1 medium-sized onion
1 clove garlic	1 clove garlic
30ml (2tbls) oil	2tbls oil
275ml (½pt) chicken or vegetable stock	1¼ cups chicken or vegetable stock or broth
30ml (2tbls) tomato purée	
15ml (1tbls) chopped thyme	2tbls tomato paste
15ml (1tbls) chopped parsley	1tbls chopped thyme
sea salt	1tbls chopped parsley
freshly ground black pepper	sea salt
125g (¼lb) grated Farmhouse Cheddar cheese	freshly ground black pepper
	1 cup grated, aged Cheddar cheese

Heat the oven to gas mark 4 / 180°C (350°F). Soak the burghul (bulgar) in water for 30 minutes. Drain it and squeeze it dry. Remove the stalks and seeds from the peppers, keeping them whole. If necessary cut a thin slice from the bottom of each one to make them stand upright. Finely chop the walnuts. Scald, skin and finely chop the tomatoes. Finely chop the onion and garlic.
Heat the oil in a large frying-pan on a low heat. Mix in the onion and garlic and cook them until they are soft. Take the pan from the heat and mix in the burghul (bulgar), tomatoes, 60ml (4tbls) stock, tomato paste, herbs and seasonings. Mix them well and fill the peppers. Stand the peppers upright in a casserole and cover the tops with the cheese.
Cover the casserole and put it into the oven for 15 minutes. Take off the lid and continue cooking for a further 15 minutes to allow the cheese to brown slightly.

Cooking time : 1 hour 10 minutes (including soaking)

Stir-braised Cashew Nuts with Celery and Fennel

This stir-braised dish is subtly sweet and sour. It looks light and delicate but is nevertheless very substantial. Serve it with a savoury brown rice, such as steamed rice with tamari (Shoyu) sauce.

METRIC/IMPERIAL	AMERICAN
6 large sticks celery	6 large stalks celery
1 medium-sized bulb Florence fennel weighing around 225g (½lb)	1 medium-sized Florence fennel or finocchio, weighing around ½lb
1 large onion	1 large onion
1 large clove garlic	1 large clove garlic
2 large oranges	2 large oranges
30ml (2tbls) cornflour	2tbls cornstarch
30ml (2tbls) tamari sauce	2tbls Shoyu sauce
15ml (1tbls) white wine vinegar	1tbls white wine vinegar
5ml (1tsp) honey	1tsp honey
275ml (½pt) chicken stock	1¼ cups chicken or vegetable stock
60ml (4tbls) oil	4tbls oil
225g (½lb) cashew nuts	½lb cashew nuts

Finely chop the fennel, celery, onion and garlic. Squeeze the juice from one of the oranges and mix it with the cornflour (cornstarch), vinegar, honey and stock and tamari. Cut the rind and pith from the remaining orange. Cut the flesh into quarters and slice it thinly.
Heat the oil and garlic in a heavy frying-pan on a high heat until the garlic sizzles. Put in the celery, fennel, onion and cashew nuts and stir them around on the heat for 2 minutes. Pour in the stock mixture, bring it to the boil and cover the pan. Turn the heat to moderate and cook for 10 minutes. Add the orange slices just before serving.

Cooking time: 30 minutes

Apple and Nut Crumble

This apple dessert relies on sultanas (white raisins or muscats) and a little honey for natural sweetness. The nut and crumb topping is crisp and slightly chewy.

METRIC/IMPERIAL	AMERICAN
700g (1½lb) cooking apples	1½lb tart apples
30ml (2tbls) clear honey	2tbls honey
30ml (2tbls) sultanas	2tbls white raisins (muscats)
5ml (1tsp) ground cinnamon	1tsp ground cinnamon
50g (2oz) hazelnuts	½ cup hazelnuts (filberts)
50g (2oz) almonds	½ cup almonds
30ml (2tbls) sesame seeds	2tbls sesame seeds
30ml (2tbls) wheatgerm	2tbls wheatgerm
25g (1oz) butter	2tbls butter

Heat the oven to gas mark 5 / 190°C (375°F). Peel, core and thinly slice the apples and put them into a bowl. Fold in the honey, sultanas (white raisins) and cinna-mon. Put the apples into a pie dish. Finely grind the hazelnuts. Blanch and split the almonds. Mix them both with the wheatgerm and sesame seeds. Melt the butter in a saucepan on a low heat, without letting it foam. Fold in the nut mixture and take the pan from the heat. Spread the nut mixture evenly over the apples. Bake the pudding for 30 minutes. Serve hot or cold; it is equally good either way.

Cooking time: 1 hour

Yogurt and Coconut Cream

This yogurt cream is light and refreshing. It looks elegant when set in stemmed wine glasses. But if you make your own yogurt (page 126), it is cheap and a good choice when you have a fresh coconut.

METRIC/IMPERIAL	AMERICAN
15g (½oz) gelatin	2tbls gelatin
60ml (4tbls) water	4tbls water
125g (¼lb) freshly grated coconut	¾ cup freshly grated coconut
425ml (¾pt) natural yogurt	2 cups plain yogurt
45ml (3tbls) honey	3tbls honey
grated rind 1 lemon	grated rind 1 lemon

Soak the gelatin in the water in a small saucepan. Put the coconut into a blender with one-third of the yogurt, honey and lemon rind. Work them to a cream; it will not be absolutely smooth. Turn out into a bowl and stir in the remaining yogurt.
Melt the gelatin on a low heat without letting it bubble, and quickly stir it into the rest of the ingredients. Pour the cream into either a large bowl or into individual bowls or goblets and put it into a cool place to set.

Cooking time: 40 minutes, plus setting

Date and Walnut Bread

Dates, walnuts and cheese make a light, moist, semi-sweet loaf which can be eaten plainly or spread with butter. It is also delicious with honey or cheese.

METRIC/IMPERIAL	AMERICAN
225g (½lb) fresh or semi-dried dates	½lb fresh or semi-dried dates
45ml (3oz) chopped walnuts	¾ cup chopped walnuts
225g (½lb) wholemeal flour	½lb (2 cups) whole grain flour
freshly grated nutmeg	freshly grated nutmeg
2.5ml (½tsp) sea salt	½tsp sea salt
2.5ml (½tsp) bicarbonate of soda	½tsp baking soda
75g (3oz) cottage cheese	¾ cup cottage cheese
1 egg, beaten	1 egg, beaten
150ml (¼ pt) milk	⅝ cup milk
butter for greasing 450g (1lb) loaf tin	butter for greasing 3-cup bread pan

This date and walnut bread is most unusual in that it is made with cottage cheese, rather than wholemeal flour and the usual raising agents. Compare it with the more conventional version on page 148.

Heat the oven to gas mark 4 / 180°C (350°F). If you are using fresh dates, skin, stone (pit) and chop them. Semi-dried dates can simply be stoned (pitted) and chopped. Put the dates and walnuts into a bowl with the flour and add the nutmeg, salt and soda. Make a well in the centre. Rub the cheese through a sieve (strainer) and gradually beat in the egg. Pour the cheese mixture and the milk into the flour and mix everything to a moist dough. Put it into a greased 450g (1lb) loaf tin (3 cup bread pan) and smooth the top. Bake the loaf for 1 hour and turn it onto a wire rack to cool.

Cooking time : 1 hour 20 minutes

Sesame and Hazelnut Slices

Serve these extravagant honey slices with their nut and seed topping for special occasion tea parties.

METRIC/IMPERIAL	AMERICAN
125g (¼lb) butter	8tbls butter
125g (¼lb) plus 45ml (3tbls) clear honey	½ cup honey
125g (¼lb) wholemeal flour	1 cup whole grain flour
5ml (1tsp) baking powder	1tsp baking powder
5ml (1tsp) ground cinnamon	1tsb ground cinnamon
2 eggs, beaten	2 eggs, beaten
45ml (3tbls) chopped toasted hazelnuts	3tbls chopped toasted hazelnuts (filberts)
30ml (2tbls) sesame seeds	2tbls sesame seeds
butter for greasing tin 20cm x 28cm (8 x 11in) and 3cm (1in) deep	butter for greasing 8 x 11in and 1in deep pan

Heat the oven to gas mark 4 / 180°C (350°F). Beat the butter to a cream and beat in the 125g (¼lb) or ⅜ cup honey. Mix the flour with the baking powder and cinnamon and beat it into the butter, alternately with the eggs.

Thickly butter the tin (pan) and pour the 45ml (3tbls) honey evenly into the bottom. Scatter in the hazelnuts and sesame seeds. Put in the cake mixture and smooth the top. Bake the cake for 25 minutes. Take the cake out of the oven and let it cool. Cut it into slices and carefully lift them out with a spatula. Put them on a plate, nutty side up.

Cooking time : 45 minutes, plus extra for cooling

† Try a topping of chopped walnuts and treacle (molasses) instead of hazelnuts, sesame seeds and honey.

Fish & Shellfish

Fish and shellfish are a superb natural source of high quality, animal protein. Deep-sea or salt-water fish have not been subjected to scientific breeding and are relatively free from pollution. Unfortunately this is not always true of freshwater fish from lakes and streams, although the mercury scare has not proved to be as serious as anticipated. Fish and shellfish are easy to cook, light to eat, easy to digest and full of natural goodness.

Besides protein, the main value of all fish and shellfish is in the high proportion of minerals that they contain. White fish in particular is one of the few foods that contains iodine. Fish have little or no carbohydrate in their make-up and there is very little fat in white fish, since the natural oils are contained only in the liver. In the case of oily fish, the fat is distributed throughout the body and is a mixture of saturated and polyunsaturated fat. Contained in this fat is a high level of vitamins A and D. Most fish also contain small amounts of B vitamins.

Since wholefood cooking methods are mainly light and bring out the natural flavours of the fish, instead of masking them in heavy sauces or a thick coating of batter, it is always most important to buy your fish as fresh as possible and cook it on the same day or at least the day after. If you are buying whole fish, make sure that the eyes are bright and the skin moist and glossy and unbroken. Fish fillets should be firm. If they are pulpy then they have probably been frozen and badly thawed. Frozen fish 'steaks' and fish fingers (fish sticks) covered in crumbs or batter will never taste as good as fish that is freshly caught and quickly cooked.

Smoked fish can be delicious, but very often it has been artificially coloured with a substance called BFK (meaning, simply, Brown For Kippers) that, although permitted in Britain for example, is considered unsafe by international standards. Look for uncoloured smoked kippers, mackerel and other fish, which will generally be a dull biscuit colour instead of the bright, orangey-brown colour induced by dye. Very bright yellow smoked haddock and cod could also have been artificially coloured. However, the bright red colour of some shellfish is the perfectly natural result of its having been boiled.

Cooking methods

When you buy white fish or shellfish such as prawns (shrimp) or crab, the fish skin and bones or the shells can be used to make a flavoursome stock with which you can make a sauce or a soup. Simply put them into a large saucepan with about 1.7L (3pt) or US 2qt water, a roughly chopped onion, carrot and stick of celery, 5ml (1tsp) black peppercorns and a large bouquet garni. Bring them to the boil, skim them if necessary, cover and simmer for 45-60 minutes. Strain the stock, cool it and store it in the refrigerator in a covered container. It will keep for 3 days.

Court bouillon: the lightest possible way of cooking fish is to poach it in a court bouillon flavoured with herbs and peppercorns. A dash of white wine, cider or white wine vinegar will lighten and improve the flavour. You can use this method for small, thin fillets, thicker cutlets (chunks or steaks) and small or large whole fish. Both white and oily fish can be cooked in this way. The golden rule for poaching is not to over-cook the fish. Only have as much court bouillon as will just about cover it, bring it to the boil, lower the fish in gently and cook it, with the water just trembling, until it is done. Then lift it out carefully and drain it well. White fish can be finished with a sauce made from the court bouillon, and both white and oily fish benefit from a sharp accompaniment such as capers or lemon.

Oven poaching: fish can also be oven-poached, that is, baked in a dish with a little liquid, covered with foil. White fish can be cooked in cider or white wine and flavoured with chopped herbs or a piece of lemon rind. Oily fish is most often soused, that is cooked in vinegar or a mixture of vinegar and water with vegetables and spices. It can then either be served hot or left to get cool in the liquid and served with a salad. The vinegar will not make the dish sharp but it counteracts the richness of the fish.

Dry-baking is a sure way of sealing in all the goodness in fish and enhancing its natural flavour. Before you start, season the fish with sea salt and freshly ground black pepper and let it stand for a while. Baking in a brick is a very effective way of dry-baking, but do remember to use a separate brick for fish and one for meat as the one may flavour the other. Small, whole, stuffed fish can be cooked very effectively in a brick as they become penetrated by all the flavours of the stuffing. You can also cook thick fillets, steaks or thick sections of fish such as cod on a bed of herbs. Do not heat the oven until you first put the brick inside and start timing when you first turn it on. Small fish need only 30 minutes at a high temperature, with 10 minutes extra if they are stuffed, but large fish or a thick section will need up to 1½ hours in a moderate oven.

En papillote: the other method of dry-baking is called 'en papillote', that is with the fish wrapped in foil or thick waxed or greaseproof paper. Small fish such as mackerel, herrings or whiting can be cooked whole, filled with herbs or a stuffing. White fish can be cooked in fillets or cut into squares or strips and flavoured with herbs or chopped mushrooms. A few shelled shrimp or prawns make an excellent luxury addition to a parcel of baked white fish. Take the fish, still wrapped, to the table and serve them this way so the flavoursome juices are only set free when they are on the plate.

Steaming: really fresh fish is delicious lightly steamed.

Always use a closed method of steaming so all the goodness and flavour are preserved. If you are only cooking for one or two people, fish fillets can be steamed between two enamel plates, but if you need more room, wrap the pieces of fish in foil and stack them either in a perforated vegetable steamer or a large colander standing over a pan of boiling water. Take care that the level of water does not cover the parcels of fish. For a really good flavour, season the fish well and if possible sprinkle it with lemon juice and let it stand for a while before cooking. After this the fish may be steamed quite plainly or you can add flavourings such as chopped herbs or a sprinkling of paprika. While the fish is cooking you can make a sauce with stock made from the skin, head and trimmings to which you can later add all the juices which have collected in the parcels of fish. This will ensure that none of the goodness is lost or thrown away.

Grilling or broiling is a very quick and easy way of

cooking both white and oily fish, whole or filleted. Smaller fish can be made to look very attractive if they are grilled whole. The slits that you cut in the side to ensure that they cook properly can also add to their appearance and, if you fill the slits full of herbs, to the flavour as well. Whole white fish need to be brushed with a little oil before cooking in order to keep them moist, but this is not absolutely necessary for oily fish, as they contain sufficient oil to be self-basting. White fish fillets need a little more care than those of oily fish to prevent them from drying under the heat. Brush them with a mixture of oil and orange or lemon juice or tomato purée or paste and season them at least an hour before cooking so they stay moist and succulent. You can add a chopped onion as well and some fresh herbs to turn this into a real marinade. It is not essential to marinate or coat oily fish fillets, but they can benefit from this treatment. Always make sure something sharp is added as well to counteract their

richness. Cider vinegar and grated horse radish are good with mackerel fillets; and lemon juice and a pinch of dry mustard powder work wonders with herrings. Natural (plain) yogurt can also be used for marinades for fish to give them a tangy freshness.

Stir-frying and stir-braising are two methods that can be used very effectively for white fish. Cut the fillets into thin strips and add them to the pan only after you have stir-fried the vegetables to prevent the fish from disintegrating.

Pâtés: the other use for oily fish is in pâtés and these can be made without any fat and flavoured with herbs and citrus fruits. They can be served to start a meal or as a main dish with a salad.

Shellfish are expensive to use alone to make a main dish but they can be used in a combination with other fish or with another ingredient such as eggs, milk or salad vegetables. They make superb, light and attractive first courses.

RECIPES

Crab and Tomato Soup

Serve this smooth soup made from a fresh crab as a first course on special occasions.

METRIC/IMPERIAL	AMERICAN
225g (½lb) crab meat (mixture of white and brown)	½lb crab meat (mixture of white and brown)
450g (1lb) ripe tomatoes	1lb ripe tomatoes
1 large onion	1 large onion
1 clove garlic	1 clove garlic
25g (1oz) butter	2tbls butter
5ml (1tsp) paprika	1tsp paprika
pinch cayenne pepper	pinch cayenne pepper
575ml (1pt) stock (this can be either fish or chicken stock)	2½ cups stock or broth (this can be either fish or chicken stock)
30ml (2tbls) chopped parsley	2tbls chopped parsley

Scald and skin the tomatoes. Cut them in half. Put a strainer over a bowl and scoop the tomato seeds into it. Rub them to extract as much juice as possible. Discard the seeds. Roughly chop the tomatoes. Finely chop the onions and garlic. Melt the butter in a saucepan on a low heat. Stir in the onion, garlic, paprika and cayenne pepper and cook until the onion is soft. Add the chopped tomatoes and their juices. Cover the pan and cook gently for 5 minutes so the tomatoes cook to a purée. Stir in the stock. Bring it to the boil and simmer for 5 minutes more. Stir in the crab meat.
Either pass the soup through the medium blade of a vegetable mill or work in a blender until it is smooth. Return the soup to the pan. Stir in the parsley and reheat gently without boiling.

Cooking time: 30 minutes

A fresh crab makes a luxurious soup for four people.

Prawn, Pear and Tarragon Salad

Prawns, pears and tarragon all have delicate flavours that combine superbly in an attractive salad.

METRIC/IMPERIAL	AMERICAN
225g (½lb) prawns (unshelled weight)	½lb prawns or jumbo shrimp, unshelled weight
4 medium-sized, firm Conference pears	4 medium-sized firm pears
60ml (4tbls) olive oil	4tbls olive oil
30ml (2tbls) tarragon vinegar	2tbls tarragon vinegar
10ml (2tsp) tarragon mustard (preferably the granular kind)	2tsp tarragon mustard (if available) or mustard containing seeds
125g (¼lb) curd cheese	½ cup farmer's, curd or cottage cheese
30ml (2tbls) chopped tarragon (if available)	2tbls chopped tarragon (if available)

Shell and clean the prawns. Quarter, peel, core and finely chop the pears. Mix the oil, vinegar and mustard together to make the dressing and fold it into the pears. Divide the pears between four small bowls and put a portion of the cheese in the centre of each one. Arrange the prawns around the cheese and scatter the tarragon over the top.

Preparation time : 20 minutes

Fish and Lemon Soup

Serve this substantial lemon-flavoured soup as a main course accompanied by wholemeal (whole grain) bread and a salad.

METRIC/IMPERIAL	AMERICAN
700g (1½lb) cod or haddock fillets	1½lb codfish or haddock fillets
juice 1 lemon	juice 1 lemon
sea salt	sea salt
freshly ground black pepper	freshly ground black pepper
225g (½lb) carrots	½lb carrots
2 medium-sized onions	2 medium-sized onions
225g (½lb) tomatoes	½lb tomatoes
1 medium-sized cucumber	1 medium-sized cucumber
10 black olives	10 black olives
25g (1oz) butter	2tbls butter
1.1L (2pt) fish stock	5 cups fish stock
30ml (2tbls) chopped parsley	2tbls chopped parsley
15ml (1tbls) chopped thyme	1tbls chopped thyme
4 slices lemon	4 slices lemon

Cut the fish into strips 1 x 5cm (½ x 2in). Sprinkle it with the lemon juice, salt and pepper and leave it for 2 hours, preferably not in the refrigerator.
Cut the carrots into julienne sticks, thinly slice the

Lemons and five vegetables go to make this fish soup.

Smoked mackerel has a delicate flavour; here it is combined with curd cheese and orange juice to make pâté.

onions, scald, skin and finely chop the tomatoes and thinly slice the cucumber without peeling. Stone (pit) and quarter the olives.

Melt the butter in a saucepan on a low heat. Stir in the onions and carrots and cook them until the onions are soft. Stir in the cucumber and cook for 2 minutes more. Add the tomatoes and cook until they are reduced to a purée. Pour in the stock and bring it to the boil. Add the herbs and simmer for 10 minutes. Put in the pieces of fish and any juices that have collected on the plate, Simmer for 5 minutes more. Ladle the soup into bowls and serve with a slice of lemon floating on top.

Cooking time: 45 minutes, plus 2 hours for marinating

Smoked Mackerel Pâté

Smoked mackerel and curd cheese make a simple but very impressive pâté. Serve it as a main course for 4 people or as a first course for 8. Sliced wholemeal bread and butter is the best accompaniment.

METRIC/IMPERIAL	AMERICAN
450g (1lb) smoked mackerel fillets	*1lb smoked fish*
225g (½lb) curd cheese	*½lb (1½ cups) curd cheese*
grated rind and juice 1 medium-sized orange	*grated rind and juice 1 medium-sized orange*
10ml (2tsp) tomato purée	*2tsp tomato paste*
30ml (2tbls) grated horseradish	*2tbls grated fresh horseradish*
For the garnish:	**For the garnish:**
1 orange	*1 orange*
few cucumber slices	*few cucumber slices*

Remove the skin and bones from the fish fillets. Flake the fillets and mix them with the curd cheese. Put the mixture into a blender with the orange juice and tomato paste and work it until you have a smooth purée. Turn it into a bowl and beat in the orange rind and horseradish, making sure they are well incorporated. Put the pâté into a dish, smooth the top and chill it for 1 hour. Just before serving, decorate the top with thin slices of orange and cucumber.

Preparation time: 1 hour 30 minutes

Herring and Orange Pâté

This moist, flavoursome pâté can be served as an appetizer or a main course. As a first course, it will serve 8. It can also be spread on melba toast or crackers and be served with drinks.

METRIC/IMPERIAL	AMERICAN
3 large herrings	3 sea herrings
For the marinade:	**For the marinade:**
juice ½ large orange	juice ½ large orange
5ml (1tsp) chopped chives	1tsp chopped chives
5ml (1tsp) chopped thyme	1tsp chopped thyme
5ml (1tsp) chopped parsley	1tsp chopped parsley
For the pâté:	**For the pâté:**
grated rind ½ large orange	grated rind ½ large orange
10ml (2tsp) grated horseradish	2tsp grated fresh horseradish
10ml (2tsp) Dijon mustard	2tsp Dijon-style mustard
15ml (1tbls) chopped parsley	1tbls chopped parsley
15ml (1tbls) mixed chopped chives and thyme	1tbls mixed chopped chives and thyme
30ml (2tbls) double cream (optional)	2tbls heavy cream (if desired)

Mix the ingredients for the marinade into a bowl. Fillet the herrings and cut one of the fillets into thin strips. Mix the strips into the marinade and leave them for 30 minutes.

Heat the oven to gas mark 4/180°C (350°F). Finely mince (grind) the remaining fillets. Mix in the rest of the ingredients for the pâté. Put half the mixture into a small, earthenware terrine or pâté dish. Lay the marinated strips on top. Put in the remaining pâté mixture, press it down well and smooth the top. Cover the terrine and put it in a baking tin (pan) of water. Put it into the oven for 1½ hours. Cool the pâté (preferably not in the refrigerator) completely before turning it out.

Cooking time: 2 hours 15 minutes, plus extra for cooling

Salmon-filled Lemons

Salmon tends to be expensive these days, but you need only a very little to make a luxurious first course. The yogurt gives a creamy texture but light flavour that does not at all mask that of the salmon.

METRIC/IMPERIAL	AMERICAN
4 lemons	4 lemons
175g (6oz) fresh salmon	6oz fresh salmon
bouquet garni	bouquet garni
1 blade mace	1 blade mace
6 black peppercorns	6 black peppercorns
2 hard-boiled eggs	2 hard-cooked eggs
60ml (4tbls) natural yogurt	4tbls plain yogurt

Squeeze the juice from the lemons and reserve it. Scrape the membranes from the lemon shells. Put 30ml (2tbls) of the lemon juice into a shallow pan with

Fresh salmon with hard eggs and yogurt makes a party hors d'oeuvre; serve it in lemon shells.

the bouquet garni, mace and peppercorns and enough cold water to just cover the salmon. Bring them to the boil and simmer them for 10 minutes. Lower in the salmon and with the water just trembling, poach it for 10 minutes. Remove it and let it cool.

Finely chop the eggs. Flake the salmon and remove any skin and bones. Mix the salmon and one of the eggs with the yogurt. Pile the salmon mixture into the lemon shells and top it with the remaining egg and the parsley. Serve the lemons with wholemeal (whole grain) rolls or thinly cut wholemeal (whole grain) bread.

Cooking time : 45 minutes

Mackerel Kebabs

Kebabs with plenty of vegetables always make quite small amounts of meat or fish go a long way and turn them into healthy and balanced meals. These mackerel kebabs are made all the better for being marinated, but if you are in a hurry, you may simply baste them with the dressing.

METRIC/IMPERIAL	AMERICAN
2 medium-to-large mackerel	2 medium-to-large mackerel
6 button onions	6 button onions
8 small tomatoes	8 small tomatoes
225g (½lb) flat mushrooms	½lb flat mushrooms
1 large green pepper	1 large green bell pepper
60ml (4tbls) olive oil	4tbls olive oil
juice 1 lemon	juice 1 lemon
30ml (2tbls) chopped thyme	2tbls chopped thyme
pinch cayenne pepper	pinch cayenne pepper

Fillet the mackerel and cut each fillet into four or five pieces. Peel the onions, scald and skin the tomatoes and halve the mushrooms. Remove the stalk and seeds from the pepper and cut it into 1.6cm (½in) strips. Thread a tomato onto each of four kebab skewers and then alternate the pieces of mackerel with the onions, mushrooms and pepper. End with another whole tomato. Put the kebabs onto a large, shallow dish, big enough to take them all lying flat. Beat the remaining ingredients together and pour them over the kebabs. Leave the kebabs for at least 2 hours in a cool place but preferably not the refrigerator, turning them several times.

When you are ready to cook, preheat the grill (broiler) to high. Lay the kebabs on the hot rack and baste them with any marinade remaining in the dish. Cook them for 12 minutes, turning them frequently. Serve the kebabs with a savoury brown rice.

Cooking time : 3 hours

Make fish kebabs with marinated mackerel fillets and strips of green pepper, onions and tomatoes.

Smoked fish and green pepper salad with lemon dressing.

Hot Shellfish and Celery

This first course is very quick and easy but it tastes as though you have gone to endless trouble in preparing it. The browned garlic gives it a nutty flavour.

METRIC/IMPERIAL	AMERICAN
125g (¼lb) cockles	¼lb shrimp, unshelled weight
4 large sticks celery	4 large stalks celery
1 clove garlic	1 clove garlic
30ml (2tbls) oil	2tbls oil
freshly ground black pepper	freshly ground black pepper
30ml (2tbls) malt vinegar	2tbls malt vinegar

Wash the cockles in two changes of cold water and drain them well (or peel and devein the shrimp). Finely chop the celery and garlic. Heat the oil in a frying-pan on a high heat. Put in the celery and garlic and stir-fry them until the celery is translucent and the garlic brown. Put in the cockles or shrimp and stir-fry for ½ minute. Season with plenty of pepper. Add the vinegar and let it bubble. Take the pan from the heat and serve as soon as you can in small bowls.

Cooking time : 15 minutes

Smoked Fish and Green Pepper Salad

Smoked cod or haddock, lemon and herbs make a moist, cold fish dish to serve with a light mixed salad of lettuce and tomatoes.

METRIC/IMPERIAL	AMERICAN
For the dressing:	**For the dressing:**
1 lemon	1 lemon
60ml (4tbls) olive oil	4tbls olive oil
15ml (1tbls) chopped thyme	1tbls chopped thyme
15ml (1tbls) chopped tarragon	1tbls chopped tarragon
15ml (1tbls) chopped marjoram	1tbls chopped marjoram
15ml (1tbls) chopped fennel	1tbls chopped fennel
1 clove garlic, crushed with a pinch sea salt	1 clove garlic, crushed with a pinch sea salt
freshly ground black pepper	freshly ground black pepper
For the dish:	**For the dish:**
700g (1½lb) smoked cod fillet	1½lb smoked fish, such as Finan haddie
bouquet garni	bouquet garni
1 blade mace	1 blade mace
5ml (1tsp) black peppercorns	1tsp black peppercorns
1 slice onion	1 slice onion
1 medium-sized green pepper	1 medium-sized green pepper
6 spring onions	6 scallions

Cut the rind and white tissue or pith from the lemon and slice the flesh thinly. Beat the oil and vinegar with the herbs, garlic and seasonings. Add the pieces of lemon and let the dressing stand for 4 hours at room temperature. Put the fish into a shallow pan with the bouquet garni, mace, peppercorns and onion and

102

cover it with water. Bring it to the boil and simmer for 5 minutes. Lift it out and drain it well. Flake it, remove the skin and bones and let it cool.

Remove the stalk and seeds from the pepper. Cut it into lengthways quarters and thinly slice them. Finely chop the spring onions (scallions). Fold the pepper and onions into the fish. Press down hard on the lemon slices in the dressing to extract as much juice as possible and then discard them. Fold the dressing into the fish mixture. Serve plainly or on a bed of lettuce, garnished with slices of cucumber and tomato.

Cooking time: 4 hours 15 minutes

Stir-braised Coley (Shad or Pompano)

Stir-braising with vegetables in a tasty cooking liquid is an excellent way of cooking fish. It mellows the flavour and masks the somewhat dark colour of coley which tends sometimes to make it rather unpopular.

METRIC/IMPERIAL	AMERICAN
700g (1½lb) coley fillets	1½lb shad or pompano
1 large green pepper	1 large green bell pepper
1 large onion	1 large onion
45ml (3tbls) oil	3tbls oil
1 clove garlic, crushed with a pinch sea salt	1 clove garlic, crushed with a pinch sea salt
200ml (7floz) tomato juice	1 cup tomato juice

Skin the fish and remove as many bones as possible. Cut it into pieces about 1cm (½in) wide and 5cm (2in) long. Remove the stalk and seeds and finely chop the pepper and the onion.

Heat the oil in a frying-pan on a high heat. Put in the pepper, onion and garlic and stir-fry them for 2 minutes. Pour in the tomato juice and bring it to the boil. Put in the fish, cover the pan and cook on a moderate heat for 10 minutes.

Cooking time: 30 minutes

Crab and Egg Salad

Crab on its own as a main meal can be expensive and time-consuming to prepare so, to make a light salad for four people, accompany it with hard-boiled eggs and a creamy mayonnaise-type dressing.

METRIC/IMPERIAL	AMERICAN
350g (¾lb) crabmeat	¾-1lb crabmeat
6 hard-boiled eggs	6 hard-cooked eggs
1 medium-sized lettuce	1 medium-sized lettuce
parsley sprigs	parsley sprigs
tomatoes for garnish (optional)	tomatoes for garnish (if desired)
For the mayonnaise:	**For the mayonnaise:**
1 egg yolk	1 egg yolk
2.5ml (½tsp) Tabasco sauce	½tsp Tabasco sauce
2.5ml (½tsp) ground paprika	½tsp ground paprika
grated rind ½ lemon and juice up to ½ lemon	grated rind ½ lemon and juice up to ½ lemon
pinch sea salt	pinch sea salt

Keep the white and brown (claw and body) crabmeat separate. Peel the eggs and cut them in half lengthways. Put a bed of lettuce on a large serving plate. Put the brown crabmeat in the centre and surround it with the white. Arrange the egg-halves, cut side down, around the crab.

Put the egg yolk into a bowl with the Tabasco sauce and paprika and beat it with a wooden spoon. Gradually beat in 30ml (2tbls) oil and then add 10ml (2tsp) lemon juice. Beat in the rest of the oil very gradually. Taste the mayonnaise and add as much of the remaining lemon juice as desired. Add salt to taste if necessary. Spoon the dressing only over the eggs and garnish with the parsley sprigs.

Preparation time: 30 minutes

Steamed Plaice (Flounder) with Cucumber Sauce

This sauce made with cucumber gives steamed plaice (flounder) a summery flavour.

METRIC/IMPERIAL	AMERICAN
2 large plaice	2 x 1-2lb flounder or 8 flounder fillets
little butter for greasing	little butter for greasing
sea salt	sea salt
freshly ground black pepper	freshly ground black pepper
juice 1 lemon	juice 1 lemon
30ml (2tbls) chopped fennel	2tbls chopped fennel
For the sauce:	**For the sauce:**
1 small cucumber	1 cucumber
25g (1oz) butter	2tbls butter
20ml (1½tbls) wholemeal flour	1½tbls whole grain flour
275ml (½pt) fish stock	1¼ cups fish stock
juice ½ lemon	juice ½ lemon
30ml (2tbls) chopped fennel	2tbls chopped fennel

Cut 8 fillets from the fish, skin them and make a well flavoured stock with the skins. Lay the fillets on a large piece of lightly-buttered foil and sprinkle them with salt and pepper, lemon juice and fennel. Roll up the fillets. Bring the edges of the foil together and fold them over to seal them. Steam the fillets for 15 minutes. Make the sauce while they are cooking. Finely dice the cucumber. Melt the butter in a saucepan on a high heat. Stir in the cucumber and cook it briskly for 2 minutes, stirring. Stir in the flour and cook it for ½ minute. Stir in the stock and bring it to the boil. Add the fennel and lemon juice; simmer for 2 minutes. Carefully unwrap the fish and lift the rolled fillets onto a warm serving dish. Pour the juices from the foil into the sauce. Stir the sauce, reheat it if necessary and pour it over the fish.

Cooking time: 1½ hours (including making stock)

Fennel Rollmops

These pickled herrings make a delicious salad with tomatoes for a main course. They can also be served singly as a first course.

METRIC/IMPERIAL	AMERICAN
8 herrings	8 herrings
50g (2oz) sea salt	¼ cup sea salt
575ml (1pt) cold water	2½ cups cold water
575ml (1pt) white wine vinegar	2½ cups white wine vinegar
15ml (1tbls) mixed pickling spice	1tbls mixed pickling spice
5ml (1tsp) fennel seeds	1tsp fennel seeds
1 piece dried fennel stalk about 8cm (3in) long	1 piece dried fennel stalk about 3in long
45ml (3tbls) chopped fresh fennel	3tbls chopped fresh fennel

Slit the herrings, clean them, remove the backbones and lay the fish flat. Dissolve the salt in the water and pour the brine into a flat dish. Lay the herrings in the brine, cut side down, and leave them for 2 hours. Put the vinegar, pickling spice and fennel stalk and seeds into a saucepan. Bring them gently to the boil. Remove them from the heat and leave them until the herrings are ready.

Halve and thinly slice the onion. Lift the herrings from the brine and at the head end put 5ml (1tsp) chopped fennel and a little of the onion. Roll up the herrings, starting from the head end, and secure them with cocktail sticks (picks). Pack the herrings into a wide-necked jar with any remaining fennel and onion. Strain the spiced vinegar over them making sure the fish are completely submerged. Cover tightly. Leave the herrings for not less than two days in a cool place before opening. Eat within 6 weeks.

Cooking time: 2½ hours

Sprats or Smelt with Lemon

Sprats (smelt) are rich little fish that need the sharp contrast of lemon. You can eat them whole or remove the head and gut before cooking. This will make them easier to eat and will give them a more mellow flavour.

METRIC/IMPERIAL	AMERICAN
675-900g (1½-2lb) sprats	1½-2lb smelt
juice ½ lemon	juice ½ lemon
60ml (4tbls) oil	4tbls oil
freshly ground black pepper	freshly ground black pepper
For serving:	**For serving:**
juice 2 lemons	juice 2 lemons
90ml (6tbls) chopped parsley	6tbls chopped parsley

Either keep the sprats (smelt) whole or cut off the heads taking with them most of the gut. Put the fish into a dish. Beat the oil, lemon juice and pepper together and pour them over the fish. Mix the lemon juice and parsley together. Leave everything for 2 hours at room temperature.
Divide the small fish between 4 skewers. If they are whole, push the skewer through just below the head. If you have removed the heads, push the skewer through the middle of the widest part. In each case, make sure they are all facing the same way.
Preheat the grill (broiler) to high. Lay the fish on the hot rack, belly-side down and grill (broil) them for 4 minutes without turning them.
Slide the fish from the skewers onto individual serving plates and scatter the parsley steeped in lemon over the top.

Cooking time: 2 hours 15 minutes or 2 hours 30 minutes, depending on whether the heads are removed.

Herring with Mustard Yogurt

Lemon, mustard and yogurt give a light flavour to rich herrings.

METRIC/IMPERIAL	AMERICAN
4 small to medium-sized herrings	4 small to medium-sized herring
275ml (½pt) natural yogurt	1¼ cups plain yogurt
10ml (2tsp) made English mustard	2tsp prepared mustard
grated rind 1 lemon	grated rind 1 lemon
15ml (1tbls) chopped lemon thyme (or common thyme)	1tbls chopped lemon thyme (or common thyme)
30ml (2tbls) chopped parsley	2tbls chopped parsley

Fillet the herrings and lay the fillets in a flat, heat-proof dish. Beat the rest of the ingredients together and spoon them over the fish. Leave the herrings for 4 hours at room temperature.
Preheat the grill (broiler) to high. Put the dish of herrings under the heat and cook until the fish are golden brown on top and cooked through. There is no need to turn them. Serve immediately from the dish.

Cooking time: 4 hours 30 minutes

Whiting Stuffed with Olives

Oranges and olives are mixed here into a moist and tasty stuffing for whiting. The dish is impressive, but nevertheless cheap and easy to prepare.

METRIC/IMPERIAL	AMERICAN
4 medium-sized whiting	4 medium-sized whiting
10 green olives	10 green olives
1 medium-sized onion	1 medium-sized onion
1 clove garlic	1 clove garlic
25g (1oz) butter	2tbls butter
75g (3oz) wholemeal breadcrumbs	1½ cups whole grain breadcrumbs
grated rind and juice 1 medium-sized orange	grated rind and juice 1 medium-sized orange
30ml (2tbls) white wine vinegar	2tbls white wine vinegar
15ml (1tbls) chopped thyme	1tbls chopped thyme
30ml (2tbls) chopped parsley	2tbls chopped parsley
freshly ground black pepper	freshly ground black pepper
30ml (2tbls) oil	2tbls oil

Clean the whiting if necessary and scrape away the dark skin that lines the belly. Make three diagonal slits on each side of the fish. Stone (pit) and chop the olives. Finely chop the onion and garlic.

Melt the butter in a frying-pan on a low heat. Mix in the onion and garlic and cook them until they are soft. Mix in the olives, breadcrumbs, orange rind and juice, vinegar, herbs and pepper. Take the pan from the heat. Press the stuffing into the belly cavities of each fish. Brush the whiting on both sides with oil.

Preheat the grill (broiler) to high. Lay the whiting on the hot rack and cook them for 10 minutes on each side.

Cooking time: 40 minutes

† Substitute lemon rind and juice for the orange in the stuffing and prepare small mackerel in exactly the same way.

Trout Poached with Mint

A sprig of mint placed inside trout before they are poached gives them a very fresh flavour. You can serve them quite plainly with lemon and herbs or add a little melted butter to the sauce.

METRIC/IMPERIAL	AMERICAN
4 trout	4 sea trout (grey or spotted)
4 mint sprigs	4 sprigs mint
40g (1½oz) butter (optional)	3tbls butter (if desired)
juice 1 lemon	juice 1 lemon
30ml (2tbls) chopped mint	2tbls chopped mint
30ml (2tbls) chopped parsley	2tbls chopped parsley
For the court bouillon:	**For the court bouillon:**
8 black peppercorns	8 black peppercorns
1 medium-sized onion	1 medium-sized onion
1 slice lemon	1 slice lemon
1 sprig parsley	1 sprig parsley
30ml (2tbls) white wine vinegar	2tbls white wine vinegar
150ml (¼pt) dry white wine	⅝ cup dry white wine
pinch sea salt	pinch sea salt
1L (1¾pt) water	4½ cups water

Put the ingredients for the court bouillon into a saucepan. Bring them to the boil, cover and simmer for 45 minutes. Meanwhile, clean the trout but do not cut off the fins. Scrape away any blood from down the backbone and wash the insides under cold running water. Put a sprig of mint inside each fish and lay the trout in a large oval casserole or in a roasting tin (pan). Strain the hot court bouillon over the trout. Cover the trout with a lid or foil. Bring the liquid to simmering point and cook the trout with the water just trembling for 10 minutes. Small trout should be done by this time. If you are uncertain, prick them with a skewer. They should be soft but firm.

Lift the trout onto a warmed serving dish with a perforated fish slice. Keep them warm. Melt the butter in a small pan on a low heat without letting it foam.

Take the pan from the heat and mix in the lemon juice and herbs. Spoon the contents of the pan over the trout. Alternatively, sprinkle the lemon juice and herbs over the trout without the butter.

Cooking time: 1 hour 15 minutes

Fish with Tomato and Caper Sauce

Skate, although a white fish, is very rich and lemons, tomato purée and capers make a light and contrasting dressing and a colourful dish. If you prefer, swordfish can be used instead with the same dressing.

METRIC/IMPERIAL	AMERICAN
For the court bouillon:	**For the court bouillon:**
½ lemon, thinly sliced	½ lemon, thinly sliced
8 black peppercorns	8 black peppercorns
bouquet garni	bouquet garni
pinch sea salt	pinch sea salt
1.1L (2pt) water	5 cups water
For the dish:	**For the dish:**
2 skate wings weighing together 675-900g (1½-2lb)	1½-2lb swordfish
juice 1½ lemons	juice 1½ lemon
90ml (6tbls) oil	6tbls oil
30ml (2tbls) tomato purée	2tbls tomato paste
15ml (1tbls) chopped capers	1tbls chopped capers
30ml (2tbls) chopped parsley	2tbls chopped parsley
freshly ground black pepper	freshly ground black pepper

Put the ingredients for the court bouillon into a sauce-

low heat until the butter has melted. Pour the curry mixture over the cod, turning the fish to make sure they are coated on both sides.

Preheat the grill (broiler) to high. Put the dish under the heat and cook the cod for 7 minutes on each side or until quite cooked through. Serve them immediately, from the dish.

Cooking time : 35 minutes

Marinated Cod Fillets

A tomato-flavoured marinade makes this baked cod moist and full of flavour.

METRIC/IMPERIAL	AMERICAN
700-900g (1½-2lb) cod fillets	1½-2lb cod fillets or steaks
1 large onion	1 large onion
1 clove garlic	1 clove garlic
45ml (3tbls) olive oil	3tbls olive oil
30ml (2tbls) lemon juice	2tbls lemon juice
5ml (1tsp) paprika	1tsp paprika
10ml (2tsp) tomato purée	2tsp tomato paste
sea salt	sea salt
freshly ground black pepper	freshly ground black pepper
4 large tomatoes	4 large tomatoes
30ml (2tbls) chopped parsley	2tbls chopped parsley

Skin the fish and cut it into four portions. Finely chop the onion and crush the garlic. Mix the oil, lemon juice, tomato paste and seasonings together in a large, shallow dish. Mix in the onion and garlic. Place the pieces of cod in the marinade and leave them for 2 hours at room temperature, turning them several times.

Heat the oven to gas mark 3 / 170°C (325°F). Scald, skin and roughly chop the tomatoes and put them on top of the pieces of cod. Put the dish, uncovered, into the oven for 45 minutes. Sprinkle the parsley over the top and serve immediately from the dish.

Cooking time : 2 hours 55 minutes

Haddock Baked with Mushrooms

When haddock is cooked en papillotte it becomes very firm and tasty. If you cut it into small pieces it makes a very attractive dish that is gently flavoured with lemon, mushrooms and herbs.

METRIC/IMPERIAL	AMERICAN
700-900g (1½-2lb) fresh haddock fillets	1½-2lb fresh haddock fillets
juice 1 lemon	juice 1 lemon
sea salt	sea salt
freshly ground black pepper	freshly ground black pepper
little butter for greasing	little butter for greasing
125g (¼lb) button mushrooms	¼lb small mushrooms
30ml (2tbls) chopped parsley	2tbls chopped parsley
15ml (1tbls) chopped tarragon	1tbls chopped tarragon

pan. Bring them to the boil, cover and simmer for 45 minutes. Put the skate (swordfish) into a large pan and strain the hot court bouillon over it. Bring it to the boil and simmer very gently for 15 minutes. Lift out the fish and cut each skate wing in half (or portion the swordfish). Lay the portions on a warm serving dish and keep them warm. Beat the rest of the ingredients together and spoon them over the fish.

Cooking time : 1 hour 5 minutes

Mildly Curried Cod

This fish dish has a light curry flavour and lovely golden colour.

METRIC/IMPERIAL	AMERICAN
4 cod cutlets	4 cod steaks
25g (1oz) butter	2tbls butter
10ml (2tsp) curry powder	2tsp curry powder
5ml (1tsp) ground turmeric	1tsp ground turmeric
grated rind and juice ½ medium-sized orange	grated rind and juice ½ medium-sized orange
1 clove garlic, crushed with a pinch sea salt	1 clove garlic, crushed with a pinch sea salt

If using cutlets, skin them and remove the small bones in the top. Put the fish into a flat, heatproof serving dish.

Put the butter, curry powder, turmeric, orange rind and juice and garlic into a saucepan and set them on a

Skin the fish and cut it into 1.5cm (½in) strips. Put them onto a flat plate and sprinkle them with the lemon juice and seasonings. Leave them for 30 minutes. Thinly slice the mushrooms.

Lightly butter 4 pieces of foil about 25cm (10in) square. Divide the fish between the pieces of foil and top it with the mushrooms and herbs. Seal the edges of the pieces of foil and lay them on a large baking sheet. Put them into the oven for 20 minutes. Take the foil-wrapped fish to the table on a warm serving dish and unwrap them on individual plates, so none of the juices are lost.

Cooking time : 1 hour 10 minutes

Stir-fried Whiting with Cheese

This is a light and unusual stir-fried dish, which includes summer vegetables.

METRIC/IMPERIAL	AMERICAN
4 medium-sized whiting	4 medium-sized whiting
grated rind and juice 1 lemon	grated rind and juice 1 lemon
60ml (4tbls) oil	4tbls oil
1 clove garlic, crushed with a pinch sea salt	1 clove garlic, crushed with pinch sea salt
freshly ground black pepper	freshly ground black pepper
350g (¾lb) courgettes (small, if possible)	¾lb zucchini (small, if possible)
30ml (2tbls) chopped lemon or common thyme	2tbls chopped lemon or common thyme
100g (¼lb) grated Farmhouse Cheddar cheese	1 cup grated, aged Cheddar cheese

Fillet the whiting and lay the fillets on a large, flat plate. Mix the lemon rind and juice, oil, garlic and pepper together and spoon them over the whiting. Leave the whiting for 4 hours at room temperature.

When you are ready to cook, coarsely grate the courgettes (zucchini) and cut the whiting into 1.5cm (½in) strips. Heat a heavy frying-pan (skillet) on a high heat with no fat. Put in the whiting and stir-fry them for 1 minute. Mix in the courgettes (zucchini) and thyme and cook in the same way for 1 minute more. Mix in the cheese and serve immediately.

Cooking time : 4 hours 30 minutes

Sea Bream (White Snapper) with Creamy Watercress Sauce

Sea bream (white snapper or porgy) have a very creamy texture and the stock and egg yolks make a creamy sauce to match.

METRIC/IMPERIAL	AMERICAN
675-900g (1½-2lb) sea bream	1½-2lb white snapper or porgy
butter for greasing	butter for greasing
juice 1 lemon	juice 1 lemon
1 bunch watercress	1 bunch watercress

25g (1oz) butter	2tbls butter
15ml (1tbls) wholemeal flour	1tbls whole grain flour
30ml (2tbls) chopped parsley	2tbls chopped parsley
275ml (½pt) fish stock	1¼ cups fish stock
2 egg yolks	2 egg yolks
5ml (1tsp) made English mustard	1tsp prepared mustard

Skin the fish and make stock with the skin. Cut the fish into even-sized serving pieces and lay them on a lightly-buttered ovenproof dish. Sprinkle them with lemon juice and leave them for 1 hour at room temperature.

Heat the oven to gas mark 5 / 190°C (375°F). Cover the fish with foil and bake it for 20 minutes.

While the fish is cooking, prepare the sauce. Finely chop the watercress. Melt the butter in a saucepan on a low heat. Stir in the watercress and cook it gently for 1 minute. Stir in the flour and mustard and cook them for 1 minute. Stir in the stock and bring it to the boil. Add the parsley and simmer the sauce for 2 minutes. When the fish is cooked, lift it onto a warmed serving dish and keep it warm. Pour all the juices from the cooking dish into the sauce. Beat the egg yolks together in a bowl and gradually beat in 90ml (6tbls) of the sauce. Pour the mixture back into the saucepan and reheat gently without boiling. Pour the sauce over the fish before serving.

Cooking time : 1 hour 30 minutes

Simply Baked Mackerel

METRIC/IMPERIAL	AMERICAN
4 mackerel each weighing 225-275m (½-¾lb)	4 mackerel each weighing ½-¾lb
75g (3oz) butter	6tbls butter
juice ½ lemon	juice ½ lemon
2 shallots, finely chopped	2 shallots, finely chopped
15ml (1tbls) chopped lemon thyme (or common thyme)	1tbls chopped lemon thyme (or common thyme)
30ml (2tbls) chopped parsley	2tbls chopped parsley
20ml (4tsp) grated horseradish	4tbls grated horseradish
salt	salt
freshly ground black pepper	freshly ground black pepper
wedges of lemon to serve	wedges of lemon to serve

Heat the oven to gas mark 5 / 190°C (375°F). Cut off the fins and tails of the mackerel but leave on the heads. Slit the fish open along the belly, gut them and rinse under a running tap. Pat dry.

Cream the butter and add the lemon juice, seasoning, chopped shallots, herbs, horseradish and seasoning. Stuff the fish with the mixture.

Cut four squares of foil large enough to enclose the fish comfortably and wrap the mackerel. Twist the top edges of foil together and twist the ends upwards to prevent the juices leaking out. Bake the parcels for 20 minutes, then open one to test by piercing with a fork to see if it is cooked. Serve with wedges of lemon.

Cooking time : 35 minutes

Simply baked mackerel.

Meat, Poultry & Game

The question that puzzles many people who wish to change to a wholefood or natural style of eating is 'what place does meat have in the diet and do I have to give it up'? There may be emotive or moral reasons for giving up meat but, these apart, let's look at some facts.

Meat is a high protein food and it is high quality protein, since it contains all the essential amino acids our body needs. It has other important constituents as well, so it most definitely is a highly nutritious food. But because it is so nutritious, we do not need to eat it in such large amounts as perhaps we are accustomed.

As we have seen in other chapters, vegetables, grains, pulses or dried legumes and dairy products all contain protein to a varying degree. If we eat meals based on whole and natural ingredients all the time, we are going to be eating a large selection of these in any one day. Therefore we can afford to cut down on the amount of meat that we eat. It is certainly far from essential to eat meat at every meal, or even to eat it every day; and provided you are careful over the other constituents of your diet, you can be very healthy without it. But as a part of a varied natural diet meat is a valuable food that adds to our enjoyment and our well-being.

Minerals & Vitamins

Meat, and particularly liver, is a rich source of B vitamins, chiefly B_{12}, which is essential for healthy red blood cells. This is only found elsewhere in eggs, milk, cheese, yeast extract and, to a lesser extent, in soya beans.

All red meats and game—particularly liver and kidneys—are rich in iron. Lighter meats are high in potassium and all meat contains significant amounts of sodium.

Taste the true flavour of meat, by cooking it the natural way, with as little fat as possible.

Shopping for meat

Another question is what kind of meat to buy and where to buy it. Good quality, fresh meat is essential to the wholefood cook as the most nutritious methods of cooking also bring out the natural flavours of the meat. So if meat is inferior in quality, your final dish will suffer. The best meat that you can buy is that which has been naturally reared without the use of drugs such as antibiotics and growth-promoting hormones. Buy direct from the farmer if you know his rearing methods, from butchers who specialize in naturally-reared meat or from a specialist butcher who buys high-quality meat from local farms and markets.

The meat that is probably the worst affected by 'factory farming' is the battery chicken (chicken raised on wire). From both a gourmet and a natural food point of view, a chicken that has been allowed to run free and is sold fresh is by far the best. Once you have eaten a 'real' chicken, an oven-ready frozen chicken is a tasteless substitute. You may pay more for a 'free-range' chicken, but it is far better to eat chicken less often and enjoy it, knowing that it is good for you, than frequently to eat chickens with no flavour that are full of antibiotics and polyphosphates.

Game: The most natural meat of all is game: wild duck, grouse, pheasant—and in America wild turkey—wild rabbit, hare or, if you are lucky, the bigger game such as venison. Although most game is protected, quite scarce, and therefore expensive, pigeon (prairie chicken) and wild rabbits are fairly cheap in country districts. If you are able to take advantage of this, they could easily appear on the menu quite frequently.

Fat content: game has also a lower fat content than most meats and this is something that you must also take into consideration when you buy. All meat contains fats; not just the visible fat, for example round the edge of chops, but fat that is actually in the structure of the meat. Try to buy meat with as little visible fat as possible and, when you are making a stew, cut any fat away before cooking.

Processed meat: as there are so many different kinds of meat available, there is no need to buy processed meats, which nearly always contain colouring and preservatives. Home-made pâtés and meat loaves always taste far better than any you can buy in a shop. Sausages are more difficult to make, but bought ones can be of varying quality. In continental Europe they must be 100% meat, but in some countries, Britain being the worst example, cereal additions are permitted and the bright pink, bready sausages all too often found in supermarkets should in no way be considered as wholefood. There are some small, family butchers who make excellent sausages with pork and herbs. In the US it is compulsory for them to contain preservatives. In Britain the situation is reversed: it is compulsory to put up a sign in the shop if they do.

Too many smoked and over-salty foods are not really good for you, but a little ham or bacon occasionally will do no harm and they can both brighten up the flavour of many a bland dish. They are particularly useful in vegetable combinations.

Freezing and storing meat

Fresh meat is always more desirable than frozen meat, but if you can find a good source of naturally-reared meat that you can only buy in bulk then it is worth using a freezer to store it. The nutritional loss of home-frozen meat is negligible and it will be far better than factory-farmed meat eaten fresh.

Store the meat in separate, small amounts and thaw it out gradually in the refrigerator to prevent the development of bacteria. Once it has thawed, remove the plastic wrapping immediately.

If you buy only fresh meat, then store it in an open container in a refrigerator and do not keep it for too long. Most red meats will keep for up to three days, light meat such as chicken and veal for only two days, and offal (variety meats) should really be eaten on the day that you buy it.

Making meat stock

Many meat dishes call for the use of stock and it is always worthwhile making your own. To make a simple meat stock you need beef or veal bones, a chicken carcass or giblets or even a chicken quarter. A rabbit carcass or lamb bones from a specific recipe can also be used, but pork bones are not really suitable. Put the bones into a saucepan with a roughly-chopped onion, carrot and stalk of celery. Set them dry on a low heat and brown them gently. Pour in cold water and add a few black peppercorns, a large bunch of herbs and a bayleaf. Bring everything to the boil and simmer, uncovered, for about 1½ hours. Strain the stock and discard the rest. Put the stock into a container and, when it is cool, cover it and put it into the refrigerator where it will stay fresh for up to a week.

Cooking meat

Meat should be cooked lightly and simply and with as little fat as possible.

Roasts: to roast a cut of meat or a whole bird, do not stand it directly in the roasting pan, but stand it on a rack in the pan, so that any fat will drip away. Do not spread the meat thickly with fat before you put it into the oven. Beef, pork and lamb can be roasted dry and uncovered, as they contain plenty of their own fats. Smaller cuts, such as chops, can be roasted in the same way. Poultry and game can also be roasted dry, but they are best if they are covered with foil for the first part of cooking to keep in all the moisture.

When your roast meat is cooked, take it off the rack and keep it warm. Then spoon out the fat from the roasting pan leaving behind the rich meat juices. Stand the pan on top of the stove on a moderate heat and pour in about 275ml (½pt) or 1¼ cups stock. Stir well and bring it to the boil and let it simmer gently while you carve the meat. This will make a good, dark gravy, full of natural flavours that does not need any thickening agent. Besides stock, you can use wine or cider for the gravy and add some chopped herbs.

A very good way of roasting meat that seals in all the flavour and goodness is in a meat or chicken brick. The inside is brushed with oil and rubbed with a clove of garlic; the meat, together with flavourings such as sprigs of herbs, is put in; the lid is put on and the brick put into a hot oven for 1½ hours. When the meat is done, skim the juices that have collected in the brick, pour them into a saucepan and simmer them with stock and chopped herbs to make a gravy.

If you have a spit-roaster attachment on your cooker, then this is another excellent way of roasting meat. It must be well basted first, but all the fat will drip away as it cooks.

Pot-roasting is a way of dealing with large cuts of meat that need to be cooked slowly for a long time. The meat does not have to be browned in fat first, but it can be put directly into a casserole with a selection of diced or whole vegetables for flavour and moistened with stock or wine and a very little vinegar to tenderize it. The juices remaining can be used in exactly the same way as those in a chicken brick, or the meat can be served quite plainly.

Parcels: a good cooking method for the leaner cuts of meat is to dice the meat and cook it wrapped in foil with diced vegetables. The best cuts for this are skirt of beef (beef flank), shoulder of lamb with all the fat removed and shoulder or, in Britain, the lean end of the belly of pork. Beef can be cooked with chopped mushrooms, lamb with root vegetables and pork with leeks.

Casseroles made with mixtures of meat and vegetables can be both wholesome and delicious. The best casserole method is the cold-start way in which the vegetables and meat are put in in layers and brought to the boil with stock before going into the oven. Using this method, no extra fat has to be used and you get a well-flavoured gravy.

Grilling or broiling: provided that you have a cut of meat that is tender enough to stand a relatively short cooking time, then grilling or broiling is an excellent, quick and easy way of cooking. Again this allows excess fat to drip away. Chops and steaks can be grilled or broiled without fat; simply sprinkle them with herbs, or you can first brush them with a little oil. Larger, tender cuts of meat can also be grilled (broiled) if they are first cut into cubes and threaded onto skewers to make kebabs. Alternate the meat with onions and perhaps tomatoes and green and red (bell) peppers.

Stir-frying is a very quick way of cooking finely-slivered meat that seals in all its natural juices. The meat does not shrink in size when cooked in this way. It is therefore possible to use less than you would for any other method and mix it with finely-sliced vegetables which remain crunchy and filling.

Poaching is an excellent, low fat way of cooking large joints of meat or whole chickens. Poached with herbs and vegetables, they remain moist and succulent and full of flavour. The poaching liquid can be used the next day as a base for a soup.

Marinating tenderizes every type of meat and makes it more easily digestible. At the same time it gives it superb flavour. Yogurt is a good tenderiser for lamb, cider for pork and red wine for beef and game. A citrus juice such as lemon, lime or orange, or a dash of vinegar added to the marinade will also help to neutralize the fats.

Cold meat: once cooked, meat can be served hot or it can be left until it is cold and served with a salad or in open-faced sandwiches. Leftovers are also best used

A summer beef soup makes a change from salads.

in salads rather than being reheated. Small amounts can be diced or cut in juliene strips and combined with cooked beans or diced or slivered hard cheese or cottage cheese for main and first courses.

RECIPES

Sweet Spiced Chicken with Cabbage and Celery

You can add a little gentle flavour to a poached chicken by rubbing spices into the skin before cooking. The cabbage and celery, cooked in the stock, make the chicken into a complete dish. Serve it with potatoes, boiled in their skins, sliced and tossed with parsley.

METRIC/IMPERIAL	AMERICAN
1x 1.4-1.5k (3-3½lb) roasting chicken	3½-4lb roasting chicken
5ml (1tsp) ground cinnamon	1tsp ground cinnamon
For poaching:	**For poaching:**
1 small onion, cut in half but not peeled	1 small onion, cut in half but not peeled
1 small carrot, cut in half lengthways	1 small carrot, cut in half lengthwise
1 stick celery and a few leaves	1 stalk celery and a few leaves
bouquet garni	bouquet garni
5ml (1tsp) black peppercorns	1tsp black peppercorns
For the final dish:	**For the final dish:**
1 small green cabbage	1 small head Savoy cabbage
4 large sticks celery	4 large stalks celery
1 medium-sized onion	1 medium-sized onion
1 large cooking apple	1 large tart apple
25g (1oz) butter	2tbls butter
5ml (1tsp) ground allspice	1tsp ground allspice
5ml (1tsp) ground cinnamon	1tsp ground cinnamon
little freshly grated nutmeg	little freshly grated nutmeg
5ml (1tsp) chopped rosemary	1tsp chopped rosemary
150ml (¼pt) poaching liquid	⅝ cup poaching liquid

Rub the ground cinnamon into the skin of the chicken. Put the chicken into a saucepan with the poaching ingredients and cover it with water to the top of the legs. Bring it gently to the boil, skim if necessary, cover and poach it gently for 50 minutes.
Take out the chicken and strain and reserve the poaching liquid. Shred the cabbage, chop the celery and thinly slice the onion. Peel, quarter, core and slice the apples. Melt the butter in a large saucepan over a moderate heat. Stir in the cabbage, celery, onion, apple, spices, rosemary and 150ml (¼pt) or ⅔ cup poaching liquid. Cover the pan and cook over a moderate heat for 15 minutes. While the vegetables are cooking, cut the chicken meat into 3cm (1in) pieces. Mix them into the sauce and lower the heat. Cook for a further 5 minutes.

Cooking time : 1 hour 40 minutes

Summer Beef Soup

This light beef and vegetable soup is a delicious main dish for summer days when you tire of salads.

METRIC/IMPERIAL	AMERICAN
700g (1½lb) lean minced beef	1½lb lean ground beef or hamburger
225g (½lb) French beans	½lb green beans
350g (¾lb) courgettes	¾lb zucchini
450g (1lb) tomatoes	1lb tomatoes
1 large onion	1 large onion
1 large clove garlic	1 large clove garlic
60ml (4tbls) oil	4tbls oil
1.15L (2pt) stock	5 cups stock or broth
150ml (¼pt) dry white wine (or use all stock)	⅝ cup dry white wine (or use all stock)
15ml (1tbls) chopped basil	1tbls chopped basil
15ml (1tbls) chopped thyme	1tbls chopped thyme
15ml (1tbls) chopped marjoram	1tbls chopped marjoram
sea salt	sea salt
freshly ground black pepper	freshly ground black pepper
60ml (4tbls) grated Parmesan cheese	4tbls grated Parmesan cheese

Top and tail (string) and finely chop the French (green) beans. Wipe and thinly slice the courgettes (zucchini). Scald, skin and roughly chop the tomatoes. Finely chop the onion and garlic.
Heat the oil in a large saucepan on a low heat. Stir in the onion and garlic and cook them until they are soft. Raise the heat to moderate and put in the meat. Break it up well and stir it around until it browns. Mix in the beans, courgettes (zucchini) and tomatoes. Pour in the stock and bring it to the boil. Add the wine, herbs and seasonings. Cover and simmer for 20 minutes. Pour the soup into a tureen and scatter the Parmesan cheese over the top.

Cooking time : 40 minutes

Chicken, Cheese and Orange Salad

This light and attractive appetizer can be made with a little left-over chicken.

METRIC/IMPERIAL	AMERICAN
125g (¼lb) cooked chicken	¼lb cooked chicken
125g (¼lb) cottage cheese	½ cup cottage cheese
5ml (1tsp) spiced, granular mustard	1tsp spiced mustard with seeds
1 large orange	1 large orange
½ bunch watercress	½ bunch watercress

Finely dice the chicken. Blend the mustard into the cheese. Peel and chop the orange. Mix the chicken and orange into the cheese. Divide the salad between 4 small side plates and garnish with watercress sprigs.

Cooking time : 15 minutes

Terrine of Pork and Veal

If the main meal is going to be a meatless one, then you can serve a pâté or terrine to begin it. Make them with as little fat as possible, such as this light one with pork and veal. It will make a first course for 8-10 people served cold with buttered whole meal (whole grain) bread. Alternatively, serve it hot or cold as a main course for 4 people.

METRIC/IMPERIAL	AMERICAN
350g (¾lb) lean pork	¾lb lean pork tenderloin
350g (¾lb) lean pie veal	¾lb lean boneless stewing veal
1 clove garlic	1 clove garlic
5ml (1tsp) chopped rosemary	1tsp chopped rosemary
10ml (2tsp) chopped marjoram	2tsp chopped marjoram
10ml (2tsp) chopped thyme	2tsp chopped thyme
15ml (1tbls) chopped parsley	1tbls chopped parsley
6 crushed allspice berries	6 crushed whole allspice
6 crushed black peppercorns	6 crushed black peppercorns
2.5ml (½tsp) sea salt	½tsp sea salt
little butter for greasing a 900g (2lb) loaf tin	little butter for greasing a 5-cup bread pan

Heat the oven to gas mark 4 / 180°C (350°F). Coarsely mince (grind) the pork and veal, adding slivers of garlic as the meat goes through the mincer (grinder). (If you buy the meat ready minced (ground), then mix the crushed garlic in well.) Put the meat into a bowl and mix in the herbs, spices and salt. Press the mixture into a lightly-greased 900g (2lb) loaf tin (or 5-cup bread pan) and stand it in a baking tin of water. Bake the terrine, uncovered, for 1½ hours. If serving hot, leave the terrine for 10 minutes. Pour away any fat from the loaf tin (pan) and turn the terrine onto a warm serving dish. If serving cold, let the terrine cool completely in the tin (pan) after pouring away the fat from the top.

Cooking time : 2 hours if eating hot, plus cooling time if eating cold.

Pigeon or Squab and Vegetable Soup

One pigeon can make a substantial, warming and tasty soup. It can be served before a light main course or as a meal on its own, with some wholemeal (whole grain) bread and a salad.

METRIC/IMPERIAL	AMERICAN
1 pigeon	1 squab or prairie chicken
3 large carrots	3 large carrots
1 large white turnip	1 large white turnip
1 medium-sized parsnip	1 medium-sized parsnip
225g (½lb) leeks	½lb leeks
3 large sticks celery	3 large stalks celery
1 medium-sized onion	1 medium-sized onion
25g (1oz) butter	2tbls butter
30ml (2tbls) wholemeal flour	2tbls whole grain flour
30ml (2tbls) tomato purée	2tbls tomato paste
1.1L (2pt) stock or water	5 cups stock, broth or water
275ml (½pt) dry cider	1 cup apple cider plus 4tbls applejack
60ml (4tbls) chopped, mixed herbs	4tbls chopped, mixed herbs
60ml (4tbls) chopped parsley	4tbls chopped parsley

Finely dice all the vegetables. Heat the butter in a large saucepan on a high heat. Put in the bird and brown it all over. Remove it and lower the heat. Mix in the vegetables, cover them and let them sweat for 10 minutes. Stir in the flour and cook it for 1 minute. Stir in the tomato paste and then the stock or water and cider. Bring the soup to the boil and add the chopped herbs. Simmer for 1½ hours.
Take out the bird. Remove all the meat from the bones and dice it finely. Return it to the soup and reheat if necessary.

Cooking time : 2 hours 10 minutes

Chicken in a Brick with Rosemary and Mushrooms

The mushrooms added to the chicken here for the last part of the cooking process steam gently on top and become moist and succulent as well as adding flavour to the chicken.

METRIC/IMPERIAL	AMERICAN
1.4-1.5kg (3½-4lb) roasting chicken	3½-4lb roasting chicken
1 clove garlic	1 clove garlic
2 sprigs rosemary	2 sprigs rosemary
sea salt	sea salt
freshly ground black pepper	freshly ground black pepper
½ large orange	½ large orange
15ml (1tbls) olive oil	1tbls olive oil
225g (½lb) mushrooms	½lb mushrooms
5ml (1tsp) Dijon mustard	1tsp Dijon-style mustard
30ml (2tbls) natural yogurt	2tbls plain yogurt

Heat the oven to gas mark 7 / 220°C (425°F). Rub the inside of the chicken brick with a cut clove of garlic

Sealed up in a 'brick', with herbs and mushrooms, a chicken needs no cooking fat whatsoever.

and put one of the rosemary sprigs in the bottom. Season the inside of the chicken. Thickly slice the orange and put it inside the bird. Truss the chicken and brush the outside very lightly with oil. Season the outside with pepper only. Put the chicken into the brick with the second sprig of rosemary on top. Put on the lid and put the brick into the oven for 1¼ hours. Thickly slice the mushrooms. Scatter them over the chicken, replace the lid and return the chicken to the oven for a further 15 minutes.

Remove the mushrooms and chicken from the brick. Skim the juices and pour them into a saucepan. Stir in the mustard and bring to the boil. Take the pan from the heat and stir in the yogurt. Carve the chicken and arrange it on a warmed serving platter with the mushrooms. Pour the sauce over the top.

Cooking time : 1 hour 50 minutes

Mustard Lamb Chops

Mustard and cheese make a tasty baste for grilled or broiled lamb chops. If you taste the sauce before the chops go into the oven it will be very hot, but this quality cooks away leaving only a good savoury flavour. Any excess fat in the chops will drip away, leaving you with a very light meal.

METRIC/IMPERIAL	AMERICAN
4 loin lamb chops	4 loin lamb chops
1 small onion	1 small onion
15ml (1tbls) mustard powder	1tbls dry mustard
30ml (2tbls) grated Parmesan cheese	2tbls grated Parmesan cheese
30ml (2tbls) natural yogurt	2tbls plain yogurt
1 bunch watercress	1 bunch watercress

Heat the oven to gas mark 7 / 220°C (425°F). Peel and

finely grate the onion. Put it into a bowl and mix in the dry mustard, cheese and yogurt. Put the chops on a rack in a roasting tin (pan) and spread the mustard mixture over the top. Put them into the oven for 45 minutes. Put them on a warm serving dish and garnish them with watercress.

Cooking time : 1 hour

Peppered Kebabs

Lamb kebabs, marinated for a long time in lemon juice, become moist and tender and cook quickly and easily.

METRIC/IMPERIAL	AMERICAN
550g (1¼lb) boned shoulder of lamb	1¼lb boned shoulder of lamb
60ml (4tbls) olive oil	4tbls olive oil
juice of 1 lemon	juice 1 lemon
1.5ml (¼tsp) cayenne pepper	¼tsp cayenne pepper
5ml (1tsp) paprika	1tsp paprika
1 clove garlic, crushed with a pinch sea salt	1 clove garlic, crushed with a pinch sea salt
2 medium-sized onions	2 medium-sized onions
2 green peppers	2 green bell peppers
8 small, firm tomatoes	8 small, firm tomatoes
Optional extras:	**Optional extras:**
pitta bread (see page 148)	pitta (Greek) bread (see page 148)
or yogurt sauce made by mixing together 150ml (¼pt) natural yogurt, grated rind ½ lemon and 5ml (1tsp) paprika	or yogurt sauce made by mixing together ⅝ cup plain yogurt, grated rind ½ lemon and 1tsp paprika

Cut the lamb into 3cm (1in) cubes. In a large bowl, mix the oil, lemon juice, cayenne pepper, paprika and garlic. Fold the lamb into the dressing and leave it for 3 hours at room temperature.
Cut the onions and peppers into 3cm (1in) squares and cut the tomatoes in half. Make the yogurt sauce if required.
Alternate the lamb, onions, peppers and tomatoes onto kebab skewers, starting and ending with a tomato half. Preheat the grill (broiler) to high. Lay the kebabs on the hot rack and grill or broil them for 15 minutes turning them several times.
Serve the kebabs accompanied by the yogurt sauce. Alternatively make pockets in warmed pitta bread and put the hot meat and vegetables inside. Serve immediately.

Cooking time : 3 hours 45 minutes

Spiced Lamb Chops with Yogurt

Yogurt makes a light, non-greasy marinade for lamb. The chops are simple in appearance but have a deliciously spiced Middle Eastern flavour.

METRIC/IMPERIAL	AMERICAN
8 small best end neck cutlets	8 rib or arm chops
275ml (½pt) natural yogurt	1¼ cups plain yogurt
2.5ml (½tsp) ground cumin	½tsp ground cumin
2.5ml (½tsp) ground coriander	½tsp ground coriander
1 clove garlic, crushed with a pinch sea salt	1 clove garlic, crushed with a pinch sea salt
freshly ground black pepper	freshly ground black pepper
1 small cucumber	1 cucumber
15ml (1tbls) chopped mint	1tbls chopped mint
2 bunches mint for garnish	2 bunches mint for garnish

Trim the chops. Mix half the yogurt with the cumin, coriander, garlic and pepper. Put it into a shallow dish. Coat the chops in the marinade and leave them for 3 hours at room temperature, turning them several times.
To make the accompanying sauce, cut the cucumber into long quarters and cut away the seeds. Finely chop the rest. Mix the chopped cucumber and mint into the remaining yogurt and season with the pepper.
Preheat the grill (broiler) to high. Lay the chops on the hot rack and cook them, close to the heat, for 1 minute on each side. Move the rack down and continue cooking for a further 5 minutes on each side. Put the chops onto a serving dish and garnish them with the mint sprigs. Serve the sauce separately.

Cooking time : 3 hours 30 minutes

Leg of Lamb with Piquant Sauce

Leg of lamb, cooked by simmering in liquid, is tender and full of flavour and is well complemented by the sharp sauce.

METRIC/IMPERIAL	AMERICAN
½ leg lamb (knuckle end)	½ leg of lamb (short cut or shank half)
For simmering:	**For simmering:**
water to cover	water to cover
30ml (2tbls) white wine vinegar	2tbls white wine vinegar
large bouquet garni which includes 2 mint sprigs	large bouquet garni which includes mint sprigs
1 large carrot, cut in half lengthways	1 large carrot, cut in half lengthwise
1 large onion, peeled and stuck with 4 cloves	1 large onion, peeled and stuck with 4 cloves
1 stick celery, broken into several pieces	1 stalk celery, broken into several pieces
10ml (2tsp) black peppercorns	2tsp black peppercorns
For the sauce:	**For the sauce:**
275ml (½pt) poaching liquid	1¼ cups poaching liquid
150ml (¼pt) white wine vinegar	⅝ cup white wine vinegar
60ml (4tbls) chopped mint	4tbls chopped mint
30ml (2tbls) chopped chives	2tbls chopped chives
15ml (1tbls) chopped thyme	1tbls chopped thyme
15ml (1tbls) chopped tarragon	1tbls chopped tarragon
4 chopped sorrel leaves, if available	4 chopped spinach leaves

Put all the simmering ingredients into a large saucepan. Bring them to the boil, cover and simmer for 10 minutes. Put in the lamb, bring it to the boil, skim, cover and simmer for 2 hours.

Fifteen minutes before it is finished, pour off 275ml ($\frac{1}{2}$pt) or 1$\frac{1}{4}$ cups of the poaching liquid. Put it into a saucepan with the vinegar and herbs. Bring them to the boil and simmer, uncovered for 10 minutes.

Lift out the lamb, carve it and arrange it on a warm serving dish. Serve the sauce separately.

Cooking time: 2 hours 15 minutes

Stir-fried Pork with Red Peppers

This recipe can be made with any cut of lean pork. Tenderloin is ideal, but any lean, boneless cut will be successful. In Britain the lean end of the belly or a gammon knuckle could be used. The dish has a sharp-sweet flavour and an excellent light texture as no thickening is added to the sauce. Serve it with a seasoned rice.

METRIC/IMPERIAL	AMERICAN
450-550g (1-1$\frac{1}{4}$lb) lean pork	1-1$\frac{1}{4}$lb lean pork
4 medium-sized red peppers	4 medium-sized red bell peppers
2 medium-sized onions	2 medium-sized onions
1 large clove garlic	1 large clove garlic
150ml ($\frac{1}{4}$pt) dry sherry (or stock or a mixture)	$\frac{5}{8}$ cup dry sherry (or stock, broth or a mixture)
30ml (2tbls) tamari sauce	2tbls Shoyu sauce
30ml (2tbls) white wine vinegar	2tbls white wine vinegar
30ml (2tbls) tomato purée	2tbls tomato paste
30ml (2tbls) oil	2tbls oil

Cut the pork into very thin slices about 3 x 6cm (1 x 2in). Cut the peppers into pieces 6 x 30mm ($\frac{1}{4}$ x 1in). Slice the onions and finely chop the garlic. Mix the sherry (or stock) with the tamari sauce, vinegar and tomato paste.

Put the oil and garlic into a large frying-pan, skillet or wok and set over a high heat. When the garlic sizzles, put in the pork and stir it around for 2 minutes. Mix in the peppers and onions and lower the heat. Continue to stir-fry for 3 minutes so the vegetables are just beginning to soften. Pour in the sherry mixture, bring it to the boil and simmer gently for 1 minute. Serve as soon as possible.

Cooking time: 30 minutes

Stir-fry pork with peppers for a Chinese treat.

Beef and Mushroom Hot-pot

This cold start casserole is flavoured simply with herbs and brown (dark) ale and given a topping of crispy potatoes. All you need to accompany it are some lightly-cooked, brightly-coloured vegetables, such as spring greens or spinach and carrots.

METRIC/IMPERIAL	AMERICAN
700g (1½lb) chuck steak	1½-2lb boneless chuck
30ml (2tbls) seasoned wholemeal flour	2tbls seasoned, whole grain flour
350g (¾lb) mushrooms	¾lb mushrooms
2 medium-sized onions	2 medium-sized onions
30ml (2tbls) chopped parsley	2tbls chopped parsley
15ml (1tbls) chopped thyme	1tbls chopped thyme
15ml (1tbls) chopped marjoram	1tbls chopped marjoram
1 bayleaf	1 bayleaf
275ml (½pt) brown ale	1¼ cups dark ale
150ml (¼pt) stock	⅝ cup stock or broth
1 clove garlic, crushed without salt	1 clove garlic, crushed without salt
700-900g (1½-2lb) potatoes	1½-2lb potatoes
25g (1oz) butter	2tbls butter
freshly ground black pepper	freshly ground black pepper

Heat the oven to gas mark 4/180°C (350°F). Cut the beef into 3cm (1in) dice and coat it in the flour. Put the mushrooms in half or quarters depending on their size and thinly slice the onions.

Layer the beef, mushrooms and onions in a flameproof casserole or dutch oven with the herbs and tuck the bay leaf into the middle. Mix the beer and stock together and stir in the garlic. Pour them into the pan. Put the pan on top of the stove on a moderate heat and bring the contents to the boil. Cover it and put it into the oven for 1 hour.

Scrub and thinly slice the potatoes (or peel them if preferred). Take the lid off the pan and arrange the potatoes on top of the beef in overlapping layers. Dot them with butter and season with the pepper. Put the pan back into the oven for 1 hour or until the potatoes are cooked and golden brown.

Cooking time: 2 hours 30 minutes

Beef hot-pot, layered with mushrooms and topped with potatoes which crisp in the oven, is a warming winter dish.

Lamb in a Parcel

Meat cooked in a parcel with diced vegetables looks and tastes fresh and natural and there is a successful exchange of flavours.

METRIC/IMPERIAL	AMERICAN
700g (1½lb) lean, boneless shoulder of lamb	1½lb lean, boneless shoulder of lamb
450g (1lb) swede	1lb rutabagas
1 large onion	1 large onion
10ml (2tsp) chopped rosemary	2tsp chopped rosemary
30ml (2tbls) tomato purée	2tbls tomato paste
little freshly grated nutmeg	little freshly grated nutmeg
sea salt	sea salt
freshly ground black pepper	freshly ground black pepper
little butter or oil for greasing	little butter or oil for greasing
4 pieces foil 40cm (15in) square	4 pieces of foil 15in square

Heat the oven to gas mark 6/200°C (400°F). Dice the lamb and swede (rutabaga) into 1cm (⅜in) pieces and finely chop the onion. Put them into a bowl and mix in the rosemary, tomato paste and seasonings. Lightly butter or oil the dull inside of the pieces of foil and divide the lamb mixture between each square. Secure the edge of the foil at the top by folding them over and fold up the sides. Put the parcels of lamb on a baking sheet and put them into the oven for 1 hour.
To serve, take the parcels to the table on a serving plate and unwrap them on individual dinner plates.

Cooking time : 1 hour 30 minutes

Pork in a Brick with Sage and Onions

Pork cooked in a chicken or meat brick becomes brown and crispy on the outside and is gently permeated with the flavours of the mustard and the sage and onions.

METRIC/IMPERIAL	AMERICAN
900g-1.4kg (2-3lb) joint lean pork (blade, rolled shoulder or lean end of the belly) without rind	2-3lb lean blade loin or boneless loin pork roast
2 large onions	2 large onions
10ml (2tsp) chopped sage	2 tsp chopped sage
about 15ml (1tbls) made English mustard	about 1tbls prepared mustard

Heat the oven to gas mark 8/230°C (450°). Quarter and thinly slice the onions and mix them with the sage. Put them into the bottom of the chicken or meat brick. Spread the meat surface with the mustard. Put the pork in the brick on top of the sage and onions. Cover and put it into the oven for 1½ hours.
Take out the pork, carve it and arrange it on a warm serving dish. Skim the onions and juices well and spoon them over the pork.

Cooking time : 1 hour 45 minutes

Spiced Beef

Look around for really lean rolled boneless brisket of beef for this recipe as it is a cut of meat that can vary tremendously in the amount of fat that is included. The vinegar and spices tenderize the beef and give it a soft, spiced flavour.

METRIC/IMPERIAL	AMERICAN
1 piece rolled brisket weighing about 1.12kg (2½lb)	2½lb rolled boneless brisket of beef
8 cloves	8 cloves
8 allspice berries	8 whole allspices
8 juniper berries	8 juniper berries
12 black peppercorns	12 black peppercorns
60ml (4tbls) malt vinegar	4tbls malted vinegar
15ml (1tbls) Barbados sugar	1tbls brown or Barbados sugar
2 bay leaves	2 bay leaves
60ml (4tbls) stock	4tbls stock or broth

Crush the spices together using a pestle and mortar. Mix them with the vinegar and sugar. Put the mixture into an enamel or earthenware casserole. Put in the beef and rub it with the spice mixture. Put a bay leaf on top and below the beef, cover it and leave it for 4 hours at room temperature.
Heat the oven to gas mark 4/180°C (350°F). Pour the stock around the beef. Cover the casserole and put it into the oven for 2 hours. Serve the beef accompanied by horseradish sauce.

Cooking time : 6 hours 15 minutes

Stir-fried Beef with Carrots and Peppers

Stir-frying is one of the best ways of making a little meat into a filling meal with vegetables.

METRIC/IMPERIAL	AMERICAN
450-575g (1-1¼lb) skirt of beef	1-1¾lb flank steak
350g (¾lb) small carrots	¾lb small carrots
2 medium-sized green peppers	2 medium-sized green bell peppers
2 medium-sized onions	2 medium-sized onions
30ml (2tbls) cornflour	2tbls cornstarch
30ml (2tbls) tamari sauce	2tbls Shoyu sauce
30ml (2tbls) sherry (optional)	2tbls sherry (if desired)
275ml (½pt) stock	1¼ cups stock or broth
2 cloves garlic	2 cloves garlic
45ml (3tbls) oil	3tbls oil
10ml (2tsp) ground ginger	2tsp ground ginger

Cut the beef into small, thin slivers. Slice the carrots paper thin. Remove the stalk and seeds and finely chop the peppers. Finely chop the onions. Put the cornflour (cornstarch) into a bowl and gradually mix in the tamari sauce, sherry and stock. Finely chop the garlic.
Heat the oil and garlic in a large frying-pan or skillet on a high heat. When the garlic begins to sizzle, put

in the beef and stir-fry until it is a good brown. Move the beef to the edges of the pan and put in the carrots. Cook them for 1½ minutes and mix in the onions and peppers. Scatter in the ginger. Lower the heat slightly and stir-fry for 2 minutes more. Stir the sauce and pour it into the pan. Let it bubble and simmer until it is glossy brown and translucent. Serve with a seasoned brown rice dish.

Cooking time : 40 minutes

Spiced Kidney Casserole

When kidneys are casseroled using the slow-start method, they become deliciously moist and tender. The yogurt thickens the sauce and lightens the flavour. Soak the pig's (pork) kidneys in milk for 2 hours before use.

METRIC/IMPERIAL	AMERICAN
12 lambs' or 6 pigs' kidneys	12 lamb or 6 veal or pork kidneys
900g (2lb) potatoes	2lb potatoes
1 large onion	1 large onion
10 black peppercorns	10 black peppercorns
6 juniper berries	6 juniper berries
6 allspice berries	6 whole allspice
pinch sea salt	pinch sea salt
1 clove garlic	1 clove garlic
850ml (1½pt) stock	3¾ cups stock or broth
150ml (¼pt) stabilized yogurt (see page 127)	⅔ cup stabilized yogurt (see page 127)

Heat the oven to gas mark 6/200°C (400°F). Cut the kidneys in half lengthwise and snip out the cores. Scrub and dice the potatoes. Quarter and thinly slice the onion. Crush the peppercorns, spices, salt and garlic together using a pestle and mortar. Mix them with the stock.
Layer the kidneys, onions and potatoes in a flameproof casserole or dutch oven and pour in the spiced stock. Put the pan on top of the stove on a moderate heat and bring the contents to the boil. Cover the pan and put it into the oven for 1 hour 15 minutes. Stir in the yogurt just before serving.

Cooking time : 1 hour 35 minutes

Liver with Herbed Breadcrumbs

This way of cooking liver makes it really soft and tender. The vinegar, breadcrumbs and herbs combine to make a slightly sharp sauce.

METRIC/IMPERIAL	AMERICAN
700g (1½lb) lamb's liver	1½lb lamb, calf or baby beef liver
1 large onion	1 large onion
1 clove garlic	1 clove garlic
60ml (4tbls) oil	4tbls oil
100g (¼lb) fresh wholemeal breadcrumbs	3-4 cups fresh whole grain

120ml (8tbls) tarragon vinegar	breadcrumbs
60ml (4tbls) mixed chopped parsley, thyme, rosemary and tarragon	8tbls tarragon vinegar
	4tbls mixed chopped parsley, thyme, rosemary and tarragon

Cut the liver into small, very thin slices. Finely chop the onion and garlic. Heat the oil in a large frying-pan on a low heat. Mix in the onion and garlic and cook them until they are just beginning to soften. Put in the breadcrumbs and cook, stirring, until they are brown and the onions completely soft. Pour in the vinegar and stir in the herbs. Add the liver, and cook it, stirring and turning occasionally, for 10 minutes.

Cooking time : 30 minutes

Roast Duck with Apples

Serve this duck for a special occasion. It is plainly roasted on a rack and stuffed with apples which cook down to a slightly sharp sauce which makes a contrast to the rich meat. A green salad is the best accompaniment.

METRIC/IMPERIAL	AMERICAN
2kg (4½lb) duck	4½lb duck
2 large cooking apples	2 large tart apples
1 small onion	1 small onion
10ml (2tsp) ground cinnamon	2tsp ground cinnamon
small pinch ground cloves	small pinch ground cloves
10 chopped sage leaves	10 chopped sage leaves
5ml (1tsp) sea salt	1tsp sea salt
275ml (½pt) dry cider	1¼ cups apple cider or applejack
1 large cooking apple for serving (optional)	1 large tart red apple to garnish (if desired)

Heat the oven to gas mark 6/200°C (400°F). Peel, core and finely chop the apples and finely chop the onion. Put them into a bowl and mix in the spices and sage. Stuff the duck with the apple mixture and truss it. Prick the duck all over with a fork and rub the salt into the skin. Put the duck on a rack in a roasting tin (pan) and put it into the oven for 2 hours, basting it 30 minutes from the end.
Put the duck onto a serving dish and keep it warm. Pour away all the fat from the roasting pan, keeping any residue. Set the pan on top of the stove on a moderate heat and pour in the cider. Bring it to the boil, stirring and simmer for 5 minutes.
If you are garnishing with apple, heat the grill (broiler). Then peel, core and thinly slice the remaining apple. Put the apple rings onto a heatproof dish and brush them very lightly with a little duck fat. Grill (broil) them under a high heat until they are golden brown and arrange them around the duck.
Carve the duck at the table and put a portion of the apple stuffing onto each plate. Serve the cider gravy separately.

Cooking time : 2 hours 30 minutes

Rabbit and Herb Fricassee

This rabbit stew is thickened with dairy sour cream which also gives it a light flavour. It goes particularly well with brown rice flavoured with turmeric.

METRIC/IMPERIAL	AMERICAN
1 medium-sized wild rabbit, skinned and jointed	1 medium-sized wild rabbit, skinned and cut into pieces
30ml (2tbls) wholemeal flour	2tbls whole grain flour
2.5ml (½tsp) ground mace	½tsp ground mace
sea salt	sea salt
freshly ground black pepper	freshly ground black pepper
2 large onions	2 large onions
225g (½lb) carrots	½lb carrots
90ml (6tbls) mixed chopped parsley, sage, marjoram and savory	6tbls mixed chopped parsley, sage, marjoram and savory
425ml (¾pt) stock	2 cups stock or broth
30ml (2tbls) soured cream	2tbls dairy sour cream

Remove the meat from the bones and cut it into 2cm (¾in) dice. Soak it in lightly-salted cold water for 30 minutes. Drain it and pat it dry with absorbent paper. Put the meat back into the bowl and fold in the flour, mace and plenty of seasonings, so all the pieces of rabbit are well-coated. Halve and thinly slice the onions and cut the carrots into julienne matchstick-sized strips.

Layer the rabbit, herbs, onions and carrots in a large saucepan and pour in the stock. Put the pan on a moderate heat and bring the contents to the boil. Cover and simmer for 1¼ hours. Stir in the sour cream just before serving.

Cooking time : 1 hour 45 minutes

Roast duck, stuffed and garnished with apple rings, and with a well-browned skin is universally popular.

Dairy Products

The very words 'dairy products' tend to inspire a picture of something that is natural and wholesome, and that is exactly what they are; although, as with many other commodities, some dairy foods are better than others. Milk, butter, cheese, yogurt and eggs are used by nearly everyone, and they can be drunk or eaten plainly or used in countless ways in the kitchen. Dairy products do contain animal fats but, provided they are eaten in moderation as part of a high fibre natural food diet, they can be very nutritious. They all contain varying amounts of high-quality proteins.

Milk

Milk is always plentiful. Most milk today goes through a pasteurisation process in which it is heated to around 72°C (161°F), held there for 15 seconds, rapidly cooled and then bottled. This treatment destroys any disease-carrying organisms which could make the milk sour quickly, but unfortunately it also destroys some of the thiamin and vitamin C. The level of the remaining vitamin C falls by 50% in pasteurised milk some twelve hours after bottling.

Minerals & Vitamins

Milk contains large amounts of calcium, as well as other minerals, such as potassium and phosphorus. It is a good source of vitamins A and D and the B vitamins, thiamin and riboflavin.

Raw milk: the milk with the most natural goodness, therefore, is raw milk which has had no heat treatment. Controls on all farms are now so tight that there is absolutely no risk of infection, and so raw milk is definitely the most nutritious. Pasteurised milk is, however, the one most readily available and the vitamin loss will almost certainly be made up from other constituents of a well-balanced wholefood diet.

Homogenised milk has been heat-treated and then processed to break up the fat globules which then stay evenly distributed in the milk instead of rising to the top as cream. This type is generally used in the United States. It can consequently be frozen successfully, but once thawed it should be used fairly quickly and should never be refrozen.

Whole milk is the best choice for Americans who want a milk that is not homogenized, but separates with a creamy layer. The upper section of the container can be used as high-cream content milk.

High cream content milk comes from cows, such as those of the Jersey and Guernsey breeds, that produce an extra rich milk. In Britain bottles of it have gold tops. This is ideal for custards and can be used instead of cream in sauces and mousses and poured over fresh or dried fruit. It is the best choice for milk puddings.

Sterilized milk has been subjected to far greater heat treatment than pasteurized—up to 112°C (235°F). As a result, it will stay 'fresh' in the bottle for up to a week. Half the vitamin C and a quarter of the thiamin are lost, the flavour is also affected and it is not really a whole food product.

UHT or ultra heat treated milk is homogenized milk heated to 135-150°C (275-300°F). Consequently it will keep for six months. It is not available in the United States (where a milk that freezes is universally available) but is a convenient refrigerator standby in other countries. The heat treatment reduces the vitamin content and affects the flavour.

Evaporated milk has had the water content reduced from around 86% to 68%. Unless it has been skimmed before evaporation it is a more concentrated product than ordinary milk. It tastes very different, has changed its nutritional value and is not a wholefood product. Neither is condensed milk which has a high proportion of added sugar.

Low fat skimmed milk (or skim milk) powder has become very popular. This has been made from skimmed milk which has been dried and given a subsequent treatment to make it readily reconstituted in warm or even cold water. The vitamin content has been reduced but if you are weight or animal fat conscious, then skimmed milk powder is ideal, especially for cooking. It can be used in all the same ways as ordinary milk but a little extra care has to be taken when heating to make sure it does not burn.

Goat's milk : if babies under 6 months' age are given cow's milk, they may, in some cases, develop an allergy which may be manifest in diarrhoea, skin rashes or a runny nose. An excellent alternative is goat's milk which is similar in many ways to mother's milk and is far more easily digested than cow's milk, since the fatty acids are smaller and evenly distributed throughout the milk. Although goat's milk is quite hard to obtain, it is becoming increasingly more available as goat-keeping becomes more popular. You can sometimes find it in healthfood shops and it can be bought direct from some farms. One of its advantages is that it can be deep-frozen and will keep for up to five months. So if your supplier lives some way away, you can buy your milk in bulk.

All the vitamins and minerals that milk contains are available from other foods and so it is not, as many British people believe, at all essential to drink 'a pint a day'. So a little milk and some nuts or sesame seeds will give a greater variety of nutrients and fibre than a milk-rich diet and no nuts.

In the kitchen, milk can be made into custards and delicious whole grain puddings; and a basic béchamel sauce made with flour, butter and milk can be flavoured with cheese, herbs, tomato purée, mushrooms, onions and other flavourings. Use the sauce to top dishes such as lasagne or to turn lightly-boiled or steamed vegetables into a complete meal. Milk can also be used in baking to make breads, cakes and scones (biscuits) soft and cakes light.

Yogurt

Yogurt, which is now enjoying great popularity is easily made from milk. Yogurt was first made in the Balkans, but the countries to the west are only just beginning to realise how good it is. Yogurt is made by introducing a harmless bacteria into the milk and allowing it to feed on the milk sugars. In doing so, it creates a slight acidity which then sets the protein content of the milk. So we are left with a thick, tangy white, creamy-textured substance which has almost equal food value to milk and like milk is easy to digest. It is an excellent food for young children and old people who may have digestive troubles. The bacteria in the yogurt also set up home, as it were, in our digestive systems and help digest other food. Yogurt is therefore a tremendous help in restoring health after a person has taken a course of anti-biotics, which destroy the good and helpful bacteria as well as the harmful ones.

**Yogurt is easily made at home.
You can use a commercial
yogurt set, or just a Thermos flask.**

A little yogurt every day will greatly help in keeping you healthy, although it may not be the wonder food that it is sometimes claimed to be.

Besides all these healthy advantages, yogurt is definitely a delicious and versatile food. It can be eaten quite plainly or flavoured with chopped nuts or fresh, dried or stewed fruit. You can also spoon it over fruit and puddings as a healthier substitute for cream; and it can be mixed into mousses and gelatin-set puddings and desserts and used instead of milk on muesli and other whole grain cereals. Yogurt can also be mixed into soups and main dishes just before you serve them. It can also be stabilized to prevent it from curdling when heated and mixed into dishes as they cook. Another use is to mix it into bread, cake and scone (biscuit) mixes.

Yogurt makes excellent salad dressings. It can be used just as it is with the addition of chopped herbs, freshly ground pepper and crushed garlic, or you can beat in 30ml (2tbls) oil per 150ml ($\frac{1}{4}$pt) or $\frac{2}{3}$ cup to make the dressing thicker. If you find oil-based mayonnaise too heavy, you can lighten it considerably in texture and flavour by mixing it with an equal quantity of yogurt. In the Middle East, where yogurt is still used more than in the West, a delicious drink called ayran is made by mixing yogurt with an equal quantity of cold water and adding crushed ice or small ice cubes, finely chopped mint and parsley and some freshly ground pepper. You can also make a refreshing, light cheese with yogurt by simply hanging it up to drip in a cheesecloth or clean linen cloth. In its country of origin it is known as quark or laban.

There are many different types of yogurt on the market and each has its own individual flavour and texture. Those to be found in whole food shops are generally made only from milk, either whole or skimmed; but the large, commercial varieties may well be made from milk, skimmed milk powder and liquid sucrose and although they have many of the beneficial qualities they are not as good nutritionally as those made with milk alone. Flavoured yogurts vary in quality; when buying them it is always best to read the label first. Avoid those that contain artificial colourings and flavourings and added sugar.

Home-made yogurt: the one way of ensuring that you are always kept well-supplied with a superb-quality yogurt, that is also low in cost, is to make it yourself. All you need is fresh milk and a starter which can either be a bought carton of unpasteurized yogurt or a yogurt culture. Yogurt is extremely easy to make and you have the added advantage of knowing exactly what it is made of. If you want a flavoured yogurt, then the combination of fruits, nuts and sweeteners such as molasses and honey that you can add after it is made are endless.

Buttermilk

A product in a way very similar to yogurt is cultured buttermilk. It is more liquid than yogurt, is made in a similar way, and is generally sold in cartons of large quantity. You can drink it just as it is or dilute it with water as for ayran. If you use it in cakes and scones (biscuits) instead of milk it makes them extremely light-textured.

Cream

Cream has a high fat content and should really be used sparingly in a wholefood diet. Better for you is dairy sour cream which has been specially soured under controlled conditions again in a very similar way to yogurt, and so is more easy to digest. It also has a much lighter flavour than single (light) or double (heavy) cream.

Butter

There has been much confusion over the question of whether butter or margarine is better for you. Both are fats and in terms of calories there is no difference, unless you buy a low-fat spread. The difference is generally in the type of fats. Butter contains animal fats and all margarines contain varying amounts of vegetable fats. The better-quality ones contain all vegetable fats and the poorer ones contain a mixture of vegetable fats, beef tallow and perhaps whale fat. The hard types of margarines contain saturated fats. Margarine, whatever kind you use, is a processed product that could not be made without the aid of chemicals. The natural food lover may find it difficult to make a choice between butter and margarine, but butter is the more natural product and we have been eating it for centuries. Spread thinly and used in moderation in cooking it will do you no harm.

Cheese

The product which features in nearly every pure food diet is cheese, and there are so many different kinds from which to choose, It is impossible ever to be bored with it either in the kitchen or at the table. There are low-fat, medium fat and full fat cheeses, soft, creamy ones and solid crumbly ones. They obviously vary in their constituents but all contain more protein than milk and weight for weight more than meat, fish or poultry. They are a useful source of vitamins A and D and the B vitamins, riboflavin, biotin and B_{12} and also of phosphorus. However, calcium is the most significant nutrient. Cheese is a very concentrated food and the hard types in particular go much further by weight than any of the other protein foods.

Soft cheeses are sold plain or flavoured and they may or may not contain a preservative, so read the label before you buy. It is probably best to buy a natural soft cheese and flavour it with chopped herbs or crushed garlic to your own taste. Cottage cheese is the slimmer's favourite as it is made from skimmed milk. It can taste fairly bland on its own but it can be made into quite tasty dishes by the addition of other ingredients such as diced green peppers and tomatoes, chopped apples and celery or grated beetroot (beet) with horseradish. You can serve these mixtures cold with a salad or put them into a hot oven for 20 minutes to make a light dish for a cold day.

Curd cheese (large-grained cottage or curd) is a medium fat soft cheese and is delicious flavoured with chopped herbs. To begin a meal you can put a spoonful on top of cut grapefruit or a slice of melon, or on a tomato salad. In main course salads, curd cheese is best eaten with other protein foods such as chopped nuts with sliced avocados. Cream cheese is a very rich, full fat cheese and should be used sparingly.

Hard cheeses are made in many different countries. Some such as the Dutch Edam, are made from skimmed milk and contain less fats. Others, such as Cheddar, are made from whole milk. The best hard English cheeses are the Farmhouse types. As their name suggests, they are literally made on the farm and left to mature for long periods so they are rich and mellow when they are sold. In America look for aged cheeses, which are additive free: names such as Longhorn or Brick. If you can, avoid buying processed cheeses as these could contain additives and are not a natural product.

The hard cheeses have various uses. They can be grated or chopped and made into salads, mixed into pastries and sauces, scattered over braised vegetables or incorporated with them in dishes such as potato pies or vegetable patties. Grated cheese can be mixed into bread and scone (biscuit) recipes and mixed with eggs to make quiches. Sliced cheese can be melted on top of pizzas or melted over wholemeal (whole grain) toast. And what better quick meal is there than a lunch with wholemeal bread, a small salad and a chunk of cheese, affectionately known in Britain as 'a ploughman's lunch'?

Eggs

Eggs are an excellent source of protein. This protein contains a perfect balance of amino acids for our body-building needs. One egg will supply a tenth of the average adults daily protein needs. Eggs are relatively low in calories and as they are digested slowly you do not get hungry again too soon after you have eaten them. They are therefore a valuable food for the slimmer.

Minerals & Vitamins

Eggs contain vitamins A and D, thiamin, riboflavin, vitamin B_{12} and biotin, smaller amounts of other B vitamins and a little vitamin E. The minerals they contain include iron, calcium, potassium and magnesium.

As so much goodness is packed into a tiny shell eggs are also ideal for those with small appetites such as old people or invalids. Eggs do contain a certain amount of cholesterol, but one a day will not hurt a healthy person so eggs are included, to great advantage, in a natural food diet.

The overwhelming majority of eggs are produced by chickens which either live in wire-mesh cages— 'battery chickens'—or are deep-littered, which means that they are free to walk around but are always kept inside in artificial light. Grain-fed hens' eggs are also preferable to chemically-fed hens' eggs. Free-running or 'free-range' chickens live the more natural existence, both in terms of living quarters and food. and it is this which appeals to many people when it comes to buying their eggs.

In Britain look for 'free-range' eggs, in America for 'strictly fresh' eggs, which are farm produced; there is a difference in their nutritive content. The levels of fat, protein and some B vitamins are more or less equal in eggs produced under any conditions; but iron is substantially higher in eggs from caged birds and this is thought to be the result of the chickens pecking at their cages and feeding troughs. Calcium and sodium are higher in eggs from caged birds, while potassium is higher when the chickens run free. The amount of vitamin E is different in these two types. The most significant difference is in the vitamin B_{12} content which is twice as high in eggs from free chickens, and, in folic acid, which is 50% higher. This could be very important to vegetarians, since the only other product containing these in large amounts is meat.

Eggs can be served at any meal of the day and they can be made into sweet and main dishes. A lightly-boiled, or poached egg with wholemeal (whole grain) toast makes an ideal breakfast. For lunch you can have scrambled eggs or an omelet and in the evening you can make more elaborate dishes. Boiled eggs can be made into salads for first and main courses and you can also chop them and mix them into lightly-cooked vegetables to make a quick and easy main dish. Poached eggs can be served on a bed of vegetables and coated with grated cheese or a cheese sauce. You can also bake eggs either simply in a lightly-greased dish or, again with vegetables and cheese. Omelets can be made just with beaten eggs and chopped herbs and folded round a tasty filling, or they can be made thick and hearty and include diced vegetables, meat or grated cheese in the mixture. For special occasions you can make a light soufflé omelet by beating the egg whites separately and these can be made sweet or not. A beautiful, risen soufflé will grace any table as well as being good to eat; you can also make a more unusual roulade. Eggs form the base of many a tasty quiche, extra whipped whites can make crêpe mixtures light and the yolks can be used to thicken soups or sauces or to make mayonnaise.

RECIPES

Home-made Yogurt

Once you have got your yogurt-making established, you can use your own, home-made yogurt for a culture. To start the first batch you will need unpasteurized yogurt or, if this is not available, buy yogurt culture (*Lactobacillus bulgaricus*).
The cheapest and easiest way of making yogurt is to use a wide-necked Thermos flask. If the yogurt is going to be heated later to any great extent, it should first be stabilized (see following recipe) to prevent it curdling.

METRIC/IMPERIAL	AMERICAN
575ml (1pt) milk	*2½ cups milk*
15ml (1tbls) unpasteurized, natural yogurt	*1tbls home-made yogurt or yogurt culture*

Put pasteurized, homogenized or raw milk into a saucepan and bring it gently to the boil. Let it boil until it rises up the sides of the pan. Cool the milk to 46°C (115°F) by standing the pan in cold water.

Put the yogurt into a bowl and gradually stir in about 150 ml (¼ pt) or ½ cup of warm milk. Stir the contents of the bowl back into the saucepan. Pour the milk and yogurt mixture into a wide-necked Thermos flask. If the flask is liable to lose heat, put it into a warm place, such as a clothes-drying cupboard. Leave the yogurt for 8 hours.

Pour the yogurt into individual containers and refrigerate them immediately.

Cooking time: about 8 hours

† If you are using pasteurized or raw milk, 15 ml (1tbls) skimmed milk powder may be added with the yogurt to make a thicker set.

† Another way of obtaining a thick set is to boil the milk until it has reduced by about two-thirds, but this reduces the nutritive value rather more.

Stabilized Yogurt

METRIC/IMPERIAL	AMERICAN
575ml (1pt) natural yogurt	2½ cups plain yogurt
either 1 egg white	either 1 egg white
or 15ml (1tbls) cornflour	or 1tbls cornstarch

Put the egg white or cornflour (cornstarch) into a saucepan and stir in the yogurt. Put the saucepan on a low heat and stir until the mixture boils. Simmer gently for 10 minutes, stirring frequently. Cool the yogurt and put it into containers for storing.

Cooking time: 10 minutes plus cooling

Yogurt and Mint Soup

Yogurt, onions and mint make a light and refreshing soup.

METRIC/IMPERIAL	AMERICAN
2 medium-sized onions	2 medium-sized onions
1 large clove garlic	1 large clove garlic
60ml (4tbls) olive oil	4tbls olive oil
15ml (1tbls) wholemeal flour	1tbls whole grain flour
575ml (1pt) stock	2½ cups stock or broth
60ml (4tbls) chopped mint	4tbls chopped mint
275ml (½pt) natural yogurt	1¼ cups plain yogurt

Finely chop the onions and garlic. Heat the oil in a saucepan on a low heat. Stir in the onions and garlic and cook them until they are soft. Stir in the flour and cook it for 1 minute. Stir in the stock and bring it to the boil. Add the mint and simmer, uncovered, for 20 minutes. Take the pan from the heat and cool the soup for 1 minute. Stir in the yogurt and reheat very gently, without boiling.

Cooking time: 35 minutes

Make this curd cheese dip to eat before a meal.

Curd Cheese Dip

Curd cheese is ideal for making simple dips which are delicious with crudités at the start of a meal. These can be made in large quantities for parties.

METRIC/IMPERIAL	AMERICAN
225g (½lb) curd cheese	½lb fresh curd or farmer's cheese
60ml (4tbls) soured cream	4tbls dairy sour cream
15ml (1tbls) chopped chives	1tbls chopped chives
15ml (1tbls) chopped parsley	1tbls chopped parsley

Put the cheese into a bowl and beat in the sour cream so that the mixture becomes smooth and creamy. Fold in the herbs. Put the dip into the middle of a large serving plate and surround it with a selection of finely-cut raw vegetables.

Cooking time: 15 minutes

† Beat chopped mint and a little crushed garlic into the cheese and sour cream mixture and surround it with sticks of cucumber.

† Use only mint and spoon the cheese over cut grapefruits or chopped watermelon.

Yogurt Cheese

A pure white, creamy cheese with a light flavour can be made by hanging yogurt up in a cloth to drip. It is also known as laban or quark. This makes about 125g (¼lb) or ½ cup of cheese.

METRIC/IMPERIAL	AMERICAN
575ml (1pt) natural yogurt	2½ cups plain yogurt

Scald and cool an old glass cloth or piece of cheese-cloth or fine muslin. Stand a colander in a dish and spread out the cloth inside it. Pour in the yogurt. Gather the corners of the cloth together and tie them. Hang the yogurt up to drip, with a dish underneath, for 12 hours.
Take down the cloth and untie it. Turn out the cheese, mix it well with a spoon and put it into a container. Save the whey for scones (biscuits) and breads.

Preparation time : about 12 hours

Yogurt Cottage Cheese

A little yogurt can be used to curdle milk to make a cheese of the cottage type. This makes about 225g (½lb) or 1 cup cheese.

METRIC/IMPERIAL	AMERICAN
30ml (2tbls) natural yogurt	2tbls plain yogurt
1.15L (2pt) milk	5 cups milk

Put the yogurt into a large bowl and gradually stir in the milk. Cover the bowl and leave it in a warm place for 4 days.
Scald and cool an old glass cloth or piece of cheese-cloth or fine muslin. Stand a colander in a large dish and lay the cloth inside. Pour the soured milk into the cloth. Tie the corners of the cloth together and hang it up with a dish underneath so that the whey can drip out. Leave it for 24 hours.
Unwrap the cheese, turn it into a bowl and mix well with a spoon.

Preparation time : about 5 days

Fresh Curd Cheese

Lemon juice can be used to curdle milk, to make a fresh, soft, creamy-textured, unripened cheese. This makes 175-225g (6-8oz) or ¾-1 cup cheese.

METRIC/IMPERIAL	AMERICAN
1.15L (2pt) milk	5 cups milk
juice 2 lemons	juice 2 lemons

Put the milk into a bowl and stir in the lemon juice. Leave it for 24 hours or until it separates and looks like curds and whey.

Scald and cool an old glass cloth or piece of cheese-cloth or fine muslin. Stand a colander in a dish and lay the cloth on top. Pour in the curds and whey and gather the edges of the cloth together. Hang the cheese to drip for 24 hours. Mix it together and put it into a container.

Preparation time : about 2 days

Low-fat Liptauer Cheese

The favourite German, Liptauer cheese, made with curd cheese instead of butter, has a lighter flavour but is just as delicious as the original. Serve it as a dip to begin a meal, with a selection of crudités, such as spring onions (scallions), sticks of cucumber, olives and radishes.

METRIC/IMPERIAL	AMERICAN
¾lb cottage cheese	¾lb cottage cheese
150g (¼lb) curd cheese	¼lb (⅔ cup) curd cheese
1 large pickled Hungarian gherkin	1 large dill pickled gherkin
15ml (2tbls) chopped chives	2tbls chopped chives
10ml (2tsp) paprika	2tsp paprika
5ml (1tsp) German mustard	1tsp German mustard
10ml (2tsp) dill seeds	2tsp dill seeds
sea salt	sea salt
For serving:	**For serving:**
radishes	radishes
black olives	black olives
sticks of cucumber	sticks of cucumber
capers	capers

Rub the cottage cheese through a sieve and gradually beat it into the curd cheese. Finely chop the gherkin and mix it into the cheeses with the chives, paprika, mustard and dill seeds. Season lightly with the salt.
Put the cheese into a serving bowl, smooth the top and make patterns on it with a fork. Put the bowl onto a plate and surround it with olives, radishes, short sticks of unpeeled cucumber and a pile of capers.

Cooking time : 25 minutes

Carrot and Cream Cheese Soup

Cream cheese can be added to blended soups to make them thick and creamy. The flavour of this one is lightened by the small amount of tomato paste.

METRIC/IMPERIAL	AMERICAN
175g (6oz) carrots	1½ cups carrots, sliced thinly
1 large onion	1 large onion
1 clove garlic	1 clove garlic
25g (1oz) butter	2tbls butter
850ml (1½pt) stock	3¾ cups stock or broth
bouquet garni	bouquet garni
50g (2oz) sweet cream cheese	4tbls unsalted cream cheese
15ml (1tbls) tomato purée	1tbls tomato paste

Thinly slice the carrots and the onion and finely chop

Low-fat Liptauer cheese.

the garlic. Melt the butter in a saucepan on a low heat. Stir in the carrots, onion and garlic, cover them and let them sweat for 10 minutes. Pour in the stock and bring it to the boil. Add the bouquet garni. Cover and simmer for 20 minutes. Remove the bouquet garni. Put the soup into a blender with the cheese and tomato paste and work it until it is smooth. Reheat it before serving if necessary.

Cooking time : 35 minutes

Spiced Eggplants with Yogurt

Yogurt and mint are used in this first course recipe to lighten the flavour of rich aubergine (eggplant) slices.

METRIC/IMPERIAL	AMERICAN
450g (1lb) aubergines	1lb eggplant
15ml (1tbls) sea salt	1tbls sea salt
275ml (½pt) natural yogurt	1¼ cups plain yogurt
1 clove garlic, crushed with a pinch sea salt	1 clove garlic, crushed with a pinch sea salt
30ml (2tbls) chopped mint	2tbls chopped mint
freshly ground black pepper	freshly ground black pepper
60ml (4tbls) olive oil	4tbls olive oil
5ml (1tsp) ground cumin	1tsp ground cumin
5ml (1tsp) ground coriander	1tsp ground coriander

Cut the aubergines (eggplant) into 1cm (½in) thick slices. Put them into a colander and sprinkle them with the salt. Leave them to drain for 30 minutes. Rinse them with cold water and pat them dry with absorbent paper. Mix the yogurt, garlic, mint and pepper together.
Heat the oil in a large frying-pan on a moderate heat. Put in the aubergine (eggplant) slices and sprinkle them with half the cumin and coriander. Brown the underside, turn them, then sprinkle them with the remaining spices. When they are done, arrange them on a serving plate and spoon the yogurt over the top.

Cooking time : 40 minutes

Foil-baked Parsnips with Cheese

A little curd, cottage or farmer's cheese can make simple baked parsnips into a special dish to serve with meat or fish. If you pile more cheese onto them, they could also make a light main course.

IMPERIAL/METRIC	AMERICAN
450g (1lb) medium-sized parsnips	1lb medium-sized parsnips
50g (2oz) curd cheese	⅓ cup curd, farmer's cheese
freshly grated nutmeg	freshly grated nutmeg
little oil for greasing foil	little oil for greasing foil

Heat the oven to gas mark 3/180°C (350°F). Cut the parsnips in half lengthwise and remove the cores. Cut the halves across into two pieces. Fill the centre cavities with a very little cheese and grate a little

nutmeg over the top. Wrap the pieces of parsnip together in a large piece of oiled kitchen foil, making sure they all stay together in pairs. Lay the parcel on a baking sheet and put it into the oven for 1¼ hours.

Cooking time : 1 hour 30 minutes

Spinach and cheese are combined with oatmeal and potatoes for these original vegetarian patties.

Spinach and Cheese Patties

Spinach, cheese and potatoes, made into oatmeal-coated patties make a substantial main course.

METRIC/IMPERIAL	AMERICAN
450g (1lb) spinach	1lb fresh spinach
225g (½lb) potatoes	½lb potatoes
1 small onion	1 small onion
225g (½lb) grated Farmhouse Cheddar cheese	2 cups grated aged Cheddar cheese
2 egg yolks	2 egg yolks
45ml (3tbls) chopped parsley	3tbls chopped parsley
large pinch ground mace	large pinch ground mace
sea salt	sea salt
freshly ground black pepper	freshly ground black pepper
2 eggs, beaten	2 eggs, beaten
50g (2oz) fine oatmeal	⅔ cup fine oatmeal
60ml (4tbls) oil	4tbls oil

Wash the spinach and break off the stalks where they join the leaves. Put the spinach into a saucepan with just the water that clings to it after washing. Cover it and set it on a moderate heat for 10 minutes, turning it once. Drain it well, pressing down hard to remove as much water as possible.

Scrub the potatoes, cut them into chunks and put them into a saucepan of lightly-salted water. Thinly slice the onion and put it with the potatoes. Boil until the potatoes are tender. Drain and peel the potatoes. Mash the potatoes and onion together and mix in the spinach. Either put them all through a vegetable mill or blend in a blender to a thick purée.

Turn the purée into a bowl and beat in the cheese, egg yolks, parsley, mace and seasonings. Form the mixture into 8 round, flat patties about 2cm (¾in) thick. Put them onto a flat plate or board and refrigerate for 30 minutes, so they set into shape. Dip the patties in the beaten eggs and coat them in oatmeal. Fry them in the oil on a moderate heat until both sides are golden brown.

Cooking time: 1 hour 10 minutes

Cottage Cheese, Apple and Celery Salad

Slimmers do not have to suffer tasteless meals. All kinds of chopped ingredients can be mixed into cottage cheese to make it really appetising.

METRIC/IMPERIAL	AMERICAN
450g (1lb) cottage cheese	1lb cottage cheese
2 medium-sized Bramley apples	2 medium-sized tart apples
6 large sticks celery	6 large stalks celery
2 boxes cress	½ x 1lb jar sprouted alfalfa seeds
10ml (2tsp) mustard seeds	2tsp mustard seeds
2 sweet eating apples	2 sweet red apples
30ml (2tbls) chopped celery leaves	2tbls chopped celery leaves

Put the cheese into a large bowl. Quarter, core and finely chop the tart apples, finely chop the celery and cut the cress from the boxes or prepare the watercress. Mix the apples, celery, cress and mustard seeds into the cheese. Put the salad into a bowl and garnish it with slices of apple and the chopped celery leaves.

Cooking time: 20 minutes

132

Cheese, onion and potato pie.

Red Cheese Quiche

This quiche is moist and tasty and delicious hot or cold. It is a lovely reddish colour, flecked with herbs.

METRIC/IMPERIAL	AMERICAN
For the pastry:	**For the pastry:**
175g (6oz) wholemeal flour	1½ cups whole grain flour
pinch of sea salt	pinch of sea salt
100g (3½oz) butter	7tbls butter
cold water to mix	cold water to mix
For the filling:	**For the filling:**
4 eggs	4 eggs
275ml (½pt) milk	1¼ cups milk
30ml (2tbls) tomato purée	2tbls tomato paste
30ml (2tbls) Worcestershire sauce	2tbls Worcestershire sauce
30ml (2tbls) chopped parsley	2tbls chopped parsley
30ml (2tbls) chopped chives	2tbls chopped chives
125g (¼lb) grated Farmhouse red Cheshire cheese	1 cup grated Poona or aged English Cheshire cheese

Heat the oven to gas mark 6/200°C (400°F). Make the pastry and chill it. Beat the eggs with the milk, tomato paste, Worcestershire sauce, and herbs. Mix in the cheese.

Roll out the pastry and line a 20cm (8in) diameter flan tin (quiche pan). Pour in the egg mixture, making sure the cheese is evenly distributed. Bake the quiche for 40 minutes.

Cooking time: 1 hour 10 minutes

Cheese, Onion and Potato Pie

Cheese and potato pie is a filling family meal. The lemon rind and crushed garlic in this one give the thick sauce topping an unusual light flavour.

METRIC/IMPERIAL	AMERICAN
700g (1½lb) potatoes	1½lb potatoes
3 large onions	3 large onions
275ml (½pt) milk	1¼ cups milk
6 black peppercorns	6 black peppercorns
1 blade mace	1 blade mace
1 bay leaf	1 bayleaf
25g (1oz) butter	2tbls butter
30ml (2tbls) wholemeal flour	2tbls whole grain flour
grated rind 1 lemon	grated rind 1 lemon
1 clove garlic, crushed with a pinch sea salt	1 clove garlic, crushed with a pinch sea salt
225g (½lb) grated Farmhouse Cheddar cheese	2 cups grated aged Cheddar cheese
large pinch cayenne pepper	large pinch cayenne pepper
8 green olives, stoned and chopped	8 green olives, pitted and chopped
60ml (4tbls) chopped parsley	4tbls chopped parsley
little butter for greasing large pie dish	little butter for greasing large pie dish or casserole

Heat the oven to gas mark 6/200°C (400°F). Boil the potatoes in their skins in lightly-salted water until they are just tender. Quarter and thinly slice the onions.

Put them into a saucepan with the milk, peppercorns, mace and bayleaf. Bring them to the boil and simmer for 15 minutes. Drain the onions, pressing down well to extract as much liquid as possible. Reserve the milk and discard the peppercorns, mace and bay leaf.

Melt the butter in a saucepan on a moderate heat. Stir in the flour and cook for 1 minute. Stir in the milk, bring it to the boil, stirring, and let the sauce simmer for 2 minutes.

Take the pan from the heat and beat in the lemon rind and garlic and 75g (3oz) or ¾ cup of the cheese. Put half the potatoes into the bottom of a large, greased pie dish or casserole and sprinkle them with a little cayenne pepper, one-third of the remaining cheese and half the olives and parsley. Put in all the onions, the remaining olives and parsley and another third of the cheese. Sprinkle this with a little cayenne pepper and then top with the remaining potatoes. Spoon the sauce over the potatoes and scatter the remaining cheese on top. Put the dish into the oven for 30 minutes so the cheese is melted and bubbling and just beginning to brown.

Cooking time: 1 hour 10 minutes

Curried Cabbage and Eggs

Hard-boiled eggs are sliced and mixed into curry-flavoured cabbage with almonds and sultanas (raisins) to make an easily-prepared, colourful and substantial main dish.

METRIC/IMPERIAL	AMERICAN
8 hard-boiled eggs	8 hard-cooked eggs
1 large green cabbage	1 large head Savoy cabbage
1 large onion	1 large onion
1 clove garlic	1 clove garlic
50g (2oz) almonds	2tbls almonds
60ml (4tbls) oil	4tbls oil
15ml (1tbls) hot Madras curry powder	1tbls hot curry powder
120ml (8tbls) stock	8tbls stock or broth
50g (2oz) sultanas	¼ cup white raisins (muscats)
75g (3oz) fresh wholemeal breadcrumbs	2-3 cups fresh whole grain breadcrumbs

Peel the eggs. Shred the cabbage, quarter and thinly slice the onion and finely chop the garlic. Blanch and split the almonds.

Heat the oil in a large saucepan on a low heat. Mix in the onion garlic and curry powder and cook until the onion is soft. Mix in the cabbage and pour in the stock. Cover and cook for 10 minutes. Slice the eggs into rounds. Toss the almonds and sultanas (white raisins) into the cabbage and put half the mixture into a 1.45L (2½pt) or 6-cup heatproof dish. Arrange half the eggs on top. Put in the remaining cabbage and top with the rest of the eggs. Scatter the breadcrumbs over the eggs and put the dish under a high grill for the eggs to brown.

Cooking time: 45 minutes

Courgette (Zucchini) Omelet

Sliced courgettes (zucchini) and eggs make a thick, hearty omelet which can be eaten hot or cold.

METRIC/IMPERIAL	AMERICAN
450g (1lb) small courgettes	1lb small zucchini
1 medium-sized onion	1 medium-sized onion
1 clove garlic	1 clove garlic
6 eggs	6 eggs
30ml (2tbls) chopped chervil or parsley	2tbls chopped chervil or parsley
sea salt	sea salt
freshly ground black pepper	freshly ground black pepper
25g (1oz) butter or 60ml (4tbls) oil	2tbls butter or 4tbls oil

Wipe and thinly slice the courgettes (zucchini). Quarter and thinly slice the onion and finely chop the garlic. Beat the eggs with the herbs (if you are using them) and seasonings.
Melt the butter or heat the oil in an omelet pan on a low heat. Stir in the courgettes (zucchini), onions and garlic and cook them until they are soft. Preheat the grill (broiler) to high.
Pour the eggs into the pan and cook until they are almost set, tipping the pan and lifting the edges of the omelet with a spatula, so as much of the egg as possible reaches the sides and base of the pan. Put the omelet pan under the grill (broiler) and continue cooking until the eggs are set and the top of the omelet is risen and golden.
Either cut the omelet into four portions and serve it hot or slide it onto a plate and leave it until it is completely cold.

Cooking time: 30 minutes

Egg and Avocado Salad

An avocado, puréed with a little yogurt, will have the same texture as a thick mayonnaise. With eggs, it makes an attractive salad to begin a meal. You can also double all the ingredients for a main course.

METRIC/IMPERIAL	AMERICAN
4 hard-boiled eggs	4 hard-boiled eggs
1 ripe avocado	1 ripe avocado
45ml (3tbls) natural yogurt	3tbls plain yogurt
15ml (1tbls) tomato purée	1tbls tomato paste
few drops Tabasco sauce	few drops Tabasco sauce
1 small lettuce	1 small lettuce
4 tomatoes	4 tomatoes
30ml (2tbls) chopped coriander or parsley	2tbls chopped coriander or parsley

Peel the eggs, cut them in half lengthwise and cool them. Peel the avocado and mash it to a purée. Work in the yogurt, tomato paste and Tabasco sauce.
Arrange a bed of lettuce on 4 small plates and put the eggs, cut side down, on top. Spoon the avocado dressing over the eggs and garnish with the tomatoes cut in slices. Sprinkle the coriander or parsley over the eggs.

Cooking time: 25 minutes

† Omit the tomato paste and Tabasco sauce and add an extra 15ml (1tbls) yogurt. Use chopped chervil instead of coriander.

Yogurt and Blue Cheese Salad Dressing

Yogurt and blue cheese make a refreshing salad dressing that is excellent with cucumber and with watercress and tomatoes. Try it also spooned into an avocado half to begin a meal.

METRIC/IMPERIAL	AMERICAN
50g (2oz) soft blue cheese	½ cup crumbly blue cheese
150ml (¼pt) natural yogurt	⅝ cup plain yogurt
1 clove garlic, crushed with a pinch sea salt	1 clove garlic, crushed with a pinch sea salt
few drops Tabasco sauce or freshly ground black pepper	few drops Tabasco sauce or freshly ground black pepper

Rub the cheese through a strainer. Gradually beat in the yogurt about 30ml (2tbls) at a time. Add the garlic and Tabasco sauce.

Cooking time: 15 minutes

Eggs Baked with Tomatoes and Cheese

The texture of this attractive dish is smooth and creamy and the flavour goes well with the gentle spiciness of the cinnamon.

METRIC/IMPERIAL	AMERICAN
8 eggs	8 eggs
1 large onion	1 large onion
1 clove garlic	1 clove garlic
450g (1lb) ripe tomatoes	1lb tomatoes
5ml (1tsp) ground cinnamon	1tsp ground cinnamon
15ml (1tbls) chopped thyme	1tbls chopped thyme
125g (¼lb) grated Farmhouse Double Gloucester cheese	1 cup grated Double Gloucester, Longhorn or Velveeta cheese

Heat the oven to gas mark 6/200°C (400°F). Thinly slice the onion and finely chop the garlic. Scald, skin and roughly chop the tomatoes. Melt the butter in a frying-pan on a low heat. Mix in the onions and garlic and cook them until they are soft. Add the tomatoes, cinnamon and thyme and cook until the tomatoes are pulpy. Spoon the mixture into a large, flat, ovenproof dish and break the eggs on top. Cover the eggs with the cheese and bake them for 25 minutes.

Cooking time: 45 minutes

Smoked fish and herbs give this soufflé extra interest.

Smoked Fish and Herb Soufflé

Smoked haddock makes a very tasty soufflé. The herbs add flavour and also give an attractive, layered effect when the soufflé is spooned out of the dish.

METRIC/IMPERIAL	AMERICAN
butter, crumbs, greaseproof paper and string for preparing a medium-sized soufflé dish	butter, crumbs, waxed paper and string for preparing a medium-sized soufflé dish
275g (10oz) smoked haddock fillets	¾lb smoked fish or Finan haddie fillets
275ml (½pt) milk	1¼ cups milk
1 bay leaf	1 bayleaf
1 blade mace	1 blade mace
6 black peppercorns	6 black peppercorns
25g (1oz) butter	2tbls butter
15ml (1tbls) wholemeal flour	1tbls whole grain flour
2.5ml (½tsp) ground mace	½tsp ground mace
2.5ml (½tsp) nutmeg	½tsp nutmeg
grated rind ½ lemon	grated rind ½ lemon
freshly ground black pepper	freshly ground black pepper
4 eggs, separated	4 eggs, separated
60ml (4tbls) chopped parsley	4tbls chopped parsley
15ml (1tbls) chopped thyme	1tbls chopped thyme
15ml (1tbls) chopped fennel	1tbls chopped fennel or celery
4 chopped sage leaves	4 chopped sage leaves

Heat the oven to gas mark 6/200°C (400°F). Grease the inside of the dish with butter and coat with crumbs, then tip out the excess. Tie a greaseproof or waxed paper collar round the dish standing about 8cm (3in) above the dish rim. Skin the fish if necessary and put it into a shallow saucepan with the bay leaf, blade of mace and peppercorns. Bring it to the boil and simmer gently for 5 minutes. Lift out the fish with a perforated fish slice. Strain and reserve the milk.

Flake the fish. Melt the butter in a saucepan on a low heat. Stir in the flour and cook it for 1 minute. Stir in the reserved milk and bring it to the boil, stirring. Simmer for 2 minutes. Take the pan from the heat and beat in the mace, nutmeg, lemon rind and pepper. Beat in the flaked fish and then the egg yolks, one at a time. Stiffly whip the egg whites and fold them into the fish mixture. Pile one-third of the mixture into the soufflé dish. Scatter in half the herbs in an even layer. Repeat and top with the remaining soufflé mixture. Put the soufflé into the oven and immediately turn the oven to gas mark 5/190°C (375°F). Bake the soufflé for 30 minutes, until well-risen golden and puffy. Serve immediately.

Cooking time: 1 hour

Egg and Nut Bake

Eggs, nuts and breadcrumbs make an interesting textured and tasty main dish. Serve it with a salad and baked potatoes.

METRIC/IMPERIAL	AMERICAN
6 eggs	6 eggs
125g (4oz) ground mixed nuts of your choice	⅔ cup ground mixed nuts of your choice
1 large onion	1 large onion
1 clove garlic	1 clove garlic
25g (1oz) butter or 45ml (3tbls) oil	2tbls butter or 3tbls oil
50g (2oz) fresh wholemeal breadcrumbs	1-2 cups fresh whole grain breadcrumbs
10ml (2tsp) yeast extract	2tsp yeast extract
little extra butter or oil for greasing 20cm (8in) diameter ovenproof dish	extra butter or oil for greasing 8in diameter ovenproof dish

Heat the oven to gas mark 6/200°C (400°F). Beat the eggs and fold in the nuts. Thinly slice the onion and finely chop the garlic. Melt the butter or heat the oil in a frying pan on a low heat. Mix in the onion and garlic and cook them until they are soft. Take the pan from the heat and mix in the breadcrumbs and yeast extract. Mix the contents of the pan into the eggs. Put the mixture into the greased dish and bake the pudding for 30 minutes.

Cooking time : 50 minutes

Sweet Apple Omelet

Omelets can make delicious desserts and this sweet soufflé omelet is light and airy and melts in your mouth.

METRIC/IMPERIAL	AMERICAN
350g (¾lb) cooking apples	¾lb tart apples
45ml (3tbls) water	3tbls water
little freshly grated nutmeg	freshly grated nutmeg
45ml (3tbls) honey	3tbls honey
4 eggs, separated	4 eggs, separated
15g (½oz) butter	1tbls butter

Peel and finely chop the apples. Put them into a sauce-pan with the water and nutmeg and set them on a low heat. Cover, and cook them for 15 minutes or until they can be beaten to a purée. Stir in the honey and cool them.
Beat one-third of the apples into the egg yolks. Stiffly whip the whites and fold them into the yolks and apples.
Melt the butter in an omelet pan on a moderate heat and pre-heat the grill (broiler) to moderate. Pour the egg mixture into the pan and spread it out. Cook it for 2 minutes. Put the pan under the grill (broiler) about 10cm (4in) away from the heat for the omelet to set and brown. Slide the omelet onto a large plate and top it with the remaining apple purée. Alternatively, top it in the pan, fold and slice into 4 for serving.

Cooking time : 30 minutes

Cheese and Celery Seed Crackers

These plain, cheese and celery-flavoured crackers are good eaten instead of bread with an appetizer. They are also excellent with cheese, at the end of the meal or as a snack.

METRIC/IMPERIAL	AMERICAN
225g (½lb) wholemeal flour	2 cups whole grain flour
5ml (1tsp) baking powder	1tsp baking powder
2.5ml (½tsp) salt	½tsp salt
25g (1oz) butter	2tbls butter
50g (2oz) grated Farmhouse Cheddar cheese	½ cup grated, aged Cheddar cheese
30ml (2tbls) celery seeds	2tbls celery seeds
120ml (8tbls) water	8tbls water
60ml (4tbls) milk	4tbls milk

METRIC/IMPERIAL	AMERICAN
5ml (1tsp) ground cinnamon	1tsp ground cinnamon
5ml (1tsp) ground ginger	1tsp ground ginger
50g (2oz) butter	4tbls butter
225g (½lb) molasses	1 cup molasses
225ml (8floz) buttermilk	1 cup buttermilk
125g (¼lb) chopped pressed dates	¼lb chopped, pressed dates
butter for greasing 900g (2lb) loaf tin	butter for greasing 5-cup bread pan

Heat the oven to gas mark 4 / 180°C (350°F). Toss the flour in a mixing bowl with the soda, salt and spices. Cream the butter in a bowl and gradually beat in the molasses. Beat in the flour, alternately with the buttermilk. Fold in the chopped dates. Put the mixture into a greased 900g (2lb) loaf tin (bread pan) and smooth the top. Bake the cake for 50 minutes and turn it onto a wire rack to cool.

Cooking time: 1 hour 10 minutes

† Raisins or sultanas (dark or white raisins) or a mixture of the two may be substituted for the dates.

Tipsy Raisin Cheesecake

Cottage cheese makes a light and fluffy filling for a cheesecake and the small amount of thick cream gives an added body to make it set. The raisins provide flavour and natural sweetness. Do not throw away the soaking liquid. Use it in a dried fruit salad.

METRIC/IMPERIAL	AMERICAN
125g (¼lb) raisins	⅔ cup raisins
125ml (4floz) port	½ cup port
125g (¼lb) digestive biscuits	¼lb graham crackers
125g (¼lb) plain wheaten biscuits (such as Macvita)	¼lb plain wholewheat cookies
75g (3oz) butter or vegetable margarine	6tbls butter or shortening
5ml (1tsp) mixed spice	1tsp mixed spice
225g (½lb) cottage cheese	1 cup cottage cheese
275ml (½pt) natural yogurt	1¼ cups plain yogurt
30ml (2tbls) double cream	2tbls heavy cream

Soak the raisins in the port for 6 hours or overnight. Crush the biscuits (cookies). Melt the butter or margarine (shortening) in a saucepan on a low heat and stir in the crushed crumbs and spice. Press the mixture into the sides and base of an 18-20cm (7-8in) flan tin (quiche pan). Put it into the refrigerator to chill.
Rub the cottage cheese through a strainer and gradually beat in the yogurt and double (heavy) cream. Drain the raisins and fold them into the cheese mixture. Spoon the mixture into the crumb shell and smooth the top. Put the cheesecake into the refrigerator for 1 hour. If you are using a flan tin with a removable base, remove the cheesecake just before serving.

Cooking time: 2 hours 30 minutes

† If you do not wish to use port, use natural dark red grape juice to soak the raisins.

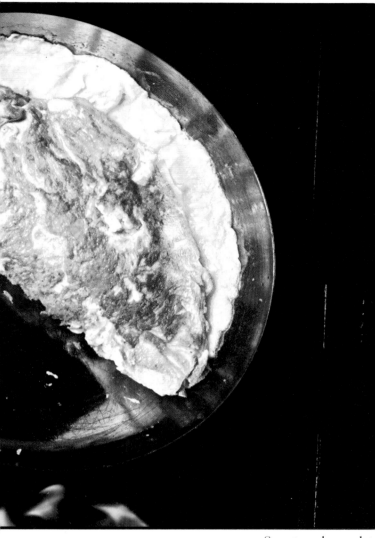

Sweet apple omelet.

Heat the oven to gas mark 7 / 220°C (450°F). Sift the flour into a bowl with the baking powder and salt and rub in the butter. Toss in the cheese and celery seeds with your fingers. Make a well in the centre, add the water and milk and mix everything to a dough. Roll it out to 3mm (⅛in) thick and cut it into circles with a biscuit cutter. Lay the circles of dough on floured baking sheets and prick them all over with a fork. Bake them for 15 minutes and immediately lift them onto wire racks to cool. They keep very well in an airtight container.

Cooking time: 35 minutes

Buttermilk Spice Cake

This cake is based on an old colonial American recipe. It is very light and moist.

METRIC/IMPERIAL	AMERICAN
275g (10oz) wholemeal flour	2½ cups whole grain flour
7.5ml (1½tsp) bicarbonate of soda	1½tsp baking soda
5ml (1tsp) salt	1tsp salt

Baking

The cook who bakes with wholemeal (whole grain) flour can be every bit as successful as the one who always uses white flour, and the produce of her kitchen will be far tastier and full of natural goodness. The deep brown appearance of pastries, breads, cakes and puddings may seem a little strange at first, but you will be used to it in no time at all and then the bland-looking white loaves and pastries will be the ones that seem unusual.

Wholemeal (whole grain) flour can be used with great success in any recipe that was first written for white flour, so you can still use your old cookery books. There is little difference in the way it has to be treated and you should have no difficulty at all once you have learned a few tips. If you would rather make the progression from white to wholemeal flour gradually, then start by using the 81% and 85% wheatmeal (whole wheat) flours which have only the bran removed. Once you have mastered this you can go on to the 100% flours. If your old cake recipes require self-raising (self-rising) flour then you will still be able to make them as both kinds of wheat flours can be bought as self-raising (self-rising).

Whole grain pastry

Contrary to what many people believe, wholemeal (whole grain) pastry need not be heavy and unappetizing. It can be just as light and crumbly as white. Use a proportion of half fat to flour and rub it in with cool, light fingers. A good idea, unless of course you are using a soft, vegetable margarine or the climate is very warm, is to take the fat straight from the refrigerator and grate it into the flour on a fine grater. This enables you to rub it in quickly and evenly. You can use all butter or all vegetable magarine for pastry; or a mixture of half butter or margarine to half lard or a pure vegetable fat. The best white vegetable fats can be found in natural food shops. If you make your own dripping, this will make a very light and crumbly pastry for meat pies, quiches etc. Season the flour with fine sea salt (a coarse salt will not be incorporated evenly) and for meat pies, a little pepper as well. You can also flavour the pastry with a little grated cheese, tossed in after the fat has been rubbed in.

When you mix wholemeal (whole grain) pastry you will probably find that you will need slightly more water than for white pastry to make the dough hold together adequately. It will also make it handle better when you roll it out. Once the pastry has been formed into a ball, coat it with a dusting of flour and put it into a plastic bag. Then put it into the refrigerator for 15 minutes. Freshly-made pastry will tend to fall apart when it is rolled out, but if it is chilled the problem will be lessened.

Use a fixed rolling pin rather than a revolving one and flour both it and your work top well. Then roll out your pastry in the usual way and to lift it, roll it round the rolling pin to transfer it to the pie dish, flan tin or quiche pan that you are using. If it falls apart, then pinch it together again and re-roll it and this time it will hold together. This method may not be in any rule book but it works perfectly. If you constantly have trouble, then roll your pastry onto a sheet of grease-proof, waxed paper or foil, lift it up, still on the sheet, and gently slide it onto your dish. Glaze the top of a pie in the usual way with milk or a beaten egg and bake it for 30-40 minutes in a hot oven gas mark 6/200°C (400°F).

You can also make flaky and rough puff pastry (half-puff pastry) with wholemeal (whole grain) flour using any recipe for white flour. The final result will not be as puffy, but the pastry will be light and rich and well worth the trouble. It is best used as a cover for both sweet and main-course pies. It will not really work for things like vol au vent cases and mille feuilles.

Whole grain cakes

Cake baking with wholemeal flour is very little different from using white flour; but perhaps the most significant difference in wholefood baking is in the type of sugar or sweetener that you use.

Sugar: no sugar is really tremendously good for us, and an excessive consumption causes tooth decay, but some types are definitely better than others. All manufactured sugar comes from either sugar cane or sugar beet.

Sugar cane, when it is harvested contains only 7-20% sucrose, which is what we eventually refine out as sugar. The rest is made up of vitamins (particularly those of the B group), minerals including iron, potassium and calcium, and fibre, as well as a large proportion of water. White sugar which is the final product of refining, is more or less pure sucrose with no fibre, vitamins or minerals. It is not a wholefood product.

The next step down in the refining process is a type of raw sugar, called Demerara sugar, because it once came only from Demerara County in Guyana. It comes in the form of large brown crystals and is not such a concentrated product as white sugar. It contains small amounts of vitamins and minerals. It is difficult to find in the United States and the nearest to it is raw sugar, left after the molasses has been removed. At one time only real Demerara (raw) sugar was available, but now there are other types, for example London Demerara, which is in fact coloured white sugar. When you buy Demerara, look on the packet. If it gives the country of origin then it is genuine, but if it lists ingredients (for example: white sugar, caramel) then it is not. Demerara sugar can be used to sweeten tea and coffee, and it can be sprinkled over fruit or used for jam. It can also be used in baking but it may

Eat wholemeal (whole grain) bread for wheat goodness.

give a slightly crunchy texture to light cakes.

The next least-refined sugar is the dark, soft, brown Barbados or Barbadoes sugar, sometimes called Muscovado in Britain, which means 'bottom of the pan'. It has a higher vitamin and mineral content than Demerara. Use it for all baking; cakes and breads made with it will be a darker colour than usual and will be very moist.

Molasses sugar, that is the richest of all in minerals and vitamins, is sugar which can be almost black and tastes like treacle (molasses) toffee. It is also referred to as black Barbados and Demerara molasses. Use it in ginger cakes, fruit cakes and dark tea breads. You may find the flavour a little too pronounced for the lighter sponge cakes.

Do not confuse refined, soft, brown sugars with Barbados. They are made from fine-grain refined sugar and sugar syrups.

Molasses (blackstrap): at the opposite end of the refining process to white sugar is molasses, the uncry-stallized syrup obtained from raw sugar. It contains a trace of protein, a number of different minerals, some B group vitamins—and only about two-thirds of the calories of white sugar. It is a thick, black syrup with a fairly strong flavour. Because of this it must be used carefully in baking, and is often best used in con-juction with one of the raw sugars. Like molasses or maple sugar, it is best in ginger cakes, rich fruit cakes, tea breads and coffee cakes.

Honey: the other sweetener much favoured in wholefood baking is honey. Like molasses and the dark sugars it contains vitamins, small amounts of B_2 and niacin and traces of a wide range of minerals. The main sugar that it contains is fructose or fruit sugar which is considered to be better for you than sucrose. Honey provides energy that is quickly available to the body and contains fewer calories than any of the sugars except molasses. Its delicious flavour is imparted to any cake or tea bread into which it is mixed. The best honey is that which has been locally produced as it has not been overheated, a process which changes its flavour and food value.

Changing from white sugar: if you are following a cake recipe originally intended for white sugar, use an equal amount of (raw) Demerara, (dark brown) Barbados or (maple) molasses sugar; or three-quarters one of the sugars and one-quarter molasses syrup; or three-quarters the amount of honey alone. You will find your honey cake will be rich and sweet enough. When making the cake, cream the butter in a bowl first and then beat in your chosen sweetener, just as you would normally.

Recipes for sponge cakes are inevitably rich, containing large amounts of butter or vegetable margarine and a sweetener. However, wholemeal (whole grain) flour and dark sugar, molasses or honey will make a rich, moist cake that is full of flavour. You will find that whereas a cake made with refined flour and white sugar has to be 'dressed up' with icing (confectioners') sugar or jam and cream, a plain wholemeal sponge is tasty enough on its own.

Carob: if you like chocolate cake but feel that chocolate bars or even cocoa should not be included in a natural food diet, then try carob powder as a substitute. It looks exactly like cocoa powder and has a similar flavour. It is derived from the pod of the carob tree and although fairly high in natural sugar it is very much lower in fat than cocoa. It also contains valuable B vitamins, calcium, phosphorous, iron and copper. For decorating cakes you can also buy carob bars which can be melted in a similar way to chocolate and spread over the top of your cake.

Whole grain bread

Because it is sometimes difficult to buy really good wholemeal (whole grain) bread, many cooks prefer to make their own. There is a certain mystique about yeast baking, but there is really no need for it at all. There is only one basic method for all breads and other, more elaborate, recipes are variations on a theme. The other misconception is that bread-making is time-consuming. It is true that bread needs time to rise twice, but the actual time that you spend working with it is relatively short.

Flours: some European wholemeal (whole grain) flours contain a certain proportion of imported wheat with a high gluten content to make sure that your bread rises well; but it is just as possible to make a good, light loaf from flour made only from home-grown wheat even if this is not high gluten, if you make it slightly on the moist side, knead it well and give it plenty of time to rise. To add variety to wholemeal (whole grain) wheat flour, you can use half rye or barley flour or one-quarter fine oatmeal. To avoid your loaf having a slightly sweet taste, always add 10 ml (2tsp) salt to every 450 g (1lb) or 4 cups flour.

Yeast: the raising (rising) agent used for bread is yeast, and you can use either fresh or dried. Fresh yeast comes in a moist compressed cake and it can be bought by the ounce (25g) from a baker who bakes his own bread, and from some grocers, delicatessens, health food stores and even supermarkets. It will keep fresh in a plastic container in the refrigerator for up to 10 days and it can be frozen for a short while. Active dried yeast takes the form of large granules, is available in packages and tins (cans) and keeps almost indefinitely. Half the amount of dried yeast is needed than fresh. Yeast is a living substance and must be treated with respect: if you do not warm it sufficiently it will not work and if the liquid that you use is too hot it will be killed. Ideally, it should be at blood heat, but a few degrees either way will make little difference. Yeast also needs to be fed with something sweet to get it to work. You can use (dark brown) Barbados or (raw) Demerara sugar, malt extract (maple sugar in the US), honey or molasses. Molasses will colour the loaf slightly, even if only 5 ml (1tsp) is used to 450 g (1lb) flour and it will give a very slight molasses taste.

Liquid: warm liquid is needed to mix the dough. A good working proportion for wholemeal (whole grain) flour is 275 ml ($\frac{1}{2}$pt) or 1$\frac{1}{4}$ cups per 450 g (1lb) or 4 cups flour. Generally, the yeast is first mixed with the sweetener and half the liquid, and when it is mixed into the flour the remaining liquid is added. Plain water is quite sufficient to make an excellent loaf, but if you want a lighter, softer texture, then you can use equal proportions of water and milk. You can also use eggs to make the dough and make up the remaining amount with water.

Fat: it is not necessary to add fat to bread, but again this will tend to make a softer and richer loaf. You can rub butter, lard, vegetable fat or vegetable margarine into the flour or add a good quality oil when you add the liquid.

Kneading: when the liquids and yeast have been mixed into the flour, the dough will be very lumpy, so turn it out onto a well-floured work top, flour your hands well and knead it. Everyone develops their own style of kneading, but the basic way it to push the dough away from you with the palms of your hands and then pull it back with the tips of your fingers, folding the top over as you do so. Do this several times and then pull out the sides of the dough and fold them over. Repeat these two actions until the dough is smooth, even-textured and elastic, flouring your hands every time they get sticky. Then form the dough into a ball, return it to the bowl and make a cross-cut in the top. Either cover the bowl with a clean cloth or put it into a large plastic bag and leave it in a warm place for one hour for the dough to double in bulk. Preheat the oven while the dough is rising.

Shaping: after rising, the dough is ready for shaping. Knead it again but not for as long as the first time. 450g (1lb) flour will make loaves in either two 450g (1lb) loaf tins or one 900g (2lb) tin (two 3-cup or one 5-cup bread pan). Grease the tins then, roughly shape the dough and lightly punch it down into the tins (pans) first, with the floured back of your hand.

Loaves can also be baked in terracotta flower pots. Make sure the pots are clean, grease them well and bake them empty. Do this three times and after that do not wash them or the bread will stick. Grease them every time that you use them. For extra effect, you can coat the sides with cracked wheat.

All kinds of different shaped loaves can be baked on a floured baking sheet. You can form the dough into a round, or a long round-sided shape, called a 'bloomer' in England. Make the shapes high and narrow at first, otherwise they will spread and flatten too much in the oven. For extra effect you can cut slashes in the top with a sharp knife. To make a two-tier cottage loaf with a bigger round underneath, divide the dough into one-third and two-thirds pieces and form them into rounds. Put the small one on top of the large one and push the handle of a wooden spoon down through both. This will join them together and make a characteristic dumpy shape. You can also make the dough into twists by making long oblong sausage shapes and either twisting or plaiting (braiding) them together.

After shaping the loaf you can give it an attractive glaze by brushing it with beaten egg and sprinkling it with poppy or sesame seeds or cracked wheat.

Second rise: stand the shaped loaves on top of the heated stove, or in a warm place, cover with a clean cloth or again use a plastic bag. Leave them for 20-40 minutes depending on the warmth. If the bread is in a tin (pan), it should rise about 1.5 cm ($\frac{1}{2}$in) above the edge before it goes into the oven. Do not leave the bread too long at this stage, or it may rise too high and then flop and develop a wrinkly surface when it is moved. This is called proving (proofing) as the bread is tested at this point because it must achieve its final shape before being baked.

Baking: after proving the bread is baked, usually the smaller loaves for 40 minutes and the larger ones for 10 minutes longer. The best temperature is gas mark 6/200°C (400°F). When the loaves are done, turn or lift them onto wire racks and leave them to cool completely. It is a real temptation to cut into freshly-baked warm bread, but the texture is never as good as when you leave it standing. Ideally, the plainer breads are best left for 12 hours and the richer ones for four.

Variations: once you have mastered the basic bread making method, there are many variations that you can experiment with. Try adding flavourings to the dough such as caraway seeds, or a spice such as paprika. For a savoury loaf, mix in chopped herbs, grated onion or grated cheese; or for a semi-sweet taste, some cinnamon and dried fruits.

Later on, you can experiment with richer breads and yeasted buns and cakes. Try the basic recipes first and make your own additions. You can try soft rolls, pitta bread for slitting open and filling with chunks of meat grilled on skewers and, the most satisfying thing of all to make, a large bubbling pizza.

RECIPES

Light Egg Rolls

These small rolls are very light and moist and best eaten on the day they are made. They are so good that you may not even need butter with them.

METRIC/IMPERIAL	AMERICAN
25g (1oz) fresh or 15g ($\frac{1}{2}$oz) dried yeast	1 oz cake compressed yeast or 1tbls dry yeast granules
5ml (1tsp) honey	1tsp honey
200ml (7floz) warm water	$\frac{7}{8}$ cup warm water

Make your own rolls using this light egg roll recipe.

450g (1lb) wholemeal flour plus extra for kneading	1lb whole grain flour, plus extra for kneading
10ml (2tsp) sea salt	2tsp sea salt
2 eggs	2 eggs
For the topping:	**For the topping:**
1 egg, beaten	1 egg, beaten
little cracked wheat	cracked wheat grains

If you are using fresh (compressed) yeast cream it in a bowl with the honey and water; use within 5 minutes. If using dried yeast, dissolve the honey in the water and scatter the yeast on top. Leave the yeast in a warm place to froth—about 10 minutes.

Put the flour and salt into a bowl. Make a well in the centre, beat the eggs and pour them into the flour with the yeast mixture. Mix everything together with a flat-bladed knife and turn the dough onto a well-floured work surface. Knead it until it is smooth. Return it to the bowl and make a cross-cut in the top. Either cover the bowl with a clean cloth or put it into a large plastic bag. Put the dough into a warm place for an hour to double in bulk.

Heat the oven to gas mark 6/200°C (400°F). Knead the dough again and form it into 16 round rolls. Lay them on a floured baking sheet. Brush them with beaten egg and scatter cracked wheat over the top. Put them on top of the stove and cover them with the clean cloth. Leave them for the second rise for 15-20 minutes. Bake the rolls for 20 minutes and lift them onto a wire rack to cool.

Cooking time: 2 hours

† Scatter the tops with poppy seeds instead of cracked wheat.

† For semi-sweet buns add 125g ($\frac{1}{4}$lb) or $\frac{1}{2}$ cup currants and 10ml (2tsp) caraway seeds.

† For cheese buns, add 125g ($\frac{1}{4}$lb) or 1 cup grated Cheddar cheese and some chopped parsley and chives.

Paprika Cheese Savouries

These crisp, golden-brown pastry fingers are good for parties or for nibbling before a meal. You can eat them piping hot from the oven or cold.

METRIC/IMPERIAL	AMERICAN
225g (½lb) wholemeal flour	½lb (2 cups) whole grain flour
pinch fine sea salt	pinch finely crushed sea salt
15ml (1tbls) paprika	1tbls paprika
125g (¼lb) butter	¼lb (½ cup) butter
1 egg, separated	1 egg, separated
cold water to mix pastry	cold water to mix pastry
30ml (2tbls) tomato purée	2tbls tomato paste
100g (¼lb) grated Farmhouse Cheese	1 cup grated aged Cheddar cheese

Heat the oven to gas mark 6/200°C (400°F). Put the flour into a bowl with the salt and paprika and rub in the butter. Add the egg yolk and enough cold water to mix the pastry. Form the dough into a ball, put it into a plastic bag and chill it.

Divide the dough into two equal halves and roll each one out into an oblong. Spread each one all over with tomato paste and spread the grated cheese over one long half of each piece. Fold the other half over the top. Cut each piece into strips 1.5cm (½in) wide. Lay the pieces on a large, floured baking sheet and brush them with the egg white. Bake them for 25 minutes and cool them on a wire rack if desired.

Cooking time: 1 hour

Curried Wheat Biscuits

The basic pastry method is also used for these light, crispy biscuits or bars, except yogurt is used instead of water to mix them.

METRIC/IMPERIAL	AMERICAN
100g (¼lb) wholemeal flour	1 cup whole grain flour
5ml (1tsp) curry powder	1tsp curry powder
50g (2oz) butter	4tbls butter
45ml (3tbls) natural yogurt	3tbls plain yogurt

Heat the oven to gas mark 6/200°C (400°F). Put the flour and curry powder into a bowl and rub in the butter. Make a well in the centre and add the yogurt. Mix everything to a dough and roll it out thinly. Cut it into small, square bars and lay them on a well-floured baking sheet. Prick them all over with a fork and bake them for 20 minutes. Cool on a wire rack.

Cooking time: 40 minutes

Mushroom and Herb Pie with Cream

Putting the mushrooms raw into this pie heightens the flavour as their juices seep into the rich, creamy filling.

METRIC/IMPERIAL	AMERICAN
For the pastry:	**For 1-crust pastry:**
175g (6oz) wholemeal flour	1½ cups whole grain flour
pinch fine sea salt	pinch finely crushed sea salt
40g (1½oz) butter	3tbls butter
40g (1½oz) lard or a white vegetable fat	3tbls shortening
cold water to mix	cold water to mix
beaten egg for glaze	beaten egg for glaze
For the filling:	**For the filling:**
75ml (3floz) clotted cream	6tbls Devonshire cream
2 eggs, beaten	2 eggs, beaten
30ml (2tbls) chopped mixed herbs	2tbls chopped mixed herbs
1 medium-sized onion	1 medium-sized onion
15g (½oz) butter	1tbls butter
225g (½lb) open mushrooms	½lb large mushrooms
sea salt	sea salt
freshly ground black pepper	freshly ground black pepper

Make the pastry and chill it. Heat the oven to gas mark 6/200°C (400°F). Put the cream into a large bowl and gradually beat in the eggs. Mix in the herbs. Thinly slice the onion. Melt the butter in a frying-pan on a low heat. Mix in the onion and cook it until it is golden. Cool it a little. Thinly slice the mushrooms and mix these and the onion into the eggs and cream. Season, using more pepper than salt.

Line a 20cm (8in) diameter flan tin or ring (pie or tart pan) with two-thirds of the pastry. Put in the filling and cover it with the remaining pastry. Seal the edges. Brush the pie with the beaten egg and bake it for 35 minutes. This pie is delicious hot or cold.

Cooking time: 55 minutes

Honey and Nut Pastries

These sweet, munchy pastries are excellent for picnics and packed lunches. If one is too big for one person to manage, you can cut each one in half.

METRIC/IMPERIAL	AMERICAN
For the pastry:	**For 1-crust pastry:**
125g (¼lb) wholemeal or wheatmeal flour	1 cup whole grain flour
pinch salt	pinch salt
15ml (1tbls) Barbados sugar	1tbls brown or Barbados sugar
50g (2oz) butter	4tbls butter
cold water to mix	cold water to mix
For the fillings:	**For the fillings:**
30ml (2tbls) clear honey	2tbls honey
125g (¼lb) unroasted peanuts	¼lb fresh peanuts
beaten egg or milk for glaze	beaten egg or milk for glaze

Heat the oven to gas mark 6/200°C (400°F). Make the pastry, adding the sugar to the flour with the salt. Chill it.

Divide the pastry into four pieces and roll each one into a circle. Mix·the peanuts with the honey. Lay the pastry rounds on a floured baking sheet and divide the peanuts between them, putting them on one side only. Fold the other side of the pastry over the top and seal the edges. Brush the pastries with beaten egg or milk and bake them for 30 minutes. Eat them hot or cold.

Cooking time: 55 minutes

Carob Cake

Carob powder added to a cake mixture makes a really deep brown, crumbly-textured cake which can be served plain or decorated for special occasions.

METRIC/IMPERIAL	AMERICAN
225g (½lb) butter	½lb (1 cup) butter
225g (½lb) Barbados sugar or molasses sugar	1 cup brown Barbados or maple sugar
5 eggs, separated	5 eggs, separated
150g (5oz) carob powder	1½ cups carob powder
225g (½lb) wholemeal flour	½lb (2 cups) whole grain flour
10ml (2tsp) baking powder	2tsp baking powder
butter for greasing 20cm (8in) cake tin	butter for greasing 8in cake pan

Heat the oven to gas mark 2/150°C (300°F). Cream the butter and sugar in a bowl and beat in the egg yolks. Mix the carob powder with the flour and baking powder and gradually add them to the butter mixture (the mixture will become very stiff at this point). Stiffly beat the egg whites and fold them into the mixture. Put everything into a greased 20cm (8in)) cake tin (pan) and bake the cake for 1 hour 15 minutes. Turn it onto a wire rack to cool.

Cooking time: 2 hours 5 minutes

† Add 100g (¼lb) or 1 cup chopped walnuts to the mixture.
† To make a cake for special occasions, break up a 100g (¼lb) carob bar and put it into a bowl. Stand it in a saucepan of warm water and melt it over a low heat. When the cake is completely cool, spread the melted carob over the top and sides and leave it to set.

Carob powder will give you a delicious, moist, dark cake with the full taste of chocolate.

Basic Sponge Cake

This is the basic recipe for a wholemeal (whole grain) sponge cake. It is moist and tasty and needs neither jam nor cream to make it enjoyable.

METRIC/IMPERIAL	AMERICAN
175g (6oz) butter or vegetable margarine	¾ cup butter or shortening
175g (6oz) Barbados or molasses sugar	¾ cup brown, Barbados or maple sugar
175g (6oz) wholemeal flour	1½ cups whole grain flour
7.5ml (1½tsp) baking powder	1½tsp baking powder
3 eggs, beaten	3 eggs, beaten
butter or margarine for greasing 20cm (8in) cake tin	butter or margarine for greasing 8in cake pan

Heat the oven to gas mark 4/180°C (350°F). Beat the butter or margarine until it is light and fluffy and beat in the sugar. Mix the flour with the baking powder and beat it into the butter alternately with the eggs. Put the mixture into a greased 20cm (8in) prepared cake tin (pan) and bake it for 40 minutes. Turn the cake onto a wire rack to cool.

Cooking time : 1 hour

† Use 125g (¼lb) or ⅓ cup honey instead of the sugar.
† Add spices such as ground cinnamon, grated nutmeg or mixed spice (ground allspice) to the flour.
† Add 175g (6oz) or 1 cup mixed dried fruit to make a moist and tasty fruit cake.

Whey Cakes

Save the whey as it drips and separates from your home-made yogurt cheese to make these exceptionally light little cakes.

METRIC/IMPERIAL	AMERICAN
225g (½lb) wholemeal flour	½lb (2 cups) whole grain flour
5ml (1tsp) mixed spice	1tsp ground allspice
2.5ml (½tsp) bicarbonate of soda	½tsp baking soda
2.5ml (½tsp) salt	½tsp salt
100g (¼lb) vegetable margarine	¼lb (½ cup) shortening
50g (2oz) sultanas	¼ cup white raisins (muscats)
50g (2oz) raisins	¼ cup raisins
200ml (7floz) whey from yogurt cheese (see page 128)	⅞ cup whey from yogurt cheese (see page 128)

Heat the oven to gas mark 6/200°C (400°F). Put the flour into a bowl with the spice, soda and salt and rub in the margarine. Toss in the fruits with your fingers. Make a well in the centre of the flour and pour in the whey. Form the mixture into a sticky dough.
Flour a baking sheet and drop small portions of the dough onto it (it should make 16 small cakes). Bake them for 20 minutes and lift them onto a wire rack to allow them to cool.

Cooking time : 35 minutes

Sugarless Carrot Cake

Grated carrots combined with dried fruits provide all the sweetness you need for this spicy cake. It will not, however, be quite as moist as one made with sugar or honey. Its texture is like a cross between a fruit cake and a rich bun.

METRIC/IMPERIAL	AMERICAN
75g (3oz) butter	6tbls butter
175g (6oz) wholemeal self-raising flour	1½ cups whole grain self-rising flour
5ml (1tsp) ground cinnamon	1tsp ground cinnamon
freshly grated nutmeg	freshly grated nutmeg
2 eggs, beaten	2 eggs, beaten
90ml (6tbls) sherry or natural apple juice	6tbls sherry or apple juice
75g (3oz) raw grated carrot	¾ cup raw grated carrot

Use grated carrots and apple juice to make a spicy cake.

METRIC/IMPERIAL	AMERICAN
50g (2oz) currants	¼ cup currants
50g (2oz) sultanas	¼ cup white raisins (muscats)
25g (1oz) raisins	⅛ cup raisins
butter for greasing 18cm (7in) cake tin	butter for greasing a small, 8in cake pan

Heat the oven to gas mark 3 / 160°C (325°F). Cream the butter in a mixing bowl. Mix the flour with the cinnamon and nutmeg. Beat the eggs with the sherry or apple juice. Gradually beat the flour and the egg mixture into the butter, beating well after each addition. You should end up with a mixture a little stiffer than the average cake. Mix in the carrot and fruits. Put the mixture into a greased 18cm (7in) cake tin (pan or dish) and smooth the top. Bake the cake for 1 hour 45 minutes. Turn it out onto a wire rack to cool.

Cooking time : 2 hours 10 minutes

Dairy-free Vinegar Cake

If vinegar is used instead of eggs as a raising (rising) agent, the resulting cake will be light and very crumbly. This one is in texture like a cross between cake and shortbread (shortbread cookies).

METRIC/IMPERIAL	AMERICAN
225g (½lb) wholemeal flour	½lb (2 cups) whole grain flour
2.5ml (½tsp) bicarbonate of soda	½tsp baking soda
125g (¼lb) vegetable margarine	¼lb (½ cup) shortening
125g (¼lb) Barbados sugar	½ cup brown or Barbados sugar
50g (2oz) raisins	⅓ cup raisins
50g (2oz) sultanas	⅓ cup white raisins (muscats)
30ml (2tbls) malt or cider vinegar	2tbls malt or cider vinegar
90ml (6tbls) natural apple juice	6tbls apple juice
extra margarine for greasing 450g (1lb) loaf tin	extra shortening for greasing 3-cup bread pan

Heat the oven to gas mark 4 / 180°C (350°F). Put the flour and soda into a bowl and rub in the margarine. Toss in the sugar, raisins and sultanas (white raisins) with your fingers. Make a well in the centre and pour in the vinegar and apple juice. Mix everything to a dough and press it into a greased 450g (1lb) loaf tin (3 cup bread pan). Put the cake into the oven for 1 hour. Turn the heat to gas mark 2 / 150°C (300°F) and continue cooking for a further 15 minutes. Very carefully turn out the cake onto a wire rack. It will be very crumbly, but will hold together better as it cools.

Cooking time : 1 hour 35 minutes

Upside-down Orange and Honey Cake

This cake is light and rich and pretty enough to be served as a sweet on special occasions.

METRIC/IMPERIAL	AMERICAN
125g (¼lb) butter	¼lb (½ cup) butter
125g (¼lb) honey	⅓ cup honey
grated rind 1 medium-sized orange	grated rind 1 medium-sized orange
125g (¼lb) wholemeal flour	1 cup whole grain flour
5ml (1tsp) mixed spice	1tsp ground allspice
5ml (1tsp) baking powder	1tsp baking powder
2 eggs, beaten	2 eggs, beaten
For the topping:	**For the topping:**
2 medium-sized oranges	2 medium-sized oranges
30ml (2tbls) clear honey	2tbls honey
butter for greasing 20cm (8in) diameter cake tin	butter for greasing 8in cake pan

Heat the oven to gas mark 4 / 180°C (350°F). Beat the butter until it is fluffy and beat in the honey and orange rind. Toss the flour with the spice and baking powder and beat it into the butter alternately with the eggs. Cut the rind and white fibres or pith from the oranges and cut them both into thin, round slices.

Put the 30ml (2tbls) honey into the bottom of a greased 20cm (8in) cake tin (pan) and arrange the orange slices in a pattern on top. Spoon in the cake mixture and smooth the top. Bake the cake for 30 minutes. Turn it out onto a round plate to cool.

Cooking time: 1 hour

Wholemeal Soda Bread

If you have never made bread before, you will not fail to be successful with soda bread, because it is very easy and does not need yeast. There are all sorts of variations that you can make on the original method such as scones (biscuits).

METRIC/IMPERIAL	AMERICAN
450g (1lb) wholemeal flour	1lb (4 cups) whole grain flour
5ml (1tsp) sea salt	1tsp sea salt
5ml (1tsp) bicarbonate of soda	1tsp baking soda
50g (2oz) butter, lard, vegetable margarine or vegetable fat	4tbls butter or shortening
275ml (½pt) soured milk, natural yogurt, or cultured buttermilk	1¼ cups soured milk, plain yogurt or buttermilk

Heat the oven to gas mark 6/200°C (400°F). Put the flour into a bowl with the salt and soda and rub in the fat. Make a well in the centre and pour in your chosen liquid. Mix everything to a dough. Turn it onto a floured work-surface and knead it very lightly just to make it smooth.
For soda bread, form the dough into a slightly flattened round shape. Put it onto a floured baking sheet and make a cross in the top with a sharp knife. Bake it for 45 minutes and lift it onto a wire rack to cool.
For scones (biscuits), roll the dough out to about 2cm (¾in) thick and either cut it into squares or triangles or stamp it into rounds with a biscuit cutter. Put the cut shapes onto a floured baking sheet and bake them for 20 minutes.

Cooking time: 1 hour or 35 minutes

† For savoury scones (biscuits) dissolve 10ml (2tsp) yeast extract (Marmite or Savita) in 150ml (¼pt) ⅔ cup hot water. Let it cool and add it to the flour with 150ml (¼pt) or ⅔ cup yogurt. 125g (¼lb) or 1 cup grated cheese can be added as well.
† For walnut and herb scones, add 125g (¼lb) or 1 cup chopped walnuts and 60ml (4tbls) chopped mixed herbs to the flour.
† For sweet scones, add 50g (2oz) or 4tbls Barbados or molasses sugar to the flour and 5ml (1tsp) ground cinnamon.
† For fruit scones, add 125g (¼lb) or ½ cup currants, sultanas or (white or dark) raisins or a mixture.

Apple and Raisin Pudding

Spiced apples, sweetened with sultanas (white raisins) and Barbados or brown sugar are topped with a light and crumbly scone mixture to make a satisfying pudding.

METRIC/IMPERIAL	AMERICAN
450g (1lb) cooking apples	1lb tart apples
50g (2oz) sultanas	⅓ cup white raisins (muscats)
pinch ground cloves	pinch ground cloves
50g (2oz) Barbados sugar	¼ cup brown or Barbados sugar
For the topping:	**For the topping:**
225g (½lb) 81% or 85% wheatmeal self-raising flour	½lb (2 cups) whole grain self-rising flour
50g (2oz) Demerara sugar	¼ cup raw sugar
1.5ml (¼tsp) ground cloves	¼tsp ground cloves
pinch sea salt	pinch sea salt
50g (2oz) butter	4tbls butter
1 egg, beaten	1 egg, beaten
60ml (4tbls) milk plus extra for glaze	4tbls milk plus extra for glaze

Heat the oven to gas mark 4/180°C (350°F). Peel, core and thinly slice the apples and mix them with the sultanas (white raisins), cloves and Barbados sugar. Put them into the bottom of a flat, 1.1L (2pt) or 5 cup ovenproof dish. Put the flour into a bowl with the sugar, ground cloves and salt and rub in the butter. Make a well in the centre and pour in the egg and milk. Mix everything to a stiff dough. Roll the dough out to the size of the dish and put it on top of the apples. Brush the top with a little milk and bake the pudding for 45 minutes.

Cooking time: 1 hour 5 minutes

Steamed Honey Pudding

Even if you eat only natural foods, you can still enjoy a rich sticky, steamed pudding occasionally. This one is very light in texture and is excellent with home-made yogurt spooned over the top.

METRIC/IMPERIAL	AMERICAN
75g (3oz) butter or vegetable margarine	6tbls butter or shortening
90ml (6tbls) honey	6tbls honey
1 egg	1 egg
90ml (6tbls) milk	6tbls milk
125g (¼lb) wholemeal self-raising flour	1 cup whole grain self-rising flour
butter or margarine for greasing	butter or shortening for greasing
natural yogurt for serving	plain yogurt for serving

Put the butter into a bowl and beat it until it is soft. Beat in 30ml (2tbls) of the honey. Beat the egg with the milk and beat it into the butter and honey alternately with the flour. Put the remaining honey in the bottom of a light-greased 850ml (1½pt) or 4 cup heatproof bowl and put the mixture on top. Cover the bowl with buttered greaseproof or waxed paper and a piece of foil.
Bring a saucepan of water to the boil and lower in the

pudding. Steam it for 2 hours, checking occasionally to make sure it does not boil dry.

Turn the pudding into a dish and serve the yogurt separately to spoon over the top.

Cooking time: 2 hours 20 minutes

Walnut Tea Bread

This dark, chewy tea bread has the slight hint of orange to lighten the flavour.

METRIC/IMPERIAL	AMERICAN
350g (¾lb) wholemeal flour	3 cups whole grain flour
5ml (1tsp) salt	1tsp salt
10ml (2tsp) baking powder	2tsp baking powder
75g (3oz) Barbados or molasses sugar	6tbls Barbados or maple sugar
45ml (3tbls) molasses	3tbls molasses
175ml (6floz) water	¾ cup water
60ml (4tbls) natural yogurt	4tbls plain yogurt
grated rind 1 orange	grated rind 1 orange
125g (¼lb) chopped walnuts	1 cup chopped walnuts
butter for greasing 900g (2lb) loaf tin	butter for greasing 5-cup bread pan

Heat the oven to gas mark 1 / 140°C (275°F). Put the flour, salt and baking powder into a bowl and toss them together with your fingers. Make a well in the centre.

Warm the sugar, molasses and water gently in a saucepan until the molasses and sugar have melted. Pour them into the flour. Add the yogurt and orange rind and gradually stir in the flour from the sides of the bowl. Mix in the walnuts and make sure they are evenly distributed. Transfer the mixture to a greased 2lb (900g) loaf tin (5-cup bread pan) and smooth the top. Bake the loaf for 1¾ hours, or until a skewer inserted into the centre will come out clean. Cool the loaf in the tin (pan) for 5 minutes and then turn it onto a wire rack to cool completely.

Cooking time: 2 hours 5 minutes

Pitta Bread

A pitta, or pitta bread, is a traditional Greek and Middle Eastern bread for one person.

METRIC/IMPERIAL	AMERICAN
25g (1oz) fresh or 15g (½oz) dried yeast	1oz cake compressed yeast or 1tbls dry yeast granules
5ml (1tsp) honey	1tsp honey
275ml (½pt) warm water	1¼ cups warm water
450g (1lb) wholemeal flour	1lb (4 cups) whole grain flour
10ml (2tsp sea salt)	2tsp sea salt

If you are using fresh (compressed) yeast, crumble it into a bowl and cream it with the sugar and half the water. If using dried yeast, dissolve the sugar in half the water and sprinkle the yeast on top; put the yeast in a warm place to froth for about 10 minutes.

Put the flour and salt into a bowl and make a well in the centre. Pour in the yeast mixture and the remaining water and mix everything together with a flat-bladed knife. Turn the dough onto a well-floured work surface and knead it until it is smooth. Put it into a large plastic bag and leave in a warm place for 1 hour to rise.

Heat the oven to gas mark 8 / 230°C (450°F). Knead the dough and divide it into 6 pieces. Roll each one into an oval about 20 x 12cm (8 x 5in). Lay them on a floured board or baking sheet, cover them with a clean cloth and put them on the top of the stove or other warm place for 15-20 minutes for the second rise.

Thickly flour another large baking sheet and put it into the oven to get really hot. Quickly lay the risen pittas on it and bake them for 15 minutes or until they are just beginning to turn brown. Either serve them immediately or wrap them in a thick cloth to keep them soft and warm.

Cooking time: 2 hours 5 minutes

Spiced Currant Buns

This is a richer bread mixture with a slightly more complicated method. The buns are soft and gently spiced and are delicious eaten with butter. When they are a day old they are excellent split and toasted.

METRIC/IMPERIAL	AMERICAN
25g (1oz) fresh yeast or 15g (½oz) dried yeast	1 oz cake compressed yeast or 1tbls dry yeast granules
30ml (2tbls) honey	2tbls honey
275ml (½pt) warm milk	1¼ cups warm milk
450g (1lb) wholemeal flour	1lb (4 cups) whole grain flour
2.5ml (½tsp) sea salt	½tsp sea salt
10ml (2tsp) mixed spice	2tsp ground allspice
75g (3oz) butter	6tbls butter
2 eggs, beaten	2 eggs, beaten
225g (½lb) currants	½lb currants or raisins
For the glaze:	**For the glaze:**
1 egg beaten with 90ml (6tbls) milk	1 egg beaten with 6tbls milk

If you are using fresh (compressed) yeast, crumble it into a bowl and cream it with the honey and milk; use within 5 minutes. If using dried yeast mix the honey and milk together and sprinkle the dried yeast on top. Leave the yeast in a warm place to froth—about 10 minutes.

Put the flour into a mixing bowl and toss in the salt and spice. Make a well in the centre. Melt the butter in a saucepan on a low heat. Cool it a little. Pour the yeast mixture, butter and eggs into the flour and mix everything to a moist dough. Turn it onto a floured work-surface, knead it and work in the currants about a quarter at a time. Return the dough to the bowl and either cover it with a clean cloth or put it into a large plastic bag. Put the dough into a warm place for 1 hour to rise.

Wholemeal bread is best home-made and can be an important source of protein in a wholefood diet.

Heat the oven to gas mark 6/200°C (400°F). Knead the dough again and divide it into 16 small round buns. Place them on a floured baking sheet and brush the tops with the egg and milk glaze. Put them on top of the stove and cover them with a clean cloth. Leave them for 15-20 minutes for the second rise.

Bake the buns for 20 minutes and lift them onto a wire rack to cool.

Cooking time: 2 hours 20 minutes

Basic Wholemeal Bread

This is the basic recipe for plain wholemeal (whole grain) bread.

METRIC/IMPERIAL	AMERICAN
25g (1oz) fresh or 15g (½oz) dried yeast	1oz cake compressed yeast or 1tbls dry yeast granules
5ml (1tsp) Barbados sugar	1tsp brown or Barbados sugar
275ml (½pt) warm water	1¼ cups warm water
450g (1lb) wholemeal flour, plus extra for kneading	1lb (4 cups) whole grain flour, plus extra for kneading
10ml (2tsp) sea salt	2tsp sea salt
butter or oil for greasing either one 900g (2lb) or two 450g (1lb) loaf tins)	butter or oil for greasing either one 5-cup or two 3-cup bread pans

If you are using fresh (compressed) yeast, crumble it into a bowl and cream it with the sugar and half the water; use within 5 minutes. If using dried yeast, dissolve the sugar in half the water and sprinkle the yeast on top. Put the yeast into a warm place to froth—about 10 minutes.

Put the flour and salt into a bowl and make a well in the centre. Pour in the yeast mixture and the remaining water and mix everything together with a flat-bladed knife. Turn the dough onto a well-floured work surface and knead it until it is smooth. Return it to the bowl and make a cross-cut in the top. Either cover the bowl with a clean cloth or put it into a large plastic bag. Leave the dough in a warm place for one hour to double in bulk.

Heat the oven to gas mark 6/200°C (400°F). Grease a 900g (2lb) loaf tin (5-cup bread pan) or two 450g (1lb) loaf tins (3-cup bread pans). Knead the dough again and either keep it in one piece or divide it into two. Roughly shape it and press it lightly into your bread tin(s) (pans). Put the bread on top of the stove and cover with a clean tea cloth. Leave for the final rising for 15 minutes, or until the dough has risen 1.5cm (½in) above the edge of the tin(s). Bake the large loaf for 50 minutes and the small ones for 40 minutes.

Turn the bread onto a wire rack to cool and leave it for 12 hours before cutting.

Cooking time: 2 hours 30 minutes or 2 hours 20 minutes

† For a wheatgerm loaf, add 1oz (25g) or ⅛ cup wheatgerm to the flour and about 90ml (6tbls) more water.

Index

Picture Credits